The Century of the
TEDDY BEAR

The Century of the
TEDDY BEAR

CONSTANCE KING

ANTIQUE COLLECTORS' CLUB

Frontispiece: A large Chad Valley bear enjoying the summer sunshine.
c.1950. Ht. 30in. (76.2cm). *Courtesy Constance King Antiques*

British Library Cataloguing-in-Publication Data
A catalogue record for this book is available from the British Library

Printed in England
by the Antique Collectors' Club Ltd., Woodbridge, Suffolk
on Consort Royal Era Satin paper
supplied by the Donside Paper Company, Aberdeen, Scotland

Contents

The Antique Collectors' Club

The Antique Collectors' Club was formed in 1966 and quickly grew to a five figure membership spread throughout the world. It publishes the only independently run monthly antiques magazine, *Antique Collecting*, which caters for those collectors who are interested in widening their knowledge of antiques, both by greater awareness of quality and by discussion of the factors which influence the price that is likely to be asked. The Antique Collectors' Club pioneered the provision of information on prices for collectors and the magazine still leads in the provision of detailed articles on a variety of subjects.

It was in response to the enormous demand for information on 'what to pay' that the price guide series was introduced in 1968 with the first edition of *The Price Guide to Antique Furniture* (completely revised 1978 and 1989), a book which broke new ground by illustrating the more common types of antique furniture, the sort that collectors could buy in shops and at auctions rather than the rare museum pieces which had previously been used (and still to a large extent are used) to make up the limited amount of illustrations in books published by commercial publishers. Many other price guides have followed, all copiously illustrated, and greatly appreciated by collectors for the valuable information they contain, quite apart from prices. The Price Guide Series heralded the publication of many standard works of reference on art and antiques. *The Dictionary of British Art* (now in six volumes), *The Pictorial Dictionary of British 19th Century Furniture Design, Oak Furniture* and *Early English Clocks* were followed by many deeply researched reference works such as *The Directory of Gold and Silversmiths,* providing new information. Many of these books are now accepted as the standard work of reference on their subject.

The Antique Collectors' Club has widened its list to include books on gardens and architecture. All the Club's publications are available through bookshops world wide and a full catalogue of all these titles is available free of charge from the addresses below.

Club membership, open to all collectors, costs little. Members receive free of charge *Antique Collecting*, the Club's magazine (published ten times a year), which contains well-illustrated articles dealing with the practical aspects of collecting not normally dealt with by magazines. Prices, features of value, investment potential, fakes and forgeries are all given prominence in the magazine.

Among other facilities available to members are private buying and selling facilities and the opportunity to meet other collectors at their local antique collectors' clubs. There are over eighty in Britain and more than a dozen overseas. Members may also buy the Club's publications at special pre-publication prices.

As its motto implies, the Club is an organisation designed to help collectors get the most out of their hobby: it is informal and friendly and gives enormous enjoyment to all concerned.

For Collectors — By Collectors — About Collecting

ANTIQUE COLLECTORS' CLUB
5 Church Street, Woodbridge Suffolk IP12 1DS, UK
Tel: 01394 385501 Fax: 01394 384434

——— or ———

Market Street Industrial Park, Wappingers' Falls, NY 12590, USA
Tel: 914 297 0003 Fax: 914 297 0068

Acknowledgements

Teddy Bears are with us from our very first days and few people are without their stories and reminiscences about a favourite toy and companion. "Chad Valley" was one of the first names I was able to read and my love of bears grew from the soft toys of my infancy. Alfred Bestall, with his wonderful interpretations of Rupert in the colourful annuals, transported me to other worlds and adventures. Once I began collecting antique toys, I was regaled with bear stories from old and young, many of which had sad endings, with the loss of the Teddy in a fire, jumble sale or at the hands of a murderous brother with an airgun. I acknowledge the help of all these in increasing my knowledge of people's emotional attachment to a toy that, above all others, mirrors nursery life in the twentieth century.

During the writing of this book, my husband Andrew worked tirelessly at photography as well as proof-reading and without his unstinting help the work would not have been possible. Oliver Holmes of Merrythought kindly gave access to old material and catalogues, as did Neil Miller of Dean's. Much of my research at Dean's was undertaken when the firm was under the management of Ian Scott at Rye in the 1970s and it is tragic that so many items have been lost each time the firm changed hands. Golden Bear, Nounours and Clemens have all assisted, especially in supplying details of their current ranges and to all these toy makers I extend my thanks. Phillida Gili, whose delicate illustrations brought John Betjeman's 'Archie' to life, very generously lent her original artwork for the book, so that the colours could be as true as possible.

At Sotheby's, Kerry Taylor and Sue Duffield helped me to obtain photographs, as has Leyla Maniera of Christie's, who catalogues the largest number of bears each year. Camilla Young at Christie's Images, Emma Sully and other members of Christie's Press Office were readily helpful, as was Leigh Gotch of Bonham's. Dominic Winter and Ludlow Antique Auctions also gave access to material, as did John and Margaret Burrows, who ran the toy museum in Bath. Bernard Beech, of Bears on the Square in Ironbridge allowed me to take photographs and Marie Robischon of Robin der Bär provided examples of her work.

The staff at the Antique Collectors Club have worked enthusiastically to get the book to press, always with good humour and an understanding of the needs of collectors that is often absent from less dedicated publishers.

Without the help of all these people, the book would not have been possible but, above all, it is Richard Steiff, the inventor of the Teddy Bear, who has most to be acknowledged for giving posterity one of the most lovable and enduring toys.

Introduction

With their sad eyes, soft coats and gentle expressions, Teddy Bears were created to demand caresses and love. While other antique toys can be classified and their value assessed, bears remain curiously superior to the vulgarities of the financial market. Performing amazing antics in the salerooms and fetching much less or far, far more than was estimated because of their individual and almost indefinable appeal, they are collected for a myriad of reasons. The compelling desires of love, loneliness, fun, greed and even novelty jostle together wherever bears are exhibited and they can arouse passions as primitive as any found in their original nursery habitat.

Collectors of bears were once regarded as amiable eccentrics, who assembled a range of amusing, but worthless, soft toys from feelings of pure nostalgia. The last quarter of the twentieth century has seen bears move into the realm of respectable antiques, with every price record featured in the national press and with magazines, postcards and books promoting the image. To admit to an enthusiasm for bears is acceptable in any circle and clothes, household linen, furnishing fabrics and wallpaper with images ursine are now as likely to be targeted at the adult as at the infant market. That this phenomenon should have occurred at the end of the century, when radical changes in family life and the global economy have made life insecure for so many people is not surprising. In times of stress, we all look to our childhood comforts of warmth, love and the uncritical devotion of animals. Teddy Bears fulfil all these criteria without the problems of living creatures. Here is a soft, furry shoulder to cry on, a sympathetic paw, a kindly pair of brown glass eyes to make life more tolerable.

FACING PAGE.
When the artist Arthur Rackham illustrated the story of *The Three Bears* in 1933, he portrayed the characters as wild animals, rather than the anthropomorphic cuddly creatures evolved by the artists who worked for Raphael Tuck and Ernest Nister.   *Courtesy Jane Vandell Associates*

Steaming into the future. Bears attract people of all types and ages and have an intrinsic appeal that crosses national frontiers.

Courtesy Constance King Antiques

The dual personality of bears, at once a child's toy and a mascot, has existed since the character was introduced early in this century. After a period of relegation to the nursery in the 1940s and '50s, he re-emerged as an adult companion in the 1970s and has not looked back. Some large toy manufacturers now admit that their survival depends on a healthy international bear market and each year artists and craft makers produce new variations of the traditional toy so that even though its 100th birthday approaches, the image is never tired or jaded.

Unlike other collectables, such as porcelain or automata, where old and new are rarely mixed, modern and antique bears appear together in many shows and collections. Special editions are created by the leading toymakers and there is a steady flow of expensive, individually made items for the luxury and specialist markets. Mink, gold, jewelled and silver teddies all have a place alongside smart shoulder bags, topped with a fluffy teddy-head, bear rings and necklaces, birthday cards, cakes and slippers.

People who stray into things ursine are always unprepared for the zany world in which they find themselves. Staid city gentlemen write letters from their companion bears to those of equally grand businessmen in New York. You are told at a party that "Archibald Bear is resting at home with a large brandy and a Corona Corona". Some bears have their own language and write notes to their owners to remind them how lonely they are. A few great favourites are taken to shoe shops for their winter wellies or to a hatter for a specially made top hat for their master's wedding and one rode in a royal carriage at the marriage of the Duke of York. Every collector has their favourite story: my own is a visit to No. 10 Downing Street, not to visit Margaret Thatcher, but to have tea with her bear, Humphrey, a shaggy, sociable fellow, who wore proletarian blue dungarees and lived with Mrs Bear, blissfully unaware of Things going on around him.

Though old bears have always had a following, they were slow to emerge as collectable in the field of antique toys and were not included in the specialist

Bear collecting developed into a passion for many people around 1980, fostered by the growth of clubs, magazines and special events, such as picnics. "Judith", one of the first bear makers and collectors, with an armful of her friends. *Courtesy Jane Vandell Associates*

Bears of all ages are often seen together in modern collections. This group clusters around a
Swallow Toys costermonger's cart of the 1930s. *Courtesy Constance King Antiques*

catalogues of the leading salerooms. The publication of Peter Bull's *Bear with Me* in
1969 did much to change attitudes, though he was primarily fascinated by the
influence of bears on the lives of ordinary people. There were few photographs
included in his book and little suggestion of the antiques scene. The text encouraged
many adults, who had kept their furry friends since childhood, to admit their
devotion. In *Bear with Me*, Peter Bull wrote of how some were taken on railway
journeys: the devastation when one was lost and the horror of the unspeakable things
that parents could do to bears that had become dirty and unhygienic. In a number
of lectures and television appearances, Bull popularised the image of bears, at the
same time making his own 2½ inch pocket bear, Theodore, very famous.

Colonel Henderson, of Good Bears of the World, must have been the first great
collector, as he owned several hundred examples, with related items, like bear-
shaped vesta cases, scent bottles, cruets, puppets and tea pots. When serving in the
Second World War on General Montgomery's staff, Henderson carried his own
miniature bear with him as a mascot. He spent his life promoting the value of bears
as companions for humans, though, in several telephone conversations with me, he
bemoaned the ever-increasing commercialisation of bear collecting.

Collectors such as Colonel Henderson and Peter Bull revered old bears, no matter how moth-
eaten and loved to pieces. This early Steiff with boot button eyes would have appealed to either
of the great enthusiasts. *Courtesy Constance King Antiques*

Auction realisations for Teddy Bears can both surprise and disappoint, as individual bears have a sometimes indefinable appeal. This group is typical of the variety to be found in one of the leading auction houses.

Top, left to right:

A black Steiff with boot button eyes mounted on red discs. Recorded in the Steiff archive as "Original Teddybär Schwarz Nr. 5325,2". Only seventeen bears of this size were made in 1917. It is thought that the 1930s coat was later supplied by Steiff. Ht. 12in. (30.5cm). £4,025.

A small Steiff, c.1920, with its button in ear, a stitched snout and claws. Ht. 8¾in. (22.2cm). £322.

Made c.1910 in blond plush, this Steiff type has an unusual horizontally embroidered nose. Ht. 11in. (28cm). £1,092.

A German-made bear on metal wheels with boot button eyes. Ht. 10in. (25.4cm). £200.

Made c.1950, "Teddy Baby" by Steiff has a "US Zone Germany" fabric tag with a card label to the collar. Made of pale pink mohair and shaved white mohair snout and feet. With blue leatherette collar and bell. Ht. 11in. (28cm). £805.

A red and green German harlequin bear, 1925-30, with a shaved muzzle. The sides of the head with black-tipped mohair. Ht. 16½in. (42cm). £1,092.

Carrying his school satchel, a white Steiff with a button in ear and the remains of a yellow fabric label. A brown stitched nose and cream fabric pads. c.1920. Ht. 14in. (35.6cm). £862.

Probably made by Bing, this key-wound walking bear, made c.1912, has boot button eyes and weighted feet with articulated ankles. He sways from side to side as he moves forward. Ht. 13in. (33cm). £920.

With his black and white ribbon, a "Jopi" peach coloured mohair bear, made in Germany c.1930. Ht. 18½in. (47cm). £2,415.

The 1948 type white plush Steiff has the silver painted button with the long, angular "F" and the remains of a yellow back tag. He has a brown stitched nose and a good hump. Ht. 20in. (50.8cm). £1,265.

Aunt Addie's golden brown Steiff with its early plain button in ear, c.1907. He has black boot button eyes and cream felt pads. The bear was accompanied by a photograph of Aunt Addie (see below). Ht. 24in. (61cm). £8,970.

A 1979 Paddington Bear, made as an animated puppet by Filmfair in brown synthetic plush and a fully adjustable body. Ht. 8in. (20.3cm). Estimated at £6,000-8,000 but withdrawn before the sale.

A Steiff blond mohair with button in ear and boot button eyes and a very pronounced hump. The pads are re-covered with hessian. Ht. 16½in. (42cm). Withdrawn.

Bottom row, left to right:

A very fine Steiff centre seam (the seam running down the centre of the head) c.1910, in blond plush. Known as "Puw" bear, he has always lived in North Wales. Ht. 24½in. (62.2cm). £7,475.

A black Steiff, 1908-12, with his button in ear, a black stitched snout and mouth and elongated, shaped limbs. It is thought that Steiff made the black bears especially for the British market. Unusually, he does not have the normal red felt backing circles behind the eyes and, in form, looks earlier than 1912, the date usually given for this type. Ht. 13in. (33cm). £4,600.

"Growler", made in the US Zone of Germany, has a Steiff label and an extremely loud growl that once prevented him being thrown into a dustbin. Ht. 20in. (50.8cm). £1,092.

A 1950's Steiff with a button in ear and a yellow fabric tag numbered "535,02" in beige long mohair with a dark brown embroidered nose. Ht. 20in. (50.8cm) £1,380.

All sold in June 1997.

Courtesy Sotheby's London

"Aunt Addie" with her 1908 Steiff bear. Adeline was born in 1890 in Decater, Indiana, USA. The photograph shows the bear in a place of honour in the family photograph in 1908 with her mother and younger brother. The bear is shown on the facing page.
Courtesy Sotheby's London

Two German and two English-made Teddies with a Kämmer and Reinhardt character doll. As dolls became more child-like and realistic in the early years of the twentieth century, soft toys became correspondingly child-friendly. The Teddy Bear, with his jointed limbs and turning head, is closely related to dolls in form but has the irresistible appeal of a soft and cuddly animal with trusting eyes. *Courtesy Constance King Antiques*

When my first book on collectable toys was published in 1973, I included a special section on bears only after some opposition, as they were still generally considered worthless. The appearance of my Chad Valley "Rupert", otherwise known as Teddy Villers (he has a dual personality), attracted such great interest that strangers still come up to me and ask after him by name. Such is the power of bears…

A First World War U-boat captain, made by the artist-maker Marie Robischon in 1996. Artist bears have revitalized the market at the end of the century.

Courtesy Marie Robischon

Goldilocks' jumps out of the window.

By 1900, the story of *The Three Bears* had evolved into a series of charming pictures with appealing bear cubs and a pretty golden haired little girl. *Author*

By the late '70s, Teddy Bear collecting as a specialist area was flourishing, especially in America, and they began to appear in dealers' catalogues and to be individually offered at auction. In the '80s, bears boomed. In London, Christie's South Kensington hit the headlines when the first auction devoted to bears of all ages was organised, an event that attracted as many cameramen as buyers. Today the value of things ursine is known to every antique dealer, as they are collected by people of all ages and types. Japanese buyers, usually interested only in antique toys in pristine condition, have recently become converted to the bear world, despite their doubtful sawdust and kapok stuffing. That the character of bears triumphs over their problems of personal hygiene is proof of their allure.

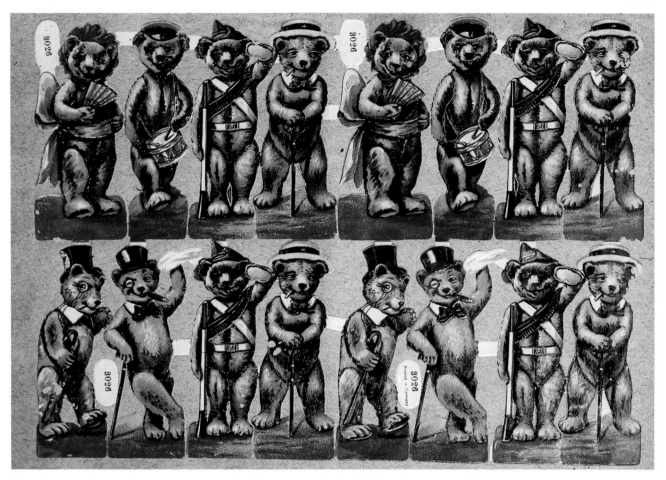

The German printers of scraps were among the first to recognise the limitless design potential of anthropomorphic bears. This set was published by Mamelok and Soehne, Germany, whose scraps are marked "M & S".
Courtesy Jane Vandell Associates

As international interest in collecting has snowballed, the price of old bears has risen dramatically, so that the finest early examples are now the province of the wealthy. Even 1970s examples can sell at over £200, taking them out of the reach of many of the eccentric, lonely people who rescued them in the past. Fortunately, toymakers have turned their attention to the enthusiasts' market and there are reproductions and artist creations. The proliferation of bears available in every country in a wide price range makes this one of the most lively collecting fields. Teddy Bears' picnics, specialist shows and fairs all contribute to the furry creature's popularity. To the delight of arctophiles, this is truly the Century of the Bear.

Bears became respectable in the early 1980s and began to appear regularly in the auction rooms in Britain and America
Courtesy Sotheby's London

CHAPTER 1
Before the First Teddy Bear

Bears gold, cinnamon tipped, brown, beige or white have exerted their influence on humans since the beginning of time. Simultaneously reviled and honoured, treated with horrific cruelty and considerable affection, bears have fascinated people because of their mystical and sometimes sinister associations. They are so completely different in appearance to any other carnivores that they form a special group of animals with a comparatively small number of species. They have always been regarded with some trepidation, not just because of our fear of the animal's size and strength but because of several unsettling resemblances to humans.

When walking, the bear places its whole foot on the ground, so that the prints resemble those of men, a fact that has given rise to many fearful stories in lonely country places. Was it an animal or a huge man that trampled the snow behind the byre at dead of night? Why are they said to react fiercely if a pregnant woman is expecting a boy? Was it a man or beast that carried off the peasant girl from the isolated footpath?

All these emotions can be discovered in European folk tales and superstitions. Sometimes werewolf-type characters resemble bears more than wolves, a feature that film-makers have always exaggerated. Bears have expressive round eyes and this sets them apart from most other animals and eventually made them ideal subjects for soft toy portraits. Many stories describe the bear's curious attraction to women. Some of the ancient superstitions regarding bears have their roots in completely natural behaviour. The comment made by Pliny the Elder, that bears mate facing each other, rather than *more ferarum*, obviously fascinated better educated people, while the peasants took an earthy interest in the bear's lust. It was a short imaginative step for primitive people to spin tales of bears that made off with maidens. The mythology suggests that Bruin was a gentle ravisher and the females who returned home were unscathed by his teeth and claws. The progeny of these curious alliances were said to look perfectly normal but were of a strange, dreamy disposition: a useful creature to lurk in the forest and provide unmarried peasant girls with such an unproveable

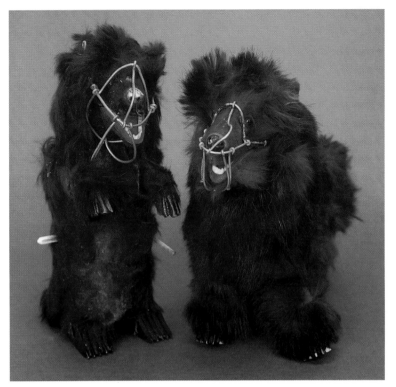

COLOUR PLATE 1
Décamps specialised in making interesting automata, such as this pair of clockwork bears that walk, turn their heads and open and close their mouths. The brass muzzles are particularly well made. They have glass eyes and the bodies are carton covered with rabbit skin fur. One stands on his hind legs, the other is on all fours. The mechanical imitation of walking is particularly difficult, because of the problems of balance. Standing bear 8in. (20.3cm) tall, bear on all fours 7½in. (19cm) tall. *Courtesy Constance King Antiques*

PLATE 1
Because bears can perform almost any human movements, they made ideal subjects for Victorian children's books. *Courtesy Jane Vandell Associates*

The Bear.

*H*E came from beyond the Equator,
And I'm certain that, sooner or later,
If he studies with care,
Though he's only a Bear,
He'll become a most
excellent waiter!

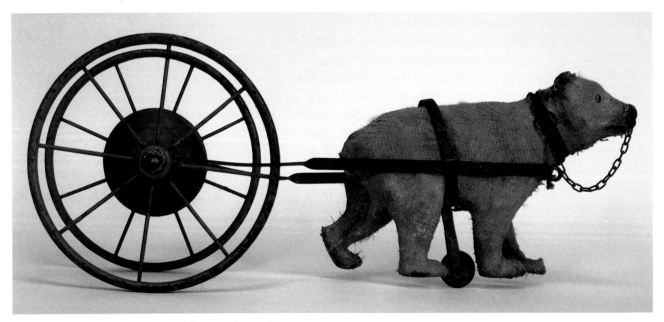

COLOUR PLATE 2
Bell toys were made in Germany, mainly for sale in America, where they were most popular. This fabric-covered carton version has glass eyes and a sealing wax nose. c.1885. Length 13in. (33cm).
Author

COLOUR PLATE 3
"Beauty and the Beast" from Father Tuck's "Plays in Fairyland". What princess could resist the handsome bear… Published by Raphael Tuck c.1905 and printed in Germany. *Author*

excuse for their loss of virginity.

Beauty and the Beast, the fairy tale with its roots firmly embedded in such traditions, has always held great appeal for children, who ignore the symbolism but savour the fear of the maiden and the loving, persuasive enthusiasm of the big, gruff animal. Perhaps because children are surrounded in books and films by images of animals, they invariably identify and sympathise with the furry-faced bear, who has to disappear before the milksop Prince can take over and marry the heroine.

Female bears come into season only once in every three years and drive away the much larger males at other times. In the summer months, when food is plentiful, the males often congregate in small packs and romp together playfully. While the males will sometimes fight ferociously, they rarely damage each other and the battles seem to be more ritual than reality. Though superstitions relate that families of bears live romantically in dens, only the sow and the cubs are together. Reflecting this fact, the collective noun, "a sloth of bears" is first discovered in a fourteenth century manuscript, describing a group of males, referred to as "a sloath of beeryes".

COLOUR PLATE 4
The Three Bears from "Father Tuck's Nursery Series. No. 1475. Published in 1895, Designed in England. Printed in Bavaria". The bears are costumed and behave as humans.   *Author*

COLOUR PLATE 5
The happy family of Three Bears, all smartly dressed and ready for their walk while their porridge cools. Raphael Tuck, c.1898.   *Author*

The perceived fierceness of bears resulted in the name being linked to the bravest men of battle and legend, such as King Arthur, whose name is derived from the Latin *Arcturus*, or Bear Guardian, while his Breton counterpart, who apparently undertook similar exploits, is named Arxur, the Breton word for a bear.

Because bears appear in so many guises in folklore and fairy tales, they have an ancient and well-established presence in the nursery. Early block-printed children's books show illustrations of wild bears, while the animal was also represented as a toy. In the eighteenth century, children were expected to show a serious, almost scientific interest in animals and they were instructed on the habitats of the various types of bears, their behaviour patterns and eating habits. This instructive approach continued into the early part of the nineteenth century but, as attitudes to children and their upbringing became less knowledge-driven, the anthropomorphic qualities of the bear were accentuated and it became less of a wild animal than an engaging and almost pet-like curiosity.

The various editions of the *Three Bears* nursery story reveal how attitudes to animals changed in the nursery between 1830 and 1900. In the 1831 version, written and illustrated by Eleanor Mure and in the 1837 Robert Southey book, the story is about wild bears whose life is disrupted by an intruder. By 1869, when "Picture Books for Small

Children", illustrated by Harrison Weir, were published, the still very realistically drawn wild bears are seen to have developed a few clothes, such as a jacket and a cloak. Despite these additions, the bears are still obviously animals, though already beginning to attract the whimsy that was to characterise many Victorian prints and advertisements that included animals. When Dean and Son of Fleet Street, London, published their untearable shaped book *The Three Bears* in the 1890s, it was common for all the animals to be anthropomorphic and wear smart, contemporary clothes, as well as lorgnettes and pince-nez.

Goldilocks and the Three Bears became one of the most popular of all children's stories, though she was a comparatively late arrival and evolved from "Silverhair" of earlier versions. The drawing of the bears represents them virtually as soft toys, with attractive, soft yellow fur and large gentle paws. Though a little girl enters their life, children see her not as a human like themselves but as an intruder into the bears' home, with its neat furniture, curtains and crockery. The story, like *Beauty and the Beast*, is a gift for psychiatrists and educationalists and has provided most adults with a perception of animals that we carry into adult life.

Late nineteenth century advertisements drew heavily on associations with animals, particularly bears, to market everything from corsets to breakfast foods, coffee and pianos. The bears were usually costumed, but were much more realistic than those seen in children's books and they work, play and eat just like humans. These advertisements are now eagerly collected by Teddy Bear enthusiasts, as are

COLOUR PLATE 7
A guide sheet from "The Three Bears" jigsaw, published by
Ernest Nister c.1895.   *Author*

COLOUR PLATE 8
By the 1890s, toy makers were producing simpler jigsaw pieces
that children could assemble easily. The Three Bears story is still
popular today.
                                                         Author

picture blocks and books of the Goldilocks story. Most enthusiasts merge bear and
Teddy Bear collecting together and include virtually anything ursine in their sphere
of interest. When collections, such as that of Colonel Henderson of Good Bears of
the World, come on the market, they are often characterised by a very wide
assortment of bear-related items, from silver charms to bear furniture.

Because images of bears were so often incorporated into family crests and coats-
of-arms and have strong links with cities, such as Berne, Warwick and Berlin, they
have always inspired gold and silversmiths. In the sixteenth and seventeenth
centuries, European craftsmen were making exquisite cast and chased models that
were sometimes embellished with precious and semi-precious stones, or decorated
with enamelling. This tradition has continued to the present, though today many
of the expensive gift items have taken the form of the Teddy rather than the wild
bear and have bows around the neck.

Even in the Middle Ages, bears were occasionally costumed like people and in
Berne two fierce bears in tunics, one carrying a stick and the other a drum, are used
on a clock jack in the Zytglogge, in a tower that originally guarded the town. The
parade of bears on the Berne city clock, installed in 1530, circle on a turntable at
the hour, some walking, some on all fours and others even riding horses,
demonstrating that, from the earliest times, bears have been anthropomorphised by

COLOUR PLATE 9
A good quality bronzed metal inkwell and penholder, made c.1860. The bear has glass eyes and
the head hinges to give access to the ink. The top of the tree lifts off so the pen can be concealed.
Probably German. Height 3in. (7.6cm).
                                        Courtesy A. Nethercott Antiques, Bath

COLOUR PLATE 10
Bear cubs at play provide a beguiling subject for woodcarvers.
This plaque was made in Canada as a souvenir piece, c.1910.
Marked on the right with a "K.P." monogram. Length 10in.
(25.4cm). *Courtesy Constance King Antiques*

COLOUR PLATE 11
Desk accessories for men were often made in bear form in the
Victorian period. This realistic spelter version was intended for
matches and spills. Probably English. *Courtesy Constance King Antiques*

craftsmen and artists.

Perhaps because of the interest in game hunting and travel, there was a sudden
fashion for bears among goldsmiths and silversmiths in the 1870s and hallmarked
English novelty pieces were produced by firms such as Robert Hennel and J.
Aldwinkle & Slater. Cruet sets were especial favourites, as the shape of a well-fed
bear, sitting on his hind quarters, made an ideal container. A collar usually neatened
the neck, where it unscrewed for filling. Virtually identical model bears were made
by various companies and are now highly regarded. The current enthusiasm for all
types of silver novelty items, such as inkstands, has made pieces of
this type very expensive and it one of the few areas where bear-
related items sell for higher prices outside the Teddy Bear world.
Among the most prestigious work, and probably made as a
presentation item, was a table lighter with a horn base, in the form
of a bear pit with silver railings, made in 1879 by William
Thornhill.

A vast range of silver and plate items related to bears was
produced after 1900 and there is an especially tempting range of
rattles and teething rings. Many of these are now reproduced, but
the originals are, fortunately, hallmarked. Pre-1900 designs
represent wild bears but once Teddies became popular, a more
chubby, soft toy image was used. In the Edwardian period, the
whole family was offered items embellished with bears: for the
men, seals, cigarette holders, vesta cases and stock pins; for ladies,
buttons, scent bottles and brooches; for children, bear handled

COLOUR PLATE 12
Bronze metal book ends with seated bears were popular long before the first
Teddy Bear appeared and were made in most countries. This pair carried the
British manufacturer's marks c.1885. *Courtesy Jane Vandell Associates*

PLATE 2
Large toy bears were available in the mid-nineteenth century, alongside elephants and lions. From *The London Toy Warehouse* published by Dean's. 1845. *Author*

cutlery, money boxes and mugs. Such a great assortment of pieces has meant that collectors can specialise in silver toys, especially those by known makers. Unmarked Continental silver pieces of lower grade metal depend more on quality, humour and subject matter for their value, though the range of objects is equally wide.

Toy and model bears were available in the toyshops in the eighteenth century and an itinerant showman with his chained bear is found in Princess Augusta Dorothea's miniature town, known as "Mon Plaisir", constructed between 1704 and 1751. The first substantial commercial production of toy bears began in Germany in the 1820s. The figures were either traditionally carved or modelled in papier mâché or composition substances. Smaller versions, such as might have inhabited Noah's Arks, can still be found, but larger pieces are harder to locate, as they were so fragile. Fortunately, their development can be traced through drawings and illustrations in toy merchants' catalogues that are proven to have been surprisingly accurate. Though the toys were constructed individually by homeworkers, they were collected together, painted and sometimes varnished by merchants, whose agents travelled the world with samples and catalogues. Today, one is as likely to find these German toys in America as in Europe.

Soft toys were the simplest playthings to produce at home and are recorded from Roman times, but as they were so fragile, few have survived, even from the eighteenth century, unless they were in a Baby House or some type of tableau. Queen Victoria, in the early years of the nineteenth century, owned a fabric elephant with a back cloth, among several other soft toys, and it is highly probable that some bears were produced at the time, though serious commercial manufacture did not begin until the last quarter of the nineteenth century, notably with Margarete Steiff in Germany and Farnell and William Terry in England. By 1890, most of the materials that were to be utilized in the manufacture of the first bears were available, including felt and artificial silk, with wood wool and kapok for filling.

COLOUR PLATE 13
A well carved German-made bear on a stick, a form of scissor toy, where the bear performs amusing antics. c.1885. *Author*

COLOUR PLATE 14
Caged bears were familiar to many children who visited the zoos and menageries that had become so popular in the second half of the nineteenth century. This fur-covered composition bear with glass eyes was made in Germany. His wood and metal cage is back opening. c.1900. 5¼in. (13.3cm). *Courtesy Constance King Antiques*

Simple mechanical bears were early arrivals in the nursery and an 1831 sample book illustrates a standing bear on a round turntable, activated by a crank mechanism. His tamer stands near him, dressed in a long green coat trimmed with fur, a conical hat and high boots. Brown bears were the easiest to train and they were used by itinerant showmen. European children, even those living in small villages, were familiar with these animals, which had travelled from Russia with their trainers and the clothes of these showmen were mirrored by the toymakers. Some form of Russian dress was used for bear-keepers until the beginning of the twentieth century, though a turban sometimes replaced the fur-trimmed conical hat in the later versions. After the Crimean War, all resemblances to Russians disappeared and, at the end of the nineteenth century, the tamers wore a form of Hungarian costume to avoid antagonising their audiences.

In early toys, the bear is restrained and controlled by a cruel ring through the nose but, by the 1860s, this is replaced by a halter of some kind. Toy bears are found with both nose rings and muzzles, though they do not help in dating toys as the manufacturers seem to have chosen the method that looked most effective on the individual model. Unlike children of today, who would be horrified at seeing an animal restrained in this way, Victorians tolerated what we would perceive as barbaric treatment of animals with equanimity.

Some of the more complex German-made toys show bears and trainers on turntables, accompanied by musicians who beat drums, by means of a simple lever mechanism, while the complete model was pulled along on a wheeled base. Brown bears were trained to "dance" when music was played and any performing bear, no matter how old and mangy, soon attracted a crowd. While stories of the cruelty that could be involved in training abound, there are other tales that recount the devotion of bears to their masters. Our appreciation of wildlife today is so completely different that it is hard to comprehend the appeal of such subjugated creatures, but within the context of eighteenth and nineteenth century daily life, with its High Street slaughterhouses, ill-treated horses and starving dogs, the performing bears provided an amusing interlude for people of all ages, who had none of the respect felt today for a wild animal's dignity.

COLOUR PLATE 15
To complete any writing table or desk: a carved bear's head, hinged at the back of the neck. When opened, there are two compartments for postage stamps. Early versions, such as this, exhibit a high standard of carving. Swiss, c.1885. *Author*

The Thuringian firm of Eduard Cramer of Schalkau was established in 1896 and produced a range of mechanical bears, the musical movement of which was activated when the bear's head was moved backwards and forwards. In America, amusing tin "Dancing" bears, usually under four inches high, were made by firms such as Hull and Stafford and Bergmann. Though the models were realistic, their only movement was provided by the wheeled base. Celluloid, which was much easier to mould, had been invented in the USA by John and Isaiah Hyatt c.1869-70, but it was only gradually introduced as a toymaking medium, though by the turn of the century, there were amusing, but fragile, bears for cake decoration and the nursery.

While mechanical bears were the most expensive toys, there was also a whole variety of carved specimens. In the area of the Gröden valley, unvarnished pine bears, with the fur defined by a few skilled chisel cuts, were sold either singly or with other animals as part of a boxed set for a menagerie. Private zoos had been fashionable among the nobility from the eighteenth century but it was in the Victorian period that a visit to the Zoological Gardens became a feature of childhood. As children in towns became familiar with wild animals, the toymakers provided lions, tigers and bears for the nursery. Because of the presence of zoos in most towns, children came to love the antics of the bears and succumbed to the great appeal of the frolicking cubs. "A Visit to the Zoo" became one of the most popular themes for the brightly coloured books and picture blocks that were flooding the market by the 1880s because of improvements in cheap lithography. The attractive, rich shades used by the makers, often using up to sixteen colours in the printing process, make these late Victorian toys ideal as background items in bear displays, though they are of course increasingly collected in their own sphere as printed toys.

Scrap books were extremely popular before the First World War, especially at Christmas, and these could be filled with the embossed reliefs that, like books and bricks, had blossomed into glorious colour. In the 1850s, the cutting dies became so advanced that factory production made coloured scraps available to the masses and this, together with the new, steam-driven lithographic presses combined, in the 1860s, to create a substantial, almost exclusively German industry. Known as chromos, these attractive cut and embossed pieces could be used to decorate anything from cakes to glove boxes and greetings cards. At first bears in their natural habitat were featured but, by the 1890s, partly or fully costumed wild bears had become the favourites, as they held much more appeal for children. It was only a short step from considering the bear as a person to converting it into a doll-like soft toy.

Even the word "Teddy" is found to have been occasionally used for bears before the advent of the first cuddly toy and in a book written by Anna Maria Ross, published in 1901, a bear in a zoo has the name. Much more widely known, however, was the true story recounted by Gustav Schröder in an 1899 book. Schröder was a well-known hunter, who both killed bears and regarded the species with affection. He told

COLOUR PLATE 16
German printers of scraps or "chromos" frequently took over other factories and imitated the designs of competitors, making it extremely difficult to attribute unmarked examples. This little waiter, wearing a top hat, comes from a late Victorian scrap book. *Author*

COLOUR PLATE 17
A page from a child's Christmas scrap book, inscribed "Gilbert L. Bridgeland from his loving Mother. 1882". In this set of chromos, the little girl is still called "Silverlocks".   *Author*

of a female bear being taken from the wild in 1865 that he called "Teddy". He described her affectionate play and mischievous escapades in his household, where she was regarded as a pet until she became too large and difficult to handle.

That the presence of a chained bear was a common sight in European daily life is evidenced by the number that were included in the model towns and markets that were carved in South Germany and widely exported. These boxed toys provide faithful vignettes of contemporary life, with the sellers and their customers in busy scenes that are depicted with convincing accuracy. The bears either walk behind

COLOUR PLATE 18
Elastolin created a wide range of wild bears and their cubs in many sizes. The smallest cubs are often unmarked. Height 2in. (5.1cm). The metal bear was made by William Britain and is marked "Br 1". *Author*

COLOUR PLATE 19
Fur-covered drinking bears were a speciality of the French firm Décamps. This example has electric bulb eyes that light up and wooden paws. The clockwork mechanism causes him to lift the decanter and pour liquid into the tumbler, which he then raises to his mouth. The liquid returns to the decanter through a tube inside the body. This example dates to the 1920s but similar models were made in the nineteenth century. 14in. (35.6cm). *Courtesy Constance King Antiques*

their masters, or are standing ready to dance for the clustering townspeople. The bear tamers, always carrying long sticks, also earned a living as showmen at fairs and, rather like the itinerant Punch and Judy men, gave performances wherever they could attract a small crowd on a village green. In one sixteenth century woodcut, a pair of bears is shown with a handler who is accompanied by two musicians. The bears were controlled by a rope that passed through the the rings in their noses.

Because the subjugation of any animal as large and supposedly fierce as a bear has always aroused awe, they were sometimes kept virtually as pets in ancient Rome and have a long tradition of being princely gifts among noblemen. When, in the eighteenth century, it became fashionable to have a small menagerie or at least a few unusual animals on country estates, the bear was again favourite, because the cubs were so friendly and appealing. This long interest engendered a manufacture of decorative and gift type bears in earthenware, metal and wood, while the advent of the zoological gardens that were open to the general public inspired a spate of related games and toys.

The advent of menageries and zoos did slowly change the public perception of animals and gradually kinder methods of management evolved. Some bears kept in captivity lived to a great age, one in the Bear garden in Berne living to the age of forty-seven. In model menageries, the bears always walk on all fours, and while they are caged, they are no longer forced to parody human behaviour or chained through the nose. In early models of zoological gardens, the bears are usually carved and painted in fine detail, while the buildings have a whimsical style. By the 1860s, composition substances were gradually replacing wood and the toys were more frequently made in the small factories around Sonneberg. Some of the composition

PLATE 3
Composition polar bears and their cubs. The more crudely modelled parents date to the 1930s, but similar models were produced over a long period.
Courtesy David Hawkins

animals were very finely made, though they are fragile. In some instances, wire armatures were used for added strength, but they have often rusted and caused the figures to split. Any pre-1900 bears of this type are of interest, though there is obviously a premium on any in fine condition.

In an attempt to create a much stronger composition figure, the firm of Hausser, founded in Stuttgart, developed a substance later patented as Elastolin. Though mainly associated with military figures, this firm included a charming range of bears that was mainly intended for use in zoos and arks. The brown bears, cleverly modelled and with realistic humps on their backs, were made in several sizes and there were charming cubs, so that groups and small scenes could be assembled. Some of the cubs lie and play in different positions, which gives a most attractive effect. While polar bears could also be purchased, these were not made in as many poses.

O. & M. Hausser had previously traded as Müller and Freyer, a firm that had made composition-type dolls in the nineteenth century. Seeing the possibilities of toy figures constructed of this material, they made animals in two part moulds with wire strengtheners embedded in the substance. The figures were heated after assembly and finally painted. The bears made by the firm can be recognised, as they are marked "Elastolin", though other firms made similar figures. Although the trade name was used before the First World War, it was not fully registered until 1926. The figures were much improved after 1925, when the Austrian firm, Pfeiffer, which made "Tipple Topple", was taken over. Pfeiffer had developed a much finer formula that enabled them to make models with greater strength but relative lightness. Unlike many other factories, the later models are often better than the early products.

Some of the Elastolin figures are up to a foot high, though most of the bears are in smaller sizes, that makes them especially suitable for cabinet displays. At first glance, they resemble wood: because of their dark colour and because they mix well with the carved "Black Forest" products, they tend to be bought by the same group of collectors. Other firms, particularly in France, made bears in composition substances, and the current value depends on the appeal of the pose and, obviously, on condition.

Some bear enthusiasts include a few early fur covered mechanical versions in their collections. The earliest examples seem to date to the last quarter of the nineteenth century, though it is probable that earlier versions, obviously prey to moths and vermin, have been lost. One of the most popular subjects was the drinking bear, who tips the contents of a bottle into a cup that is then lifted to the mouth. A tube ran through the body of the bear, passing the liquid from the cup back to the bottle, a method that has frequently caused parts of the mechanism to rust. These drinking bears were made in both France and Germany and have a carton body with metal moving parts and carved wooden noses, jaws and paws. They are rarely marked in any way, though later versions are sometimes stamped France or Germany and the metal bottles they carry are frequently found to be German.

Smaller, fur covered mechanical bears are found in walking and dancing versions and are usually black or dark brown with glass eyes and wooden feet. They have either a collar, a muzzle or a ring through the nose and are key-wound. The carton bodies, with metal clockwork mechanisms, were covered with rabbit fur. Lording it over all other makers of fur-covered bears in the second half of the nineteenth century was the French firm of Roullet et Décamps, founded in 1867 by Jean Roullet (born 1829). The beguiling variety of bears, some completely realistic, others anthropomorphised, was created in an old Paris mansion at 10 parc Royal. The most expensive figures were automated and stood on bases that contained

COLOUR PLATE 20
Victorian children must have screamed with happy horror at this fierce jumping bear, made of carved wood. He carries a board in his paw reading "Gesetzlich Geschützt". Stamped on the reverse is a Swiss cross and another registered design mark. Swiss made, c.1895. Height 16½in. (41.9cm).   *Author*

musical movements, often of Swiss origin. Occasionally, the movement was secreted within the torso of the animal itself.

Automata are invariably among the most expensive adult toys and were intended to be displayed in the drawing room or parlour. Other leading French makers, such as Lambert or Bontems, seem to have had no interest in bears, so any that appear on the market are attributed to Roullet et Décamps. Some of the finest animal automata were designed by Gaston Décamps (born 1882), whose artistic training, in combination with a period spent as a pupil of the animal sculptor Frémiet, enabled him to translate his study of animals into realistic figures.

Roullet et Décamps produced fur-covered animals for a very long period, though few seem to date after 1940. The 1878 catalogue revealed the work of an already well established firm with an assortment of automata that had gradually been introduced. The first mechanical toy made by the firm was a gardener pushing a barrow, and it is thought that this model was made at the original small workshop set up in 1866 at rue des Quatre Fils. Roullet's son-in-law and his grandson, Gaston Décamps, were all involved in the family business that, in the twentieth century, was to become primarily associated with splendid electrically-operated window and exhibition tableaux and figures.

The 1878 catalogue reveals the mechanical skill that was one of the main strengths of the firm and their ingenuity in adapting basic structures to create completely different animals and scenes: what is available as a bear is also seen as a cat or a monkey. The cheapest figures are more in the nature of clockwork toys, standing under ten inches high, and are key wound. Usually brown in colour, they have carved wooden paws and faces and glass eyes. Various models can be found, though they are now frequently inoperative. They can either walk upright or turn somersaults. A more expensive bear walked on wheels concealed beneath its feet and turned its head from side to side, and was made in three sizes, from 20-32cm. All these toy bears have characteristic fierce faces, with sharp, rather unbear-like white teeth and long red tongues. They seem to have been designed to frighten children, rather like the wolf in Red Riding Hood. One toy model, 23cm tall, has a curious long tail, rather like a dog or rabbit, walks on its hind legs and wears a collar. This range of toy bears seems to have been made in an attempt to offer products to all sections of the market, and, judging by the number that are still available, the line must have been very successful.

Perhaps the finest model was the Clown and Dancing Bear automaton. The two performers stand on a rectangular base that contains the musical movement. The bear turns its head and dances, while the clown strikes a drum and plays the cymbals, a prestige item that originally cost 130 fr., as against a simple toy mechanical bear that sold for 10 fr. Another expensive automaton was the musical bear holding a box, that opens to reveal the head of a monkey.

"Ours Sentinelle" is one of the most charming automata and is rarely found, even though it was much cheaper than the Clown and Bear. A sentry stands in his box, while a bear sits under a tree. The roof of the sentry box is raised and the soldier turns towards the bear and pokes out his tongue. The bear drops on all fours, rises on his hind legs again and turns to stare at the sentry.

Being such a popular circus act, the Bear on a Tricycle was an obvious subject for

COLOUR PLATE 21
Made principally in Switzerland, but popularly referred to as "Black Forest" carving. This well carved, trophy-like bear's head made of lime dates to the late 1880s and has glass eyes. Numbered on the back "2108". 9in. (22.9cm) high, 11in. (27.9cm) wide.

Author

Décamps and there were other toy-like pieces, such as mother bears wheeling their babies in prams, a model that is now more often found in the doll version. Many of the bears, both automata and mechanical, wear a bow of coloured ribbon around the neck, beginning a convention that has continued on Teddies.

A few particularly ferocious specimens were made by Roullet et Décamps, including a mean-looking character that stood 44in. (110cm) tall. This rather heraldic beast, wrapped about in heavy chains, beats a large drum while he opens and closes his mouth, nods and turns his head from side to side, as if looking for customers.

Several other firms in France and Germany produced large, nodding window display bears, though in later models they are sometimes costumed rather than fur-

PLATE 4
A pair of carved Swiss bears, popularly known as "Black Forest" pieces. The seated example is a tobacco jar, with a matchbox holder in one paw and an ashtray in the other. The standing bear is a match and spill holder, with a sandpaper striker on its paw. c.1890.

Courtesy Woolley and Wallis, Salisbury

covered. French makers have always claimed that their original ideas were imitated by German factories that manufactured cheaper models and, at the 1871 Exhibition in London, W. H. Cremer commented on the small, clockwork, fur-covered animals, based on earlier French designs, that were sent from the Sonneberg toy factories. Throughout the century, ideas and mechanisms were pirated by small manufacturers and there was rivalry even among neighbours. In Paris, there were many protests regarding the claims of Fernand Martin, who had opened a factory on the Boulevard de Ménilmontant in 1880, where he made skeleton-like figures with large lead feet, that were dressed to represent street characters. Martin seems to have created such a variety of mechanisms that his competitors became angry with him because of what they perceived as the theft of their inventions. Because the dancing bear was such a feature of life on the streets of Paris, he included a walking model with a chain at its neck, known to collectors as "L'Ours Martin", a toy that was first produced, according to Martin himself, in 1903. Despite the toy's atavistic appearance, it continued in production until 1920, when the business was run by Victor Bonnet et Cie. L'Ours Martin is a very cheaply made product but does have appeal and is now bought by tin toy collectors as well as arctophiles, even though it represents the most economical segment of the mechanical bear market.

No twentieth century bear maker has achieved either the realism or the verve of the individually carved figures that were produced to decorate furniture and ornamental items in the second half of the nineteenth century. Wild bears and cubs, with skilfully carved shaggy fur and fierce teeth in open mouths, clasped the legs of chairs and tables or stood with proudly outstretched forelegs on hall stands. Carved pieces of this type are usually termed "Black Forest", though they were often made in Switzerland. The more complex and improbable the object, the better it is liked by collectors: a chair leg might be hollowed out to resemble a tree-

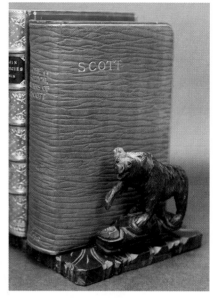

COLOUR PLATE 22
"Black Forest" carved book ends with hinged bears and a sliding extensible base. Though other subjects were carved, bears were the most popular. This was an ideal gift, as the bears folded flat for travelling. Height of bears, 4in. (10.2cm).
Courtesy Constance King Antiques

PLATE 5
An especially decorative group of Swiss carved furniture, made between 1880 and 1910. The hall seat, with its carved foliage, exhibits the highest standard of work. The bear with a raised paw would have held a tray for visiting cards, while the other bear probably supported a bowl. The bench in the foreground was a nursery piece.
Courtesy Lots Road Auction Galleries

COLOUR PLATE 23
A group of carved wooden Berne bears, representing the animal in natural positions. The most detailed carving is seen on the largest animals, which are also the earliest. c.1880-1900.   *Author*

PLATE 6
A fur-covered mechanical polar bear automaton, balancing a ball on its composition nose. The bear swivels at the waist and waves its arms when the musical movement in the base is activated. Ht. 21in. (53.3cm).

Courtesy Jane Vandell Associates

trunk, out of which peers a bear or cub; two bears with outstretched paws support a bench or occasional table. Dark wooden hall settles, such favourites of the Victorians, provided an exciting opportunity for the woodcarvers and their complex backs represent, in low relief, diverting scenes of anthropomorphic bears who play musical instruments, work as woodcutters or gambol among intricately intertwined leaves and fruits. Though the woodcarvers created furniture based on birds, dogs and even people, it is the bear images that now attract most attention.

Bear inspired furniture was principally made by the Trauffer family, who taught at the Brienz school of carving in Switzerland. F. P. Trauffer began to sell smaller pieces in the 1880s, principally to tourists, particularly the Americans, who were visiting the country in ever-increasing numbers and eager to buy what they perceived as "folk art". Most items are unmarked, though a few rare pieces do carry the maker's initials. Soon other carvers imitated the Trauffer work, though every piece was quite distinctive. Late work is often carved from pine, but the finest early examples were made of lime or even the much more expensive walnut. In general, the cheaper the piece, the more thick dark stain, varnish or even paint was applied, as this could be used to disguise joins, splits in the wood or even some mistakes.

Children's furniture, such as musical seats and potty chairs, were constructed, as well as decorative pieces, like brackets, clock cases, smokers' stands, "trophy" wall plaques and jardinières. Though much of the furniture must have been uncomfortable to use, it is coveted by lovers of the whimsical as well as by bear collectors. Many of the pieces that now appear on the market are modern copies, computer carved in the East, though these usually represent the simpler subjects, such as hall stands and the more basic settles. The original nineteenth century versions contain a wealth of incidental detail and often exhibit some breaks and

COLOUR PLATE 24
Combined inkwells and pen stands were popular with early tourists in South Germany and the Swiss Alps. The head is hinged and lifts to reveal the inkwell. c.1890. Height 5¼in. (13.3cm). *Author*

damage, as the fine lattice of leaves and branches around the bear was inevitably fragile. The structures sometimes incorporate other materials and some bears have glass eyes and painted mouths: others look in mirrors or have umbrella holders of metal or ceramics.

While the finest bear furniture was made in Switzerland, it was derived from much earlier toy-type work, made both in Russia and Germany. Craftsmen had made images of bears as souvenirs, toys and ornaments throughout the nineteenth century, most of these being left unpolished and carved in cheap pine. One particular type of souvenir was created to satisfy the tourists who visited Switzerland and these are often referred to as the "Berne bears", though they were sold across Germany and especially in Bavaria. Where the bear stands with, or on a pole, he was almost certainly a Berne or Berlin souvenir. Many of the complex versions have a more masculine appeal, as the range includes racks, tobacco boxes and pen holders. A sumptuous variety of dark, carved items was produced and there are always fresh designs to be discovered. They are usually completely unmarked but some twentieth century pieces carry a country of origin stamp.

Plain pinewood miniature bears and bear families were carved in the Bavarian

PLATE 7
Bear chessmen in brown and white carved wood. Probably Swiss, c.1895.

Courtesy Woolley and Wallis, Salisbury

villages throughout most of the twentieth century and were intended both as toys and souvenirs. Several bears are frequently included in sophisticated settings and some even represent schoolroom scenes, with cubs sitting at rows of desks or playing with toys. Occasionally other materials add to the spectacle, such as paintings, mirrors or even fabric clothes. Bears fishing, hunting, skiing or even saying their prayers are found and these offer the collector an absorbing specialist area. Because of the detail that is packed into such a small space, the structures are often fragile and though many thousands were produced, it is not easy to find perfect specimens.

Russian carved bears are, in general, much cruder and more in the nature of peasant work, obviously intended as robust nursery toys. Simple movements are often incorporated by the use of joints or a length of string and the bears saw wood or move their limbs. The Russian toy woodcarving industry developed around a monastery in Zagorsk, near Moscow, and, by the nineteenth century, a variety of wooden toys, including bears, was being manufactured. Amusing animated toys, known as *khoziaistva,* usually work on the push-pull principal, perhaps the best known of which is the peasant and bear who strike an anvil alternately. By 1900, some carved wooden toys were produced in most parts of Russia and dancing bears were among the most popular exports. These were chip carved and sold in the white and can be differentiated from the Swiss and German bears by their lack of fine detail and their much more primitive appearance. "Jumping Jack" bears in white pinewood have continued in production to the present day and are sold from Russian craft shops, so their dating is largely based on the degree of patination and the string used for articulation. In general, the Russian carved bears are less popular than those originating in Germany, though they will become more collectable as old folk industries disappear.

Almost every type of early bear has remained in production in some form to the present time and completely atavistic designs are offered for sale in gift and toy shops alongside modern versions. It is because of the continuation of tradition, especially in Europe, that the distinction between toy and novelty pieces is not adhered to by collectors, who seem to encompass everything ursine. Specialist displays not infrequently surround mohair bears with carved or moulded images, while a Décamps type automaton makes an impressive centrepiece, even though he

COLOUR PLATE 25
Some of the Berne type bears were intended to hold useful items, such as thimbles or a spool of thread. They are interesting, as the quality of the carving varies considerably. c.1900. *Author*

COLOUR PLATE 26
"The Artist Bear", originally sold as a Berne souvenir, with a painting of the city on his rustic easel. His tools lie on a tree-trunk beside him. c.1900. *Author*

COLOUR PLATE 27
Wooden skiing bears were a popular tourist souvenir of a fashionable holiday in South Germany or the Swiss Alps in the 1890s. *Courtesy Constance King Antiques*

COLOUR PLATE 28
A Russian carved blacksmith and bear helper, who beat alternately on the anvil. Simple but effective mechanical toys of this type were made in several regions. Decorated with carving and pokerwork. c.1910-20. *Author*

was originally intended for an adult rather than a nursery market. The bear has perhaps run full circle and is today designed almost as much for adults as for children; he has become a protected species and is no longer reviled but respected by humans and photographed, protected and studied. When any evidence of his exploitation is revealed, there is a huge public outcry as another link in the fragile structure that maintains the balance of nature is threatened. The captive bear no longer performs for the amusement of humans but is an accusing mirror, reminding us of the fragility of the survival chain for so many species.

CHAPTER 2
A New Toy

Long before the Teddy Bear was born in 1903, images of bears were common in the parlour and nursery. The animal had been portrayed in an upright position in tin, wood and composition, frequently with a frivolous bow around its neck. It was fitted with a growl and had glass eyes. Made of plush as well as fur, bears could talk, push a pram, nurse a baby and live in a decidedly human dwelling fitted with furniture, crockery and neat bed linen. It was only a short step for the bear to roll, hug and somersault into the twentieth century and the modern nursery, where he still reigns supreme.

Through a curious combination of circumstances, the whole subject of bears began to fascinate the public in the first years of the twentieth century. In Germany, toymakers were perfecting manufacturing methods and looking for new and realistic animal designs, while in England and America fresh, more relaxed attitudes to nursery life were encouraging parents to buy children playthings that could be loved and hugged. Toy wild bears would no doubt have pleased many children, but an animal that held some of the attributes of a doll was infinitely more attractive. Probably the catalyst that turned the bear into a Teddy came about because of a curious and otherwise completely insignificant event in American political history.

On 18th November, 1902, Clifford K. Berryman, a well-known political cartoonist, satirized a recent story about President Theodore Roosevelt, who was known to be a great lover of bear hunting. The President, on 14th November, had taken some time off from settling a dispute about the boundary line between Mississippi and Louisiana. Crowds of press photographers and reporters gathered for what was seen as a staged event, at which the President would be photographed

COLOUR PLATE 30
Small bisque figurines were popular gifts in the early 1900s. The white bear sits in his bath and could also have been used in a doll's house. German, unmarked, c.1905. 2½in. (6.4cm) x 1½in. (3.8cm).   *Author*

FACING PAGE: COLOUR PLATE 29
The industrious Steiff working at a German sewing machine has unusual brown boot button eyes and a white metal button in the ear, with the name written in capitals, a type used from 1905.   *Author*

COLOUR PLATE 31
It all began in America with a satirical cartoon in the *Washington Post* in 1902. "Drawing the Line in Mississippi", drawn by Clifford K. Berryman, the leading American political cartoonist of the period. *Courtesy Jane Vandell Associates*

No. 6. The Roosevelt Bears at the County Fair.
" They walked on ropes drawn good and tigh;
And jumped through hoops and landed right."

COLOUR PLATE 32
"The Roosevelt Bears at the Country Fair"
"They walked on ropes drawn good and tight/ And jumped through hoops and landed right."
No. 6 in the series. *Author*

with a bear that he had killed. He was later to grumble that the famous bear hunt was turned into a cross between a picnic and a hunt and that the "comic press" had jumped at his failure to slaughter a single animal.

In an attempt to satisfy the waiting reporters, local guides and hunters went in search of an animal and eventually dragged a small bear cub to the camp, that the President was invited to shoot. Being an astute politician, he immediately saw the indignity of the situation and refused to kill the animal, commenting that he drew the line at such behaviour and would never be able to face his own children again. One Berryman cartoon of the hunt shows the little bear being pulled on a rope along with the press and the presidential entourage. In the more famous version, first published in the *Washington Post* but later used all over America, the President is shown turning away from the bear cub and "Drawing the Line in Mississippi".

In another verbal account of the unhappy hunt, the local guides found an old, lame bear that was dragged, surrounded by dogs, to the President's camp. He instructed them to stop tormenting the animal, and it was later despatched with a knife. Roosevelt, in his *Outdoor Pastimes of an American Hunter*, published in 1905, wrote of his fascination with bears and how he liked to observe their behaviour. Like so many hunters, he had a curious love of his prey and commented on their half-human movements, their giant, awkward strength and "childish" demeanour. He also

No. 11. The Roosevelt Bears at the Boston Public Library.
" They took the books and down they sat,
To read Emerson and the Autocrat."

No. 12. The Roosevelt Bears Take an Auto Ride.
" ' We've broken something,' said TEDDY-G,
' It's underneath, get down and see.' "

COLOUR PLATE 33
"The Roosevelt Bears at the Boston Public Library"
"They took the books and down they sat/ To read
Emerson and the Autocrat." No. 11 in the series. *Author*

COLOUR PLATE 34
"The Roosevelt Bears Take an Auto Ride"
"We've broken something" said Teddy G/ "It's
underneath, get down and see." No. 12 in the series.
Author

observed that bears in different areas seem to have contrasting codes of behaviour.

Though the precise details of the hunting story are lost because of variations in reporting, the incident is of great importance in the history of the Teddy Bear, as it focused attention on the appeal of the animal and aroused some public sympathy for the attractive, almost cartoon-like cub that Berryman had sketched. Teddy Roosevelt and the Bear offered toymakers a range of images that could be used for a wide variety of products, that were given additional lustre by the Presidential association, a link that was cemented when the Democratic Party adopted the bear as a mascot.

President Theodore Roosevelt (1858-1919) was, beyond doubt, the greatest single influence on the development of the Teddy Bear. Though the German-made soft toy had attracted some attention, no great blaze of publicity had burst around the furry creature until it was adopted as a political mascot for the 1904 campaign. There was a widely held belief, on both sides of the Atlantic, that Roosevelt himself was the first Teddy Bear and a postcard, published in 1907, warned that, if he did not stand again, the bear himself would be finished. This interlinking of bear and President in the imagination of the public served as a publicity machine with its own momentum. It would have been hard for Teddy to fail with such an illustrious image.

Linking the President and the bear even more firmly was the series of books written by Seymour Eaton (1859-1916) and first published in 1905. T*he Roosevelt Bears, Their*

Travels and Adventures was most brilliantly and wittily illustrated by V. Floyd Campbell, who accentuated the characters of Teddy B and Teddy G by stylish costumes and impressive gestures and poses. Unfortunately, Campbell died in 1906 and several other artists assumed his established style for the subsequent volumes, *More about the Roosevelt Bears, The Roosevelt Bears Abroad* and *The Bear Detectives* (1908). Seymour Eaton, an ex-schoolteacher, knew how to keep the interest of children, with stories full of action set in interesting places, so they travel the world, visit important buildings, participate in political events, meet King Edward in England or even, rather less satisfactorily, became involved in traditional nursery rhymes.

Though the Roosevelt Bears did not represent teddies as much as wild bears, they were treated in such a beguiling style that these anthropomorphic creatures were pushed to the forefront of fashion. No other bear illustrators matched the panache of Campbell's vision of beautifully attired young gentlemen bears, equipped without thought of cost by leading tailors, sports and academic outfitters. These bears exuded style and wealth and appealed as much to adults as children.

The more sophisticated adult audience was particularly amused by postcards that showed scenes from the four basic books, which were published between 1905 and 1908 by Edward Stern and Co. Postcard collectors now regard the Roosevelt Bear scenes very highly and they are bought avidly in America and Europe. There were four separate series of cards, that also use the work of the later book illustrators F. P. Wrightman, W. K. Sweeney and R. K. Culver. Because of the great increase in travel in the first years of this century, the postcards did much to popularise bears, especially as it was so fashionable to preserve cards in albums.

So popular did the Roosevelt Bears become that their originator, Seymour Eaton, began to be criticised for jumping on the Presidential bandwagon. Obviously stung by the complaints about his success, Eaton maintained that thousands of children enjoyed the stories, for which he was claiming no great literary merit: the tales were simply to fulfil the love of incident and adventure essential to a healthy childhood.

Even Eaton must have been astonished at the enthusiasm his bears engendered in manufacturers of all kinds of novelty items. Teddy B and Teddy G appeared on everything from tin gratuity trays to pocket knife handles and cheap copper brooches. Printed on linen cloth, they could form a cushion cover or be framed as a picture: Stern and Co. offered packs of Roosevelt Bear "Stationery for Little People" with four different scenes and there were even Teddy outfits for both toys and children on sale in 1907.

Nursery pieces, such as milk glass alphabet plates, mugs and candy containers must have enlivened many a nursery meal and were made by several firms, which also produced pressed glass versions. Virtually any Roosevelt Bear related items are hugely collectable, as they appeal to so many spheres of interest, from advertising art to ceramics. Other illustrators soon imitated the anthropomorphic presentation of the Roosevelt Bears and the Cracker Jack series of eighteen slightly undersized postcards shows bears ballooning or shooting the rapids. These sets could be obtained in return for product side-panels and carry a 1907 copyright. One card begs "Mr. Teddy" to drop his gun as the bear cubs clinging to the tree are working for Cracker Jack. Deep in Yellowstone Park, they beseech the President, wearing plus fours, to save them. This

No. 13. The Roosevelt Bears at Harvard.
" These gowns and caps and scrolls you see,
We give you now as your degree."

No. 15. The Roosevelt Bears in New York City
" They spent some days in seeing the town;
Doing Fifth Avenue up and down."

COLOUR PLATE 35
"The Roosevelt bears at Harvard"
"These gowns and caps and scrolls you see
We give you now as your degree."
No 13 in the series.   *Author*

COLOUR PLATE 36
"The Roosevelt bears in New York City"
"They spent some days in seeing the town
Doing Fifth Avenue up and down."
No. 15 in the series.   *Author*

sudden American preoccupation with bears was regarded with some curiosity in Europe and it was, rather primly, felt that such passion reflected the exuberance of a young nation.

The first American soft toy maker to recognise the marketing possibilities of Clifford Berryman's pathetic little bear cub was Morris Michtom, a Russian émigré, who ran a Brooklyn stationery and candy shop. His wife, Rose, who had sometimes made soft toys for sale in their store, created a brown plush bear that was filled with wood-shavings and fitted with boot button eyes. The toy was displayed alongside a copy of "Drawing the Line in Mississippi" and labelled "Teddy's Bear". In the best rags to riches, American dream, fashion, the toy was an instant success, with the great wholesalers, Butler Bros. and Sears Roebuck, placing large orders. Michtom, seeing the advantages of an even closer Presidential association for his new toy, is reputed to have asked for permission to use the name "Teddy's Bear". Though this story is now largely discounted because of the lack of written evidence, it has all the appeal of the entrepreneurial ventures that attracted poor people from all over the world to New York at the time and supplied the history of the Teddy Bear with solid financial roots, as the first little plush animal was to burgeon into the great Ideal Toy and Novelty Company (changed in 1938 to the Ideal Toy Corporation).

Gradually, the apostrophe "s" was dropped and the term Teddy Bear became generally accepted. Soon, dozens of other small factories, especially in New York, began to include bears in their soft toy production, though several were anxious to distance the new toy from its political associations, as sales would have been damaged if its appeal was only to one section of the electorate. By 1906, Teddy Bears were big business in America, with a novelty-hungry public already looking for alternatives to the basic design of the toy.

More softly romantic, but quite simultaneously, a different species was manufactured by a frail, crippled woman, who lived in Germany. Appolonia Margarete Steiff (1847-1909), crippled by polio as an infant, unable to walk and with only partial use of one arm, learned some needlework skills at school, though her difficulty in using her arm meant that she could not produce anything really creative until she was able to afford a sewing machine. She was soon in demand as a seamstress and, despite her physical problems, was obviously a hard-working business woman who, gradually and tenaciously, in old German style, built up a solidly founded family concern. In 1877, she opened her first small factory, where warm felt petticoats and coats were produced. Presumably because of the number of useless offcuts that lay around the clothing factory, Margarete began to make a few simple toys, beginning with an elephant. Many women in the Victorian period made toys from the patterns contained in magazines, but the greater availability of brightly coloured, cheap felt meant that larger and more attractive toys could be constructed. In 1880, Margarete began to sell her elephants and, by 1883, they were mentioned in her felt catalogue, alongside curtains, coats and blankets, all made of the best woollen material, obtained from the United Felt Factory, which was owned by a relative.

Fritz Steiff, Margarete's brother, assisted in the marketing of the toys, and designed armatures of wood and metal to support the larger versions. He was also instrumental in encouraging her to publish her first toy catalogue in 1892. This catalogue, which has been reproduced by Steiff, reveals the considerable skills that were already available to the firm and there is a wide range of dogs, cats, horses and camels mounted on iron wheels. Though some of the original needlewoman-type toys were still made, most were completely sophisticated and very obviously commercially made, with traps, carriages and mail carts supplied by the world famous toymaker Märklin. Business was obviously satisfactory and the company registered its first trademark in 1898.

In 1902, velvet, plush, silk and skin were mentioned in the catalogues and the original fillings, waste felt and lambswool, were completely replaced by more hygienic wood-shavings. The public was advised to look for the elephant trademark to ensure

PLATE 8
The majority of early bears are discovered in a slightly distressed state, as the mohair was both eaten by moth and rubbed away through constant play. This early boot button eyed bear with a Steiff button has, like many others, been re-padded. *Courtesy Constance King Antiques*

good quality.

By 1903, the firm was housed in a factory conceived by Richard Steiff, the modernity of which was commented on even by the American press. The development of the company in the early years is typical of many German manufacturers, where the complete family became involved with the project and the rush of factory construction was, of course, also undertaken by members of the family who were builders.

Soon, members of the Steiff family were working hard at trade exhibitions and travelling overseas to judge the competition and achieve sales. In particular, Franz Steiff was an excellent organizer and established warehouses in Europe, England and America. All the sons of the hard-working family were trained as engineers, artists or builders but several chose to work for Margarete. Though the Teddy Bear story is always linked in public memory with this frail lady, in fact she had little to do with the original designs, that were purely the work of her inventive nephew, Richard. It was he who had conceived the avant-garde factory buildings and he also spent hours at the Stuttgart Zoo, studying animal physiology and behaviour. In the late '90s, he had made a large, traditional, fur-covered wild bear, with a ring in its nose, as a display piece and small, roly-poly, skittle-like, ring-in-the-nose bears were made in burlap at the same time. He was also experimenting with methods of articulating bears with string, which he perfected around 1902, a date he was later to claim as that of the first Teddy Bear, though he also added that it was first called "Teddy" in America. In 1903, a group of bears was included in a New York shipment, but they failed to sell well, because of the cost and weight. These first bears were completely in the idiom of wild animals, with shaggy fur, long forelegs and huge claws. Though splendid, large creatures, they were more suited as shop window display pieces than nursery toys. Fortunately, when bears were shown in the Leipzig Fair in the same year, they caught the attention of a wholesale buyer for Borgfeldt, who ordered 3,000 for the American market. Like Morris Michtom, the beginning of bear manufacture at Steiff is a slightly grey area, though it is an undisputed fact that their bear evolved from the brown mechanical and dancing bears that had already been produced for many years in Europe and mirrored the performing bears seen in the streets and circuses.

Realising that the traditional European brown bear was not going to appeal to American children, Richard changed the design, used lighter plush and improved the articulation. Though the new bear would have been unrecognizable to his ancestors in Stuttgart Zoo, he was an immediate success with children, as he was soft, fluffy, lightweight and cub-like in form, with a fat stomach, boot button eyes and a

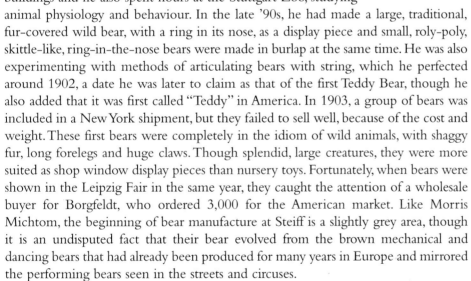

Above. Plate 9
Variations on the basic Richard Steiff design were seen from the earliest period. This button in ear, with felt pads and wood wool stuffing, has a very exaggerated humped back. As with many bears, his original growler was inoperative. He sold for £1,930 in October 1985. Ht. 24½in. (62.2cm).   *Courtesy Sotheby's London*

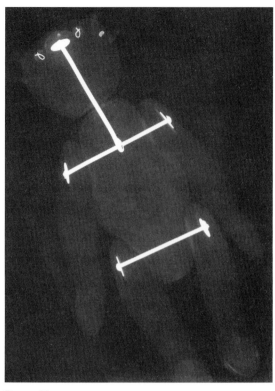

COLOUR PLATE 37
The Steiff rod bear is particularly interesting, as it is the only recorded example still to carry the very scarce elephant button. It has a brown stitched mouth, the remains of a sealing-wax nose and an early style of horizontal seam between the ears, that allowed the animal's head to be stuffed from the top. Ht. 15½in. (39.4cm). Sold for £5,175 in 1997.
Courtesy Sotheby's London

PLATE 10
An X-ray photograph showing the front view of the metal joints in a Steiff "28PB" bear, which carries the rare and early elephant button. Ht. 15½in. (39.4cm).
Courtesy Sotheby's London

shiny, dark, sealing-wax nose. The early bear is characterised by a seam that runs at the top of the head between the ears and it is also thought that this first model was always rod-jointed, so that the animal could stand on all fours. This model was first registered in 1904 and from the following year their famous "button in ear" trademark, with an embossed elephant, was used to promote Steiff toys.

Though the Michtoms at their Brooklyn candy store offer an exciting scenario for the birth of the toy bear, the serious, hard-working German family, with its technically trained young men and good track record in toy production, has the more believable claim. The Steiffs not only had a gradually evolved concept but also well established marketing channels and a fine factory. Nevertheless, the Michtom story obviously has some basis in fact and their history is typical of so many other

FACING PAGE BOTTOM LEFT: PLATE 11
Large Steiff bears of the first period invariably attract international interest. This fine example has boot button eyes and a metal button in the ear. He was made by Steiff c.1905 and has an exaggerated back hump and elongated arms, slightly upturned at the paws. He sold for £1,925 in May 1986. Ht. 30in. (76.2cm). *Courtesy Sotheby's Billingshurst*

FACING PAGE BOTTOM RIGHT: PLATE 12
In this early Steiff with long, slightly upturned arms, the seam of the head can be seen clearly. The "centre seam", made as an economy measure, makes the bear desirable because of its rarity. There is a Steiff button in the ear. The bear sold for £1,380 in 1997. Ht. 19in. (48.3cm).
Courtesy Christie's South Kensington

PLATE 13
Very early Steiffs, with the fur in such superb condition, are rare and command correspondingly high prices. This example, c.1905, is filled with wood wool, has the Steiff button in the ear and the characteristic early boot button eyes. He has tremendous appeal because of his rather wide face. He sold for £3,190 in the 1980s. Ht. 26in. (66cm).
Courtesy Sotheby's Billingshurst

COLOUR PLATE 38
A pair of uncut chromolithographed scraps, made
by Mamelok.   *Courtesy Jane Vandell Associates*

small firms, which were looking for a fresh product for a new century. It was
certainly the Michtoms who popularized the term "Teddy's Bear" as, in Germany,
he was still very much regarded as an animal and known simply as "bear".

Playthings, the American toy trade magazine was in no doubt in 1906 that the
"little old woman in Germany" was the mother of all bears and announced proudly
that "Bruin reigns". The writer went on to ask whether the President of the United
States was not the hero of every boy who would one day be old enough to hold a
gun and shoot bears, just like Teddy Roosevelt. "So Teddy the bears were named
and as Teddy they are now known the length and breadth of our country as well
as on the other side of the Atlantic."

Just why the Teddy Bear aroused such international interest in 1906 is hard to
understand. Obviously the use of a wild bear as a Roosevelt campaign item in 1904
had made things ursine of interest, but this would hardly account for elegant French
ladies in Parisian hotels sitting in restaurants with their bears, or young men carrying
smart bears in the back of their motor cars. Obviously *Playthings* invariably talked up
any new toy craze but the presence of bears as fashion accessories seems to have
been widely established and early photographs sometimes show bears used by adults
as a mascot rather than in a nursery setting. The smart young woman in Central
Park, New York, driving her Columbia electric victoria with her bear sitting
solemnly beside her was not unusual, and it was probably for this young adult market
that special Princeton, Yale and Columbia Teddy dressing jerseys were made. For less
grand customers, dungarees, outfits for the Rough Riders, in which Teddy
Roosevelt came to fame, coats and motoring outfits were available and women's
magazines offered patterns so cheaper versions could be made up at home.

Several printing companies were already manufacturing bears in 1906, including
one firm that produced sheets of heavy muslin lithographed with a 14in. (35.6cm)

standing bear and the printed directions for his assembly. Already, many of the bear jokes that are still used today had appeared, such as "Little Bear Behind", that was seen on postcards and there was a rush of enthusiasm among ceramic makers, eager to print bears on nursery crockery, ribbon plates and novelty pieces for adults, such as hatpin holders and pin boxes. Teddy Bears were already appearing on the side lamps of motor cars: "A touring car without the two brown or white bears, or a brown and a white one is considered quite out of fashion." These bears, made in several sizes, were attached to the lamps at the sides, so they looked as though they were driving. Though some of the bears were in a natural state, others wore appropriate outfits, and their motoring hats with goggles must have proved great favourites with the sporting young drivers.

Though interest in 1906 was considerable, it was as nothing compared with the explosion of energy channelled into Teddy Bear manufacture in 1907. That was truly the Year of the Bear – never again were so many novelties introduced, never again so much public interest and never again sales as high as those seen in this one great year.

The Laughing Roosevelt Bear is one of the most collectable and most engaging of

COLOUR PLATE 40
Early button in ear Steiffs sit well for their portraits. This mohair, with boot button eyes, has the Steiff lettering in capitals with an underlining final F, used from 1905. Ht. 17in. (43.2cm).   *Author*

American Teddies. He was manufactured in 1907 by Columbia Teddy Bear Manufacturers and was made of brown nettle-cloth, which contributes to his atavistic appearance. Early versions have wooden teeth and the old style, boot button eyes. When the bear's stomach was pressed, the mouth opened to reveal the fierce teeth. This New York firm promoted the Laughing Teddy in 1907 as the newest and best stuffed animal toy on the market. By 1908, mohair versions with sharp white glass teeth were made, it was said, to parody Roosevelt's toothy grin as he smiled at his critics.

Though many American Teddies were made of imported mohair, there was a well established industry that supported the lavish upholstery styles that were so popular with the furniture trade. The weavers were delighted with a completely new market to satisfy and were soon producing long pile, richly coloured plush. Salts Textile Manufacturing Co. of New York, created a special line, "Salt's Teddy fur", while, in Philadelphia, J. & J. Dobson produced similar fabrics. Tingue Manufacturing Co., of Seymour, Conn. was said in 1908 to be already the largest manufacturer of bear plush in the country, but at the time they concentrated on cinnamon, white and grey "bearskin cloth". Though fabric was easily obtainable in America, most voice and musical boxes appear to have been imported and this feature was inevitably highlighted as a selling point in advertisements, as was the use of luxurious imported mohair, usually obtained from Britain. While the Americans led in the field of innovation and novelty, they could not rival the classic mohair products of the English North country weavers, which were soft and silky to the touch.

COLOUR PLATE 41
Button in ear Steiffs have an especial appeal, as there is a sensitivity in their construction, reminiscent of much earlier toys. Both have excelsior (wood wool) stuffing and boot button eyes.

Author

COLOUR PLATE 42
A particularly well furred, light coloured Steiff with boot button eyes and a black stitched nose. The torso contains the inoperative voice box. Collectors put a high premium on any bears with such long coats. Originally belonged to the Shackleton family, with which he was photographed c.1905. Ht. 14in. (35.6cm). *Author*

In Germany, eager to satisfy the unexpected demand for the toy he had redesigned, Richard Steiff was making bears with a new, light mixture of kapok and wood wool filling and using cardboard and metal discs for joints. Between 1905 and 1906, the old embossed elephant's head had been superseded by a button marked "Steiff", still used with variations to the present day. The burgeoning demand for bears necessitated more factory space and an even greater number of the homeworkers, that were so much a feature of the German toy industry. In 1907,

PLATE 14
The elegant Shackleton brothers and sisters with their new mascot, a very fashionable Teddy Bear. Photographed in Sandown, Isle of Wight c.1905. *Author*

a stupefying 975,000 bears were produced by Steiff – still an unbroken record. Their white, light or dark brown "Bärle" were to be seen everywhere. Unfortunately, these high order book figures mask a year that was not a financial success. The USA was suffering from one of its periodic short recessions and many orders had to be cancelled and bears sold more cheaply. Even the fabric accounts were difficult for Steiff to pay. Despite the problems of over-ordering by the American market, the bears themselves were a great success and dozens of other, smaller German factories began to produce both their own versions of the Teddy Bear, as well as some virtually identical copies. Alongside great success came the accompanying problems and Steiff was constantly fighting in court to preserve its individual identity, as well as the designs of its artists.

One of the most curious features of Teddy Bear history is the fact that almost every novel idea, every product spin-off and every size and type of animal seems to have been introduced first in 1907. Throughout the century, manufacturers claimed to be producing something special or new, but there was in fact such an explosion of ideas in the early years that real novelty was hard to achieve and, when introduced, was not even liked by the children, who preferred traditional Teddies. Beating hearts, electronic voices and interchangeable heads are not appreciated in a cuddly toy and even today, among all the wizardry of super-toys, the old style bear reigns.

COLOUR PLATE 43
Birmingham silversmiths have always specialised in the manufacture of small novelty type pieces. The Teddy rattle, with a mother of pearl handle, bears the city's hallmark for 1909. It has a bone teething ring. Length 6½in. (16.5cm). *Author*

Though the Teddy is now considered one of the most conservative and traditional of toys, he was at first regarded with suspicion and there were complaints that the mothering instinct in girls was destroyed by their obvious affection for these furry animals. One great advantage of the new toy was its equal appeal to both sexes and advertising and contemporary photographs reveal boys as often as girls playing with the toy. The greatest fear of any father before the First World War was that his son should be unmanly and there were few comforting soft toys for Victorian boys. The advent of the bear coincided with a somewhat gentler approach to children with lighter, attractively decorated nurseries and bedrooms and less rigid schoolroom routines.

Teddy made it possible for boys to carry a comforting furry friend to bed, providing a willing ear for confidences, a broad shoulder to weep on and an unbreakable body that could be hurled around the room in delight, made to assume amusing positions or act as a fierce guardian against things that go bump in the night. More than any other toy, the bear freed boys from the aggressive, somewhat hard attitudes with which they were inculcated and made it acceptable for them to cuddle and caress in a decidedly unmanly way. Sometimes the affection for Teddy was so great that young soldiers during the First World War carried their old childhood friend as a mascot.

The demand for bears by boys and girls was so strong that the fabric manufacturers in America had real problems in keeping up with orders. The situation was exacerbated by a new fashion for Teddy Bear coats, sometimes known as "Northwesterns" or "bearskin coats". These were made of deep pile plush fabric and at one stage the demand for this was so great that it began to affect the furniture industry, which had previously been one of the major customers. The children's coats, available in several colours, including blue and red, were sometimes finished with bears' head buttons. Adults could also follow the fashion and men's motoring coats and ladies' jackets remained on sale into the 1930s made of "genuine" bearskin.

Though manufacturers claim that many of the ideas that have recently come on to the market are new, in fact even Teddy-printed bathrobes and pyjamas were on sale in 1907. Long hat pins with a bear's head at the top made charming gifts for young women, especially those who liked to stroll around the park carrying their Teddy friend. Boyfriends could join in the fun by anchoring their tie or scarf with a gold, silver or gold-plated stick pin. The ultimate affectation must have been to own a bear dressing-up outfit, offered by New York suppliers in all sizes. The world was really going bear mad and enjoying every minute of the new century's heedless, almost flippant disregard for the old conventions that, especially in Britain, had stifled fun in the last years of Victoria's reign. Was not King Edward, that great pleasure lover, now on the throne and was it coincidence or design that was making Teddy the most popular toy?

To write to girlfriends, there were attractive notelets, writing paper and invitation

COLOUR PLATE 44
Stick pins, that were mainly worn by men in their ties or cravats, were produced in silver and gold, as well as base metal. This gilded version was made c.1910. Length 1in. (2.5cm). *Author*

COLOUR PLATE 45
A group of silver-plated teething ring rattles, all of a slightly different design. British, unmarked, c.1908.
Courtesy Constance King Antiques

COLOUR PLATE 46
Painted spelter candlesticks in the form of Teddy Bears were the ultimate night-long comforters for Edwardian children. British, c.1908. Ht. 4½in. (11.4cm). *Author*

cards with as many as ten different illustrations, visiting cards, specially printed pictures on fabric and card, tea caddy spoons topped with a bespectacled bear and bear-shaped autograph albums so the mascots could write one another messages. *Playthings* comments that one New Yorker had her visiting cards cut in the outline of bears and used a glass bear inkstand with a fabric bear pen-wiper to clean off the surplus ink. Obviously any toy sellers were delighted to jump aboard the bear roller-coaster and his outline was used on advertisements, trade cards and promoted heavily in window displays. All the manufacturers produced a few extra-large plush bears for exhibition purposes, though few have survived, and any pieces over 30in. (76.2cm) are now at a considerable premium.

From their first days, infants were introduced to Teddy. His portraits were hung on the nursery wall or constructed as a decorative frieze. Bears sat on the handles of baby feeding spoons and were printed on bibs. To soothe an infant to sleep, brown or white plush musical bears were on offer, in sizes from 10 to 18ins. These early musical bears, with German or Swiss music boxes, were wound at the back and were produced in both Europe and America. Others, with squeeze-type musical movements were a little cheaper but must have held more appeal for very young children, as the movement to activate them is so much more organic. By 1907, the term "bear", or "Bruin", used throughout the nineteenth century in Britain, was almost completely replaced by "Teddy Bear" in Europe and America and already the manufacturers were desperate for new ideas that would put them ahead in a trade where success or failure hung on the most fragile thread.

Electric Bright Eye Teddy, manufactured at first in America, was typical of the novelties that flooded the market, but soon came to grief because the batteries concealed in the torso of the bear often failed even before the toy left the shop. On

19th February, 1907, Bright Eye Teddy Bears were patented by the Fast Black Skirt Company of 109 East 124th Street, New York. The manufacturers, from the first, obviously had many problems with weak batteries and asked buyers to send in orders for daily shipments, as they were likely to fail if kept in stock for many weeks. The bears, of traditional design, had electric bulbs instead of eyes. When the bear's paw was shaken the red or white bulbs lit up. The bears were sold in 15, 18, and 24in. sizes and there was a 36in. (91.4cm) bear that "can be used in an automobile". The dry batteries were placed in the bear's torso, with wires connecting the eyes and the paw. The body seam had to be opened for new batteries to be inserted and this must have proved an unpopular method.

A bear made by the Strauss Manufacturing Co., with a label hanging from its neck reading "I am the Strauss Self Whistling Bear", was another toy that was briefly popular. To appeal to girls, Teddy Dolls, with bisque heads set into the back of the bear's head, were sold in both Britain and America and obviously enjoyed some success, as examples still appear at antiques sales. Musical Teddy Bears were termed "an excellent novelty" in 1907. The bears were first made by Strauss, "The Toy King". The bears themselves were American-made but fitted with German musical boxes, that were wound at the back. They were sold in brown or white plush and were comparatively small, from 10-18in. (26.4-45.7cm) high, and round labels hung from the necks reading "I am the Strauss Musical Teddy".

Climbing aboard the novelty train, Steiff in Germany made a mohair hot water bottle bear, superficially a superb idea for a soft toy that kept a child warm and comfortable at night, yet this clever idea was to fail, perhaps because the process of lacing the hot water holder into the bear's torso each time it was used was simply too time-consuming. The toy shop's failure, of course, becomes a collector's prize and these early 20in. (50.8cm) Steiffs are now top rankers in the salerooms.

In 1907, almost all bears were still fitted with boot button type eyes and, when bulbs that could light up were used, these were of the smallest kind, and consequently the toys still have a distinctly animal-like facial expression. Presumably the makers used button eyes for so long as they were deemed safer than early breakable glass versions, though problems of safety were not often to the fore and dangerous wire armatures, metal handles and sharp pins were all used with careless abandon. There was already a growing concern regarding the stuffing materials used in the factories, as any kind of waste was utilized. From this year, several makers were keen to stress that they only used good excelsior, (the trade name for wood wool) and silken floss as a filler, a line that Steiff had followed much earlier.

One particularly hygiene conscious New York manufacturer advertised the "Antiseptic Bear. A new departure insuring the ultimate cleanliness". White mohair was at the time a surprisingly popular colour, perhaps because, when new, the bears looked so completely fresh and clean. The Ideal Novelty Company was, from the start, at the forefront of bear production and advised its clients that there was no

PLATE 15
An early German-made bear with boot button eyes, a plain metal ear disc, wood wool filling and the original felt pads. The back hump is not as exaggerated in the smaller versions, though the facial detail is attractive because of its delicacy. Ht. 10in. (25.4cm). *Courtesy Constance King Antiques*

COLOUR PLATE 47
Large Steiffs do not come on to the market frequently and attract a high premium, especially if the original owner is known. This fine early example, with the typically long face and elongated, slightly upturned arms, has large "spoon-shaped" pads and the very large feet typical of the first period of manufacture. His original owner was Marjorie (Billy) Webb, born in 1903 in Malvern. c.1905. Ht. 26in.(66cm). Sold for £6,900 in 1997.   *Courtesy Christie's South Kensington*

PLATE 16
Contemporary photographs reveal the variety of Teddy Bears that were available before 1910. Boot button eyed bears were made at this time in America and this example was purchased in Boston around 1906 and was sent as a gift to David Summerton, who holds him, with a monkey, in the photograph.
Courtesy Jessie Harley

need to order toys from Europe when they were available in America at half the price. Already advertising itself as the largest bear manufacturer in the country, Ideal claimed that their bear was "an exact reproduction of the foreign model and made from the finest plush." Presumably firms such as Steiff were concerned at the way their designs were already being reproduced, not just in Germany but right across the world. Though they could make some attempt in the German courts to safeguard their designs, it must have been almost impossible to protect against British and American pirates. Despite Ideal's claims, those bears thought to be early products do not resemble Steiffs but have much longer, rounded bodies and long, out-turned arms. The firm was obviously successful in the manufacture of bears and toys and began the first of its moves to larger premises.

Curiously, though larger bears were given boot button eyes, smaller mechanical versions often have round glass animal eyes, so we have to conclude that it was by choice that the buttons were used. Performing bears made of fur were now sold alongside plush or flock covered versions, though the mechanisms are frequently similar. Some swing between parallel bars and perform stunts, while others hang from rings or balance on ladders. Gillespie of New York offered weighted bear cubs in cinnamon or white that tumbled down slopes. A large brown bear, which played a drum and was clockwork driven, must have attracted much attention whenever he was displayed at trade events. Teddy on a tricycle, with wooden wheels, was another show-stopper, as the bear not only rode along but turned its head from side to side as he went. A black performing bear, standing on its hind legs, was activated by pressing a rubber bulb. Though so many mechanical bears were available before the end of the Year of the Bear, it is surprising how few have survived.

While the soft toy Teddy reigned supreme in the nursery, older children and adults, who regarded bears as mascots, were costuming the animals, possibly as a response to the extremely popular Roosevelt Bear illustrations. Automobile suits, complete with goggles, could be worn when Teddy drove in his specially made motor constructed of wood and metal, yachting suits with sailor caps, smoking

COLOUR PLATE 48
Once Teddies appeared on the market, they were imitated in wire jointed bisque by several German factories. c.1909. Ht. 2¼in. (5.7cm).
Courtesy Constance King Antiques

COLOUR PLATE 49
"Caught Again" – naughty Teddy has been caught in a speed trap by a police bear. Transfer printed porcelain, made in Germany c.1907. 5in. (12.7cm) diameter. *Author*

jackets and dressing gowns for resting bears could be purchased from toy shops and there were even home-made ensembles to be made up from the patterns that were published in magazines. Alongside prams and pullalong horses, toyshops were selling Bruin vehicles that look suspiciously like the old fashioned doll mailcarts, and some more innovative wicker bear cages on wheels, so Teddy could be taken for a walk in the park in his own transporter. Presumably some hopeful maker believed he could make Bruin vehicles the boys' alternative to dolls prams.

"Who would have thought a year or so ago that the year 1907 would start off with such an enormous Teddy Bear bonanza?" wondered a writer in *Playthings* and then went on to describe some of the items pertaining to bears that were available: candy boxes, fur covered poseable bears, rubber and celluloid versions. The wire bears that were fur covered were made especially for use as ornaments and, twisted into amusing positions, could be pinned to lapels or fixed to bags or hats. Bruin was seen on postcards, made as a Jack-in-the-box, as a wooden shoo-fly and there was talk of a Teddy version of the rocking horse. It was also in 1907 that the first mention of the very famous, and now often reproduced, Roosevelt bank is found, where the President shoots at a bear concealed in a tree trunk. Bell toys, jumping Jacks, sets of Goldilocks and the Three Bears and sand buckets for the seaside crowded the toyshop windows across America and Britain. Fortunately, from the start of his life Teddy was available in many sizes and qualities, so that children in all income brackets were able to own him; if plush versions were too expensive, there were paper dressing sets or toys that could be made up at home from blanket fabric, using patterns published in the women's magazines.

Some families combined to save tokens given away with cleaning materials or for magazine subscriptions that were then exchanged for a bear: in this way, children who would otherwise never have owned an expensive Steiff were able to acquire a splendid toy though, it must be confessed, most premium toys were of a modest size and often inferior manufacture.

"Teddy Girl", the most famous early Steiff bear of the first period, is not only large, centre seam and cinnamon coloured, but gains greatly because of a long recorded history and the fame of her original owner, Colonel T.R. Henderson, the most loved figure of the world of bears. Colonel Henderson was born in 1904, just two years after Richard Steiff designed Bär 55PB. When his elder brother Charles was given a cinnamon bear for his birthday, the younger child so coveted the new toy that

PLATE 17
Exceptionally large early Steiffs are much coveted. This well furred, button in ear, with black, boot button eyes was photographed at the Cumberland Hotel Antique Doll and Juvenilia Fair in 1984. He wore a white bow tie to celebrate the 19th event. Ht. 33in. (83.8cm).   *Courtesy Wendy Enever*

ownership was passed to him. Even as a child, Henderson loved playing soldiers and in an early photograph is shown in a child's dressing-up uniform with his bear and his older brother; in another, he teases the Teddy with the tip of his sword. As a young soldier, he was to carry miniature bears around the world with him. Like A. A. Milne, who carried a mascot dog in his pocket for company during the First World War, so Henderson carried a tiny bear in his tunic during the North West European campaign, when he served under General Montgomery.

The Colonel's daughter Cynthia, born in 1942, re-named the bear "Teddy Girl", because it was once dressed for dinner in a frilly frock. Just why bears so fascinate people began to absorb Henderson, who was a firearms expert in the Royal Scots Regiment and this fascination inspired him to launch a British den of Good Bears of the World in the early 1970s. This organisation was begun in order to bring happiness into a sometimes sad and depressing world, by offering patients in hospitals or lonely and infirm people the gift of a Good Bear. Henderson's home in Edinburgh was crammed with Teddy Bears and bear related items that he had purchased or been given as presents. He travelled everywhere with Teddy Girl at his side, though there were more than five hundred other pieces, including rattles, a bear rug and many photographs.

Bear Tracks, the newsletter of Good Bears of the World, kept Henderson in touch with arctophiles across the globe, the organisation having been chartered in Switzerland in 1973 by its founder, J. Ownby, of Ohio. The Colonel kept his family of bears completely divorced from the financial world of collectors and saw them as benign, helpful creatures which brought love and comfort to lonely people, rather than secure financial investments. I used to talk to him in the 1980s, when I was editing a magazine and he was bemused by the escalating values of antique

COLOUR PLATE 50
Colonel Henderson's adored "Teddy Girl", an impressive centre seam cinnamon Steiff, made
c.1904. She is made of thick curly mohair, has a pronounced clipped snout and elongated,
tapering arms. She was the life-long companion of T. R. Henderson and was often
photographed with him. Ht. 18in. (46cm). She sold for the world record price of £110,000 in
1994.   *Courtesy Christie's South Kensington*

bears and always anxious to emphasise that bears were for individuals who had need of them, rather than for rich collectors.

After Colonel Henderson's death in 1990, the collection stayed briefly in Australia before being returned to England by a descendant for auction at Christies. Despite their interesting history, many of the later examples, groups of china and wooden bears, money boxes and related china did not make good prices, perhaps because the bear collectors were holding their money for the star lots, "Boots" and "Teddy Girl". At this highly publicised sale in December 1994, the 23in. (58.4cm) 1912 Steiff "Boots" sold for £1,320, while "Teddy Girl" made an auction-stopping £110,000, as against a pre-sale estimate of £6,000-8,000. She sold to a Japanese museum.

The Henderson collection was historically interesting, as it revealed the taste of one of the first true arctophiles, who was acquiring bears before the sudden and financially led popularity of the field in the 1980s. This was not an exclusive display of the finest and the most expensive but a very human assortment of cheap novelties alongside conservative silver and porcelain.

In 1983, Colonel Henderson, who also had a strong interest in Christian metaphysics, wrote that Teddy Bears open the way towards an inner enlightenment of life, that leads to a fundamentally new step in human consciousness:
"It is this revelation and the Christian spirit behind and within the Good Bears of the World movement and its influence on the waters of human consciousness to which praise should be given, not the Teddy Bear itself, for Teddy is but the symbol representing the functioning of the spirit within one, and this link between the noumenal and phenomenal realms of existence."

Henderson's love of the Teddy Bear of his childhood is not atypical of that experienced by many boys of the same period, who were allowed to play with and love the animal in a manner that would have been frowned on in the 1880s.

The world just came together for Teddy in 1906-07. He was fortunate in having a Teddy on the British throne and in the White House in America and he was lucky that textile manufacturers were making pile fabrics progressively cheaper and more attractive to the touch. Perhaps he gained also from the light-heartedness of the people who crowded the shops, parks and theatres – so many writers comment on the sunny, laughter-filled years in the decade before the horror of the First World War, that we have to accept some truth in their reminiscences. Bears and their antics, whether climbing over a hat or decorating a beer mug, contributed to the joyful, hopeful spirit that characterised the early twentieth century. Ominously perhaps, it was known that in Germany children did not take to Teddy as a pet. Bears were lively toys for free, go-ahead, reckless people like the Americans. That the British took him fervently to heart was probably accidental, as the toy was designed by Richard Steiff primarily for the ever more affluent American trade, upon whose orders success depended but, from the first, this beguiling little anthropomorphic creature had a will of its own and selected its special markets.

COLOUR PLATE 51
Reading about a favourite painter, a large cork granule filled bear, with long snout and cotton pads. Probably English, c.1907 and sitting in a Victorian child's pushchair. Ht. 30in. (76.2cm).
Author

CHAPTER 3
The Edwardian Summer

European shops at first lagged behind the Americans in promotion of the new Teddy Bear but, by 1908, every good department store was including these toys in exhibition pieces and window displays. Wertheim's in Berlin, which was always extravagantly decorated for Christmas, erected a pole crowded with bears and monkeys in the centre of a toy display and drew extra attention with a model of a balloon ascent. Obviously snow scenes were popular for the winter season and the store decorations included white polar bears in the Arctic mountains. In Britain, a report in the new *Toy Trader* magazine commented that shops from Glasgow to London were following the snow scene theme, with large collections of Teddy Bears and other furry and hairy animals. So great was the demand for pile fabric that its cost rose by some thirty percent and top quality mohair was not only scarce but at a considerable premium. Despite the high demand for bears by children, it seems that they were already less popular as fashion accessories and *Playthings* reported that the craze for bears "is dead as far as women carrying them around is concerned".

Though the fickle fashionables had deserted bears, they were still thought of as new in the nursery and London children gazed in awe at William Whitely's windows, where bears of all kinds and in all sorts of poses were displayed. Movement and good articulation were of tremendous interest at this time. Possibly because the first flush of excitement at a new toy had gone and manufacturers were obviously worried that children, like their grown up sisters, might desert the bear, they channelled their energy into mechanisms, novelties and improvements in jointing.

Mechanical tumbling bears, covered in fur fabric or made of celluloid, were activated by turning the arms, while tumbling, weighted performers were sold in several colours

PLATE 18
Cicely and Molly Runnacles with their new Teddy Bears, c.1910. They were photographed at Harrods with their Farnell bears that were purchased for Christmas. Mock snowstorm scenes were a popular novelty. The photograph was kept with the bear to the last years of Molly's life. His twin now lives in Scandinavia. *Author*

FACING PAGE: COLOUR PLATE 52
Runnacles at the seaside. Still enjoying a very active social life, the 1910 Farnell bear has appeared several times on television and at charity events, as well as meeting many antique bear collectors. Ht. 22in. (56cm). *Author*

and sizes. Roullet et Décamps in France was powering some of the larger bears by electricity in 1908, though children were limited to clockwork, weights or pneumatic power for their playthings. The *Toy Trader*, in a feature on new toys, claimed that the bear had lost none of his popularity, the basic toy having been augmented by clockwork versions that were "simply splendid". These figures perform gymnastic feats, turn somersaults and "cause endless amusement to young and old alike". In Germany, Franz Steiff was more concerned with improvements to the natural movement of animals and registered a swivel head mechanism, linking the moving head to the body by means of a very secure rod that ran into the torso, a mechanism that was used on some polar bears that also had leg articulation. From this year, the Steiff button in ear was backed with a fabric label carrying the product number, a label that has changed in colour and text over the years. It was at this period that tilt growlers were offered in Steiff bears, many of these improvements being the work of Franz Steiff, who had worked so hard to promote the expansion of Margarete's business. The firm lost its early, mechanically innovative influence when he died late in the year.

COLOUR PLATE 53
Key-wound clockwork dancing bears were made both in France and Germany and usually have metal, or metal and carton, bodies, with a separate "cover" of thin plush. Published by Gutmann and Gutmann, New York in 1910.

Author

PLATE 19
A fine, early button in ear Steiff, made c.1907, with boot button eyes and elongated feet, together with a later Steiff.

Courtesy Margarete Steiff GmbH

COLOUR PLATE 54
American manufacturers were producing fine mohair bears from the earliest period. This Ideal is unusually large and his golden mohair is in fine condition. He has large, flat button eyes, a pronounced snout and a triangular face. The large, wide-apart ears are typical of Ideal. c.1910. Ht. 28in. (71cm). Sold for £4,600 in 1997.
Courtesy Christie's South Kensington

Because manufacturers were so afraid of the fickle toy market, it was believed that bright colours would help promote bears and keep them in fashion for a few more seasons. The Art Novelty Co. in America offered red, white and blue patriotic bears, while a "Yankee Doodle Bear" was a most extreme design, having a white head with red ears, blue arms and legs and a red, white and blue striped body. Though the manufacture of Teddies was well established, it is notable from advertisements that any over 20in. (50cm) high were considered very large and most, like the tumbling and patriotic versions, were between 8in. (20cm) and 12in. (30cm) tall. The problem of size is made more difficult as Steiff, in the early years, measured their bears in a sitting position. Presumably the manufacture of very large bears was limited because of fabric costs and these were the province of much richer families

PLATE 20
A well furred, good, early Steiff with original felt pads, upturned lower arms and black boot button eyes, made c.1908. He has the Steiff button in the left ear and sold for £950 in 1986.
Courtesy Phillips London.

PLATE 21
The poet and lover of England, John Betjeman, with his beloved bear, Archibald Ormsby-Gore, with his "half moon ears" and "kindly fur" that was so often wetted with his tears.

Courtesy John Murray Ltd.

or used for promotional purposes. One owner of a very splendid large bear was Princess Alice, Duchess of Gloucester (b.1901), who was photographed with him by a sundial at Drumlancraig Castle in 1910. Her bear was made of extravagant long mohair and has the very large feet associated with Steiff. Like many other children of the period, Princess Alice felt lonely and starved of affection and prayed fervently each night for her Teddy Bear to come to life so he could play with her.

Bears became so invested with personality that children believed they were alive and could feel and understand, so they needed to be put to bed at night, dressed for play and even changed into pyjamas to sleep. Patterns for bear costumes were offered in several women's magazines and there was a fashionable bathing suit with ankle length trousers and a matching waistcoat to equip the bear for the summer holidays. A few were sold complete with a suitcase of folded costumes as a "Teddy Bear Traveller". In some families, the bears were dressed in discarded baby or toddler clothes or equipped with home-made outfits, reflecting the continued anthropomorphic attitude.

Archibald Ormsby-Gore, the friend and confidant of Sir John Betjeman, dates from the sun-filled days before the First World War. For Betjeman, the fear of losing the link with his childhood, embodied in the Teddy, was a constant threat. While contact with people might engender feelings of guilt for shortcomings as a husband or son, his bear was always uncritical, ever faithful. Archibald was only known to Betjeman's personal friends until the publication in 1960 of *Summoned by Bells*, his autobiographical poem. The bear had achieved some notoriety when he accompanied his master to Magdalen College in 1925, though he was regarded merely as an affectation of his extrovert owner, and was immortalised by Evelyn Waugh, a contemporary, who renamed him Aloysius in *Brideshead Revisited*. The grave bear, whose embroidered mouth always seemed to say "They'll burn you on Judgement Day", would have felt no surprise when his owner was sent down for failing Divinity. Throughout the subsequent years of film criticism, sacking, architectural reviewing and broadcasting, the Teddy Bear always accompanied his master. Only when Betjeman left the country was Archibald separated from him, as the poet could not countenance some predatory customs official ripping

PLATE 22
Teddy Bears and automobiles forged an early link, as bears made ideal motoring mascots. The blond mohair Bruin on the left has a metal Steiff button and black, boot button eyes. He has the large feet associated with the pre-1914 Steiffs but is unusually chubby. Ht. 18in. (45.7cm).
The cinnamon coloured Steiff, also with a button in ear, was made c.1907 and still retains his long pile fur. Ht. 16½in. (41.9cm). They sold for $1540 each in 1986.

Courtesy Christie's East, New York

AUX GALERIES LAFAYETTE – PARIS

C'est de sa faute, S'il avait acheté ses jouets aux Galeries Lafayette il ne les aurait pas cassés tout de suite –

COLOUR PLATE 55
An elegant French nursery of 1911, decorated in the strong shapes and colours that were liked by the avant-garde. The Teddy, with his printed paws and round, cub-like shape, that did not become popular until the late '20s, is interesting. From a 1911 Christmas Galeries Lafayette toy catalogue. *Author*

him open in search of smuggled goods. When forced to be separated, Betjeman wrote long affectionate letters to his friend, which his secretary was instructed to read aloud.

The poet's dependence developed in early childhood, when at 31 West Hill, in Highgate, London, it was the bear who kept him company in the lonely nursery. Born in 1906, John Betjeman was a child of the pre-combustion engine era and clung, in later life, to the sounds and silences of Edwardian England. Though his childhood was, in general, not unhappy, his frequently confessed insecurity seems to have been rooted in his treatment by a sadistic nurse, who locked him in dark cupboards, smacked him across her knees and threatened him with such humiliations as being bottle fed or put back into nappies. At the tender age of five, she instructed her charge in the horrors of hell and the awful fate that awaited every human being. Only at the end of the day was there dissolution, bed and the kindly fur of "aged, uncomplaining Archibald".

In a poem, "Archibald", published in *Uncollected Poems*, those infant years so full of threats were recalled – his fear of the sound of the nursery latch, the punishments he had to undergo. The only relief was to cry over the bear's forehead and "smooth those half moon ears". The bear in this poem is not the gentle creature portrayed in *Summoned by Bells* and seems also to have been infected by the malice of the

PLATE 23

A selection of good bears that appeared in an English auction in the mid-1980s. The fine early example on the left, with upturned paws, dates from the first Steiff period. He stands 23½in. (59.7cm) and has boot button eyes. He sold for £2,310.

The pale blond bear in a jacket, also with boot button eyes and elongated feet, was made by Steiff c.1910 and measured 13in. (33cm). He made £572.

The traditional German bear on wheels, c.1912, 10½in. (26.7cm) made £418.

The example on the far right, ht. 13in. (33cm), is also Edwardian, though possibly English. He made £264. The other two date to the 1920s and made £572 and £154 respectively.

Courtesy Sotheby's Billingshurst

COLOUR PLATE 56
A Faulkner card, designed in England and printed in Germany. Postmarked 1909.   *Author*

nurse, threatening all the horrors of Judgement Day. Fortunately, John Betjeman's parents discovered the true character of the nurse and life became happy again once she was dismissed. Archie accompanied his young owner everywhere, enjoying Cornish holidays and life in the busy London house. When John reached the age of nine, Archibald was hidden away in the loft, as the boy thought his father would consider him childish for sleeping with such a threadbare companion, and only his mother remained aware of his true feelings.

Though some of the darkness of his early childhood lingered throughout adult life, it was Betjeman's exuberant love of places, people and things that made him so popular. He admired buildings, large girls, the sea, curious English characters, the aristocracy and the working classes on holiday. Throughout all his successes and campaigns for the preservation of ancient buildings, the only constant thing "sitting there, patient and hairless, is a bear". Though for Betjeman the bear's presence at

COLOUR PLATE 57
"Blanche", a Steiff button in ear with brown glass eyes and a brown embroidered nose and and mouth. She has cream cloth pads and is wood wool filled. Made c.1910, she was originally owned by a German-Jewish girl, who escaped to Britain in 1939, where she joined the Secret Service, taking Blanche with her on dangerous assignments. After the war, Blanche's owner became a freelance foreign correspondent. She died in 1974 and for a period, the bear was displayed at the Cotswold Teddy Bear Museum, whose contents were dispersed in 1995. Blanche sold for £4,140. Ht. 17in. (43.2cm).
Courtesy Bonham's, Chelsea

Oxford might have begun as an affectation, it is obvious from his writings that this approach faded as he became more aware of his dependence on the creature. There was no mannered affectation in the final lines of "Archibald", when he posed the question of what would happen should some psychologist one day take his old friend away: "Oh, my God, the dreadful void!" One of Betjeman's biographers complained that his prolonged childhood fixation was so self-conscious that it became irritating and almost a pose, in which the poet presented himself as lovable to all men because he was so weak and vulnerable. Lusting mischievously after prefect-like, unattainable girls, shambling across the floors of derelict buildings on television screens, dressed in creased, expensive clothes, writing letters to Archibald – a man of ingenuous enthusiasm or an affected poseur, trading on other people's affection for a creature, who was highly talented but charmingly vulnerable?

For the arctophile, John Betjeman is hallowed without reserve and many own a

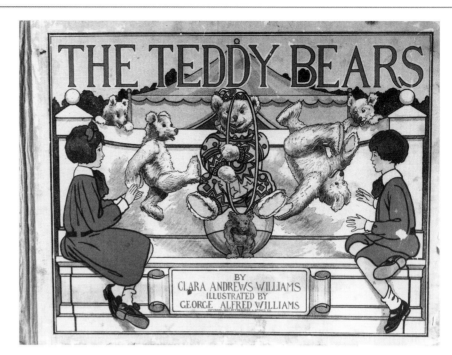

PLATE 24
Teddy clowns and tumblers at play decorate the cover of *The Teddy Bears,* illustrated by George Alfred Williams. Published in 1907 by Frederick and Stokes Co. American, with fourteen colour plates. Sold for £460 in 1997.

Courtesy Christie's South Kensington

copy of the book he wrote in the thirties for his own children, *Archie and the Strict Baptists*, published in 1977 by John Murray and illustrated by Phillida Gili. Archie developed a liking for the five hour Sunday sermons of a strict Baptist church and spent the week recounting each to Jumbo, his friend, in the hope of converting him. Though the basic narrative is light, it is alive with the character of Betjeman himself: his liking for unusual sects, an affection for churches, bells and strange names. It was no accident that Archie was a Strict Baptist, as he closely resembles the character as portrayed in "Archibald", who was so obsessed by the threats of hell and the fires of Judgement Day, the philosophy of the dreadful nursery nurse of infancy. Like his master, Archie liked long dreary sermons of the type he walked miles to hear in Cornwall or London. That those heard by Betjeman were Anglo-Catholic and those in the chapel Baptist made little difference, as it was the curiosities and the trappings of Christianity that always intrigued. Few bears of this period have as long and exhaustive a history as Archibald, whose presence at Magdalen in the 1920s among such talented intellectuals provided successive generations of students with an elegant precedent.

Toy manufacturers soon became aware that children believed the bears lived and felt human emotions and, perhaps not fully understanding a child's attraction to an animal face, they attempted to bridge the market with Teddy Dolls. Hahn and Amberg in 1908 offered celluloid faced Teddy Dolls in five different colours in their mail order catalogue, as well as bisque headed, sleeping-eyed Teddy Dolls in seven different shades. Multi-faced toys have never been great successes, because they exude an unsettling unpredictability, rather like a menacing Jeckyll and Hyde in a fluffy coat. Because of their failure as nursery toys, few have survived, which now makes them especially attractive to collectors.

The first spate of bears in literature appeared in Britain at this time, with Dean's *The Teddy Bear* and the London magazine *Butterfly* including "Bobby and the Woolly Bears" and "Willy Winks and his Bears". Other character bears soon followed, including the *Tale of Teddy Bright Eyes*, published by Humphrey Milford of London in 1909. This Teddy was such a bad-tempered boy that he was referred to as a

"Regular Little Bear", but was carried off by the Bad Boys' Fairy and turned into a real Teddy Bear. After many adventures, including having to perform as a dancing bear, he promises never again to misbehave and is turned back into a little boy called "Teddy Bright Eyes", confirming a fusing of character between child and bear. It is obvious, even at this early stage in the toy's history, that the anthropomorphic qualities of the Teddy Bear were appreciated by children and it is this element of its design that has contributed most to its longevity. While other soft toys come and go, Teddy Bears survive because real personality lurks under their fur, personality that later writers were to expand into characters like Rupert and Pooh.

By 1910, other literary bears were appearing, with the "Bruin Boys" included in Mee's *Children's Encyclopedia* and *A Bad Little Bear*, published by Henry Frowde. Just before the outbreak of the War, Harry Golding's *Tim Tubby Toes*, illustrated by M. M. Rudge, appeared. All these characters were inspired by the popularity of the new toy, which artists found amusing to draw, as they were hindered by no constraints or established traditions. One of the first Teddy cartoon strips was drawn for *The Family Journal* in 1909 and featured "Teddy the Terror of Jungleville School", a real taste of things ursine that were to come.

The English firms, Farnell's and Dean's, entered the market in 1908 with completely contrasting products. Farnell made good quality, well shaped toys, while Dean's specialized in cheap printed sheets of toys that could be cut out and sewn at home. Because soft toys were inexpensive to produce and could be assembled by

COLOUR PLATE 59
Daisy Miller's life-long friend today, with his loved-away nose and long, typically German arms. Ht. 12in. (30.5cm).

Courtesy Constance King Antiques

unskilled machinists, working in the smallest one-room factories, they were made in great numbers for the bottom end of the market. Wherever there was a sewing machine and a supply of woollen fabric, it was possible for a small bear manufactory to begin. In London, dozens of small firms, frequently operating from a single cellar or attic, sprang up in Clerkenwell and Shoreditch, though it is now virtually impossible to identify their products.

J. K. Farnell, which became the maker of the finest English bears, began operation in a similarly small way in the Notting Hill area of London in 1840, making bazaar type items, such as pen wipers and tea cosies. The founder of the firm, John Kirby, was a silk merchant who, like Margarete Steiff, probably saw the small fancy items as a useful way of using up unsold or remainders of fabrics. By 1877, the Farnell children, Henry and Agnes, were manufacturing fur toys in Acton, using, it is claimed, mainly rabbit skins. No examples of this early work are known, as rabbit is the most fragile of furs and is also soon eaten by moths. It seems unlikely that genuine fur was used exclusively until 1900, as a variety of soft toys was already produced. In 1908, it is recounted, a toy buyer suggested that they should produce Teddy Bears and this is now taken as the starting date for what was to become an important and substantial concern. It was certainly a propitious time for a British

PLATE 25
"Mr. Polly Anna", a white Steiff, originally owned by Norman Dainty, born in 1909, whose parents were tea planters in Colombo, where the bear was purchased at Cargills, a department store. The bear has cream pads and a pronounced clipped snout. Ht. 15in. (38cm). Sold for £2,070 in 1997.
Courtesy Christies South Kensington

PLATE 26
"Little Polly Anna", made by Farnell c.1910 in golden mohair. Originally owned by Norman Dainty. Ht. 8½in. (21.5cm). Sold for £632 in 1997.
Courtesy Christies South Kensington

maker to begin production. Cheap furniture for the more affluent working classes was made in many parts of the country and there was a considerable expansion of building projects. Some of the most useful by-products of all this activity were wood-shavings and sawdust, both of which were used as cheap filling materials by the toy industry. In America, wood-shavings and wood wool were known as Excelsior. Mohair plush and velveteen were both manufactured in Britain, the finest mohair being spun in the Yorkshire mills and sometimes exported to the German toymakers. Growlers and jointing equipment were made in some variety by specialist suppliers, as were glass animal eyes, that Steiff had begun fitting at an extra cost to some bears destined for the English market in 1908. Glass animal eyes had, of course, been used for many other toy animals long before this date but usually where they could be glued in position or sewn, like a button, from a shank.

Dean's Rag Book Company worked at the opposite end of the market to Farnell

PLATE 27
Daisy Miller with her favourite bear that she kept throughout her life, until she died in Saltford in 1992. Her photograph, taken c.1910, was kept in its original silver frame. *Author*

BEAR THIS IN MIND.

PLATE 28
"Bear this in Mind" warns the massively proportioned bear with a curiously structured head and large ears, probably made in England. Postmarked March 22, 1913. He has old-fashioned boot button eyes and his forearms turn upwards in imitation of German designs. The card was printed in England. *Author*

and supplied very cheap toys that could be sold through newsagents and 1d Bazaars. Though the products were inexpensive, Dean's was always a substantial firm and had come into soft toy production through their skill as printers. Dean and Son Ltd. was established in the printing and publishing centre of London in the eighteenth century and included children's picture books in their stock intended to entertain rather than inform. The early books were coloured by hand and by stencils but advances in oil colour printing around 1870 made it possible to produce richly coloured books relatively cheaply. In 1901, the firm began printing directly on to cotton and, to reassure parents that chewing or licking the books would not be harmful, claimed that the colours were both fast and hygienic. The product was marketed as highly suitable for children who "wear their food and eat their clothes".

Printed toys that could be assembled at home had been sold in America for some time, by firms such as Art Fabric Mills, but Dean's was the first to market them energetically in Europe. Dean's Rag Book Co. Ltd., a subsidiary of the old

COLOUR PLATE 60
Shopping on Wind Street, Swansea, this old lady bear struggles home from the market. She has boot button eyes and an exaggerated hump. She was made in Germany c.1909. Ht. 14in. (35.6cm).

Courtesy Constance King Antiques

COLOUR PLATE 61
A button in ear mohair Steiff, with a well shaped, long nose and a humped back. There is a large growler in the body that is inoperative. The googlie doll is by Armand Marseille.

Courtesy Constance King Antiques

publishing company, was founded in 1905 and operated from Paternoster Square in London, with the factory at 2-14 Newington Butts and showrooms in Fleet Street. One of their first toy advertisements in 1908 was for a printed 14in. (35.6cm) Mama Bear, with her children Teddy and Sissy, just 8½in. (21.6cm) tall. The advertising copy took a high patriotic attitude: "The Old Country is Best. You cannot get such enormous value with any toys made in Germany or anywhere else

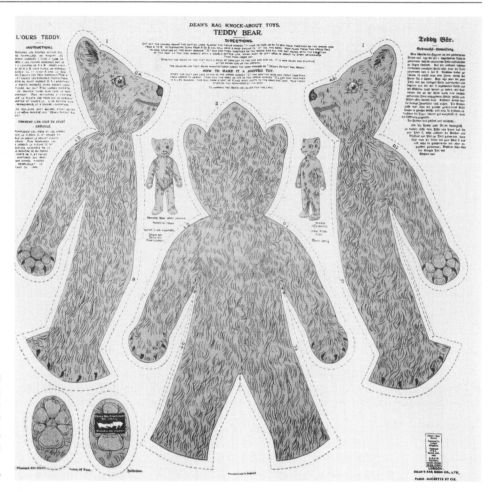
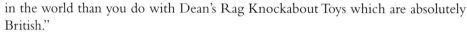

COLOUR PLATE 62
An uncut Dean's Knockabout sheet, with printed instructions for assembly. This design gave added roundness to the easily made Teddy Bears. The printed pads were progressive, as were the two-colour eyes. c.1912.

Courtesy Constance King Antiques

in the world than you do with Dean's Rag Knockabout Toys which are absolutely British."

Despite the decidedly modest and economical appearance of the bears, the self-confidence of Dean's was inspirational: "Dean's Knockabout Sheets are real works of art and make soft toys that cannot be broken, last a lifetime and are produced in artistic colours on a strong cotton cloth by the same process as Dean's Patent Rag Books: the colours are fast, washable and certified by the Institute of Hygiene." The instructions for assembling the Knockabout Sheets were printed in English, French and German. Dean's had printed the first book in two colours on a canvas-like cloth but by 1904 printing was in eight colours on bleached cotton. The early bears were produced by printing the eight colours simultaneously from hand-engraved rollers by a dye process. Dean's famous trade mark, of two dogs tearing at an indestructible book, was designed by Stanley Berkley and registered in 1909. The Knockabout Toy Sheets were manufactured under the 1905 Dean's Rag Book Patent, their title being typical of a firm whose byword was durability.

The financial problems experienced by several companies, when large orders for bears were cancelled in 1907, made them much more cautious about buying large

PLATE 29
"Dody", a dressed bear, made c.1912, with boot button eyes and felt pads. He collects coins for handicapped children at "Dolls in Wonderland" in St. Augustine, Florida. *Courtesy Vera Kramer*

COLOUR PLATE 63
A typically benign, plump, British bear, c.1912, with small round ears, brown glass eyes and a rounded humped back. He has unusually long original beige cotton pads to the front paws. Filled with wood wool. Though his maker is unknown, he is typically British. Ht. 26in. (66cm). *Author*

quantities of mohair plush and production was more restrained. Because of the nervousness of retailers, the huge December demand for Teddy Bears for Christmas was not anticipated and the *Toy and Fancy Goods Trader* commented that "Wholesale houses were quickly cleared out and wires to London only brought the response

COLOUR PLATE 64
"Here's Health, Wealth and Good Fortune". The German bears, wearing uniforms and carrying swords, sit smoking over their Biersteiner. They have short fur and boot button eyes and were made by one of the many German factories. Printed in Germany c.1910. *Author*

COLOUR PLATE 65
Novelty bears with simple squeeze-box mechanisms were produced by several German firms in the Sonneberg area. With boot button eyes and a long nose, this "clap hands", head-turning bear wears a pink cotton costume. The plush mittens are original and sewn into the side seams before assembly. 1920s versions have rounder faces and mohair paws and feet. He has a wire armature and a voice box. Ht. 10in. (25.4cm). *Author*

PLATE 30
Another version of a Sonneberg bear but without movement or the squeeze-box voice. The body is wire and wood, with separate mohair paws and feet and is re-dressed in a blue outfit. Ht. 8½in. (21.6cm). *Courtesy Bonham's, Chelsea*

that the same famine prevailed there". Obviously the widely-held belief that the toy was simply a passing fad was ill-founded and it began to be accepted as a regular player at all the international trade shows.

Steiff in early 1909 exhibited an eye-catching range of large animals at the Leipzig Trade Fair. The most striking feature was a zoo scene, with water chutes, gardens and houses lit by electricity. A snow scene was used for the Polar Bears and dolls dressed in winter sports outfits and here the mechanical tumbling bears could be wound up by visitors. The reporter was obviously impressed by the innovation of animals with "voices", so that the lions roared and the bears growled. Tilt growlers had been introduced in 1908 and Steiff was obviously eager to show off toys with these new voices. In an effort to produce completely natural-looking animals, Franz Steiff in the same year had registered patents for moving ears and ball-jointed swivel heads. The *Toy Trader* reporter went on to comment that "The beauty of Steiff's production lies in the fact that in every instance they get as near as it is possible, and where the living object is parodied this is done in a really clever and amusing, yet dignified, manner". Nearly 3,000 people were now working for the Steiff family but disaster was again looming and just a few months after the death of Franz, Margarete's death was announced on May 9th, 1909 at the age of 62. Where once a single little lady made toys for local children at Giengen am Brenz, thousands of people were associated and toys were exported across the world. Her death was reported as being the result of an operation that led to inflammation of the lungs. Fortunately, as her nephews Paul and Richard were so involved in the business, it continued with no hindrance and was turned into a limited company with a capital of 630,000 marks.

Margarete Steiff's death led to a flurry of improvements and many purchases of new equipment intended to mechanise and improve production. Her heirs were later criticised for being too fond of expensive gadgets and blamed for some temporary financial setbacks. Perhaps she had restrained the expansionist mood of her nephews and kept the business rooted in its family origins. After her death, Steiff had to be considered as a large business concern, rather than the workshop of the old lady of Giengen.

While Steiff reigns among German manufacturers, with the production lines still very active today, it does have several competitors, especially the Hermann family, who began production near Sonneberg around 1907. Various members of the family were associated with the toy industry that dominated this part of Germany: Johann Hermann's six children were all to be involved in the soft toy industry, but his second son had gained invaluable experience when he worked for Ernst Siegel in Neufang. Taking not only toymaking experience, but also his employer's daughter with him as a wife, he started his own firm with a group of close relatives, producing his first bear in 1913.

Johann Hermann Spielwarenfabrik at first marketed the bears in the traditional Sonneberg manner, by using merchants who sold the soft toys to European and American customers by means of trade fairs, catalogues and travelling salesmen. There was the briefest period for production before the 1914-18 war broke up the family group, that had worked from an attic in Johann Hermann's home. After the death of Johann in 1919, Artur moved into the town of Sonneberg and traded as Artur Hermann. Artur perhaps found trade difficult in the years after the war but his brother, Max, continued to make bears in Neufang, establishing his own firm in 1920. Though he at first worked from home, the allure of Sonneberg, with its

COLOUR PLATE 66
"Dear Little Win, Mr. and Mrs Teddy have just arrived to wish you many happy returns on your birthday. Oct. 31, 1909". Caricatures of dressed bears made ideal subjects for greetings cards.
Author

COLOUR PLATE 67
"Teddy's had a quarrel with Little Mistress Bear". Printed in Saxony, the card is postmarked 1911. It shows two completely different types of German bear, both with boot button eyes. The larger is a long-haired shaggy mohair and the smaller a cheap, simply jointed plush fabric. Were the card not dated, the smaller would be thought to date to the 1920s. *Author*

Punch is pleased with the baby.

many trade exhibitions and consortia, was considerable and he too set up business there in 1923, using the trademark "Maheso" with, eventually, a green triangle as a logo. Bernhard Hermann, the eldest son of Johann, founder of the dynasty, was also making bears in Sonneberg, using a round tag as a trademark. The three Hermann factories all produced plush mohair bears, that were much rounder and more cub-

PLATE 31
Teddy Bear "marionettes" in a "T.B." theatre. "Punch is pleased with the baby", which the white bear Judy and he toss between them. The card is postmarked August 19, 1910 and was printed in England for Davidson Bros., London and New York. The bears, both with boot button eyes, are interesting, as the heads are so dissimilar. *Author*

like than Steiff's, though early examples are almost impossible to identify when they are unmarked. The first known bear dates from the 1920s and has the smaller feet associated with a period of much greater economy. For many years, records and trade catalogues of the firm's early period were difficult to access because of the division of Germany and the early history is only slowly emerging, as documents and original catalogues are found.

One of the somewhat anonymous German makers, who came to the forefront of attention because of a legal battle with Steiff, was William Strunz of Nuremberg. A 1904 advertisement shows a standing, ring-in-the-nose bear, with the traditional long pole and long, Steiff-like limbs. It was not so much the similarity of product that upset Steiff but the use by Strunz of a button-in-ear trademark. Even though Strunz used a six-sided metal button, Steiff objected and the smaller firm was forced after 1908 to mark its bears with a fabric label secured by a metal tag. It is impossible to know whether their bear design predated that of Richard Steiff, though their 1904 advertisement proves that they were creating bears from the birth of the toy.

Though the battle for the design of the first bear was, in all probability, won by Steiff, Strunz products so closely mirror Steiff designs that it is almost impossible to believe that this could have been sheer coincidence. They used the boot button eyes, long arms, humps and rather narrow faces favoured by Steiff and even utilized rod joints that were only used by Steiff for one year in 1905, as they made the bears so heavy. Probably today many of the bears catalogued as Steiff in museums and auctions are actually Strunz look-alikes. A few examples, fortunately, are still marked, sometimes with "Präsident", used from 1910, presumably to prove the early connection with President Roosevelt, and to annoy Steiff even further, and these attract good prices because of their rarity.

Heinrich Silberstein, of Naunynstrasse, in Berlin, produced the newly fashionable

COLOUR PLATE 69
"A 'Bear'er of Best Wishes from Mumbles". "Bear'ly have I room to send/ All my views to you, my friend/ But lift me up and you will find/ My treasures I have hid behind." Published by Valentine and Sons. With views of the area c.1908. The bear appears to be British. *Author*

COLOUR PLATE 70
"Just a Line to Greet You". Three German plush bears enjoy their tea. Father wears his military uniform. The short plush coats suggest a much cheaper type of bear. The photographer "improved" the caricature by adding eyebrows to the boot button eyed animals. *Author*

PLATE 32
An early Edwardian ring-in-nose clockwork walking bear with boot button eyes, together with another bear of the same vintage that is key-wound from the centre of the stomach. Both made by Bing in Germany, c.1910. Ht. 8in. (20.3cm).

Courtesy Jane Vandell Associates

I am having a good
BLOW
at **RAMSGATE.**

COLOUR PLATE 71
Published by Wildt and Kray, London, and printed in Saxony, the card is postmarked August 20, 1910.   *Author*

Teddy Bears between 1905-10 and registered a patent in 1906 for an example with velvet paws and limbs that were jointed to the body by a double split pin. In Neustadt, near Coburg in Thuringia, Gebrüder Süssenguth had produced soft toys since the firm's establishment in 1894, but their early bears are impossible to identify. In 1896, Eduard Cramer commenced production in Schalkau, in the same poor region of Germany and included Teddies in their range of mechanical toys. Their musical bear was of interest as it played when the head was moved backwards and forwards.

The few firms which had already achieved a fully identifiable product were eager to maintain their individuality and the two German giants, Steiff and Bing, battled through the courts over the exclusive right to the button-in-ear. Steiff was already feeling vulnerable in 1909, as turnover had been disappointing and costs were up by an astonishing 300%, though it seems that this was largely because of Richard Steiff's love of buildings and progressive machinery: even though he was not consciously investing for future expansion, this was to be the eventual result. The court battle began because Gebrüder Bing had decided that their soft toys should also be marked with a button in the ear: an injunction prevented this use and Bing had to be content with a small metal button in an inconspicuous position under the arm.

Gebrüder Bing of Nuremberg is one of the most illustrious of German toymaking concerns, though their fame among collectors rests more on their superb tin toys than on their bears. The tin toy firm was founded in 1865 by Ignaz and Adolf Bing, though the partnership was modified in 1883, as there were differences about future policy and Ignaz became managing director. In 1895, the company went public and Ignaz became Chairman of the Supervisory board. By 1908, some 3,000 people were employed and Bing was known as the world's greatest toy factory. Its huge warehouse, situated in a beautiful part of Nuremberg, was visible from a great distance, as it was the highest and largest building in the vicinity. Bing owned a number of subsidiary companies, some continuing to trade under their own names, with others adopting the Bing trademark. Like Steiff, the Bings were concerned

COLOUR PLATE 72
Made by Gebrüder Bing c.1912, this example wears his original felt and cotton outfit and has
the characteristic button eyes. He rocks from side to side when key wound. Later versions have
the "BW" (Bing Werke) marked keys and labels, used after 1919. The clothes are always decorated
with these characteristic brass buttons. Ht. 8in (20.3cm).   *Courtesy Constance King Antiques*

COLOUR PLATE 73
Peek Frean delighted generations of British children with their Teddy Bear Biscuits, which had an embossed bear shape in the crisp shortcake. The small Edwardian tin was intended for children. *Author*

about the welfare of their workers and airy rooms with plenty of natural light became features of the German factories. Bing seems to have become involved in bear manufacture around 1905 and produced a typically good quality toy that is plumper in appearance than Steiffs of the same period. The bears were either marked with a small button or a metal arrow tag. Early Bings are not easy to identify, as some closely resemble Steiff products, with boot button eyes, an exaggerated hump, a long nose and over-large, ovoid shaped feet. Early labels carry the "G.B.N." mark for Gebrüder Bing Nuremberg. Though the firm produced large numbers of bears, there is little documentation, in comparison to the tin toy output and fully identifiable Bing bears are at a premium, especially when made in dark colours. Both Steiff and Bing produced somersaulting or trapeze bears in 1909, though similar mechanisms had previously been used on tin and fur-covered toys made by other firms.

Almost any mechanical bears were favourites in 1909, so there were bears that climbed trees, with foot supports at the side, bears that swung over a bar and Steiff's

Poor little chap, had such a fall
And now he cannot skate at all
Old Mr. Bruin is much bolder
So lifts him high up on his shoulder.

COLOUR PLATE 74
These roller-skating bears were certainly made in Germany, though not by Bing or Steiff. The long-haired bear is a fine example and wears the type of roller skates that was made for dolls, but could also be fitted to any kind of animal. The card, published by H.V. and Co., London, is postmarked May 31, 1910. *Author*

88

COLOUR PLATE 75
This chubby Barrow Boy in pale mohair is typical of the products of several English firms which worked in the North London area before the First World War. He is excelsior filled and has the small ears and thick arms associated with British makers. He pushes an English Swallow Toys costermonger's cart. Ht. 20in. (50.8cm). *Courtesy Constance King Antiques*

own version, that tumbled across the floor. The clockwork Steiff was arm-wound and especially suitable for children, as it was not damaged if wound in the wrong direction. The balance was very good and the bears do not fall on their side, even when set in motion today. At the Leipzig Fair, Steiff had staged a parade of their large animals, that were trundled about by men who proclaimed Steiff's position at this trade event in loud voices. The huge wheeled elephants and zoo animals are virtually impossible to find today, but the little somersaulting bears still give pleasure, as they were sold in vast numbers.

Peek Frean, the biscuit makers, brought Teddies to the London streets in some style, when they introduced their famous Teddy Bear Biscuits, which remained nursery favourites for generations of children. Each of their delivery vans was supplied with a large bear, made by Ralph Dunn and Co. of the Barbican. At first,

COLOUR PLATE 76
A 1910 Wildt and Kray postcard, printed in Saxony and caricaturing an open-mouthed Teddy Bear with a red tongue. Sent on 26th October. *Author*

thirty of these huge bears, standing five feet high, were seen on the streets and they were so successful that the number was increased to three hundred by 1909. Trade advertisements, old catalogues and even editorial mentions of the period tantalise with the names of other small companies which produced bears for a short time. The comment is often made that bears were manufactured in London in large quantities and one maker advised clients "to sample those bred at the Bear Pit, 3 St. Peter's Road, Kingsland, London, N.E."

William J. Terry also worked from Kingsland, at the new Welbury Works, 25 Middleton Road. This firm was said to be the largest British manufacturer of soft toy animals, dolls, cloth felt and plush animals, with the best value and the cheapest prices. The firm was established in 1890 in Stoke Newington and grew steadily until the 1920s. William Peacock and Co. worked from Dane Street in North London, one of the most popular factory areas, as land was still cheap. It is extremely difficult to identify the products of the smaller factories and even Peacock's only seem to have labelled their bears in the 1930s. Various attempts have been made to identify old bears by resemblances to original advertisements but this is an extremely difficult method as a line drawing almost invariably idealises the subject and early newspaper printing is often so poor that it is difficult to see real detail.

There was a serious attempt to oust the Teddy from the position of surprising popularity that it had attained in so short a time and trade magazines seem to have bidden Teddy farewell with some pleasure as "his mission has been accomplished" and a new soft toy, Billy Possum, was expected to reign. William H. Taft was Roosevelt's nominee as President in 1908 and he was represented in cartoon holding a possum. Taft was inaugurated in 1909 and cartoonists and illustrators had a lot of amusement from the subject of "Goodbye Teddy Bear, Welcome Billy Possum". One postcard showed a bear lying unwanted on the floor, while Uncle Sam played with Billy Possum. Because bears were perceived to have come into favour due to the Roosevelt association, toy sellers seem to have thought that soft toy possums would enjoy equal success. However, by September 1909, the

PLATE 33
British-made Teddy Bears appeared in an Edwardian Christmas edition of *The Lady* magazine. Though the names of the manufacturers are not recorded, the bears, with their rounded pads and plump limbs, contrast with the much leaner German products.

Courtesy Jane Vandell Associates

ISN'T HE A BEAUTY.

COLOUR PLATE 77
"Isn't he a Beauty". Published by
Wildt and Kray, London. Printed
in Saxony. The splendid German
bear appears to have a large
button in his left ear, though it is
not a type used by Steiff. c.1911.
Author

promoters of the new toy had to acknowledge that the possum was not wanted –
"The Teddy Bear is still all the rage in America".

Even the claim that Teddies had seen their day as fashion accessories was not
vindicated and a reporter at an English south coast resort commented on the
charmingly dressed young women "like lovely fashion plates in all their bravery of
embroidered white and silky gowns and frilly seaside hats were carrying immense
brown, buff or pale yellow Teddy Bears, tucked tenderly under their pretty sunburnt
arms". Making some enquiries, the reporter discovered that he had encountered the
latest, most up-to-date and smartest seaside fashion. "It is not chic, should you be a
fashionable August girl, to be seen on the sands, sea wall or pier without your Teddy
Bear. It is part of your holiday outfit this season and the big London toy shops are
selling a particular grown-up seaside brand of this popular toy."

COLOUR PLATE 78
Though perhaps not the most beautiful, the black Steiff, made of short mohair/burlap plush, is among the most rare. He has long, shaped limbs, cream felt pads and boot button eyes and was made c.1912. He is known as "Black Jack" and was discovered in 1923 in Newcastle, where his original owner discarded him when moving house. Margaret, his new owner, was never very fond of the Teddy, though she did make clothes for him so he should not feel left out in the nursery. He lived for many years in a Scottish attic. The lack of play use has meant that his condition is still very fine. Ht. 12½in. (31.8cm). Sold for £13,800 in 1997.

Courtesy Christie's South Kensington

Because owning a bear had become such a fashionable affectation with young women, their men friends joined in the fun and fixed Teddies to their bicycle handlebars or adopted him as a motorists' mascot. The light-hearted frivolity that seems to characterise the sun-filled years before the First World War is transmitted with the scents and sounds of those lost summer days in contemporary accounts.

PLATE 34
"We're off to Bed", a postcard printed in England for the Davidson Bros. Real Photographic series, London and New York. Postmarked February 1908.

Author

Perhaps even today, our affection for Teddy Bear is still coloured by our nostalgia for a life that had to end before the world became real.

A decidedly frivolous competitor for Teddy was promoted at toy trade fairs in 1910: Barbara Bear was to be yet another successor. This version was white and was believed to have derived its name from the white polar bears in the zoological

The Return from the Chase.—A Mixed Bag.

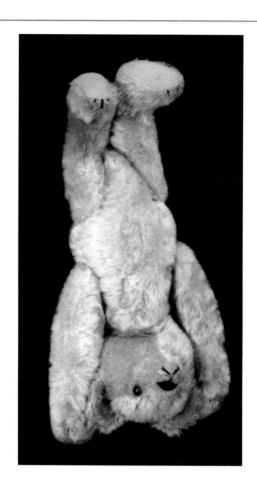

PLATE 36
A gold somersaulting Steiff type bear with boot button eyes and cream felt pads. Fully jointed and with internal mechanism. Ht. 13in. (33cm).
Courtesy Bonham's, Chelsea

COLOUR PLATE 80
A Marcuse, Day and Co. card, printed in Prussia and postmarked 1912. The girl shows off her dark plush German bear with boot button eyes. *Author*

gardens. As white bears had long been available, it is difficult to understand why this new version was innovative, especially as polar bears had been constructed alongside jointed Teddies for some time.

Because of the frequent pirating of designs, both Steiff and Décamps were careful to register mechanisms. On 12th October, 1910, E. Décamps of 10 Rue Parc Royal, Paris took out a patent for "a mechanical toy in the form of a bear which is constructed to fall about and turn somersaults. The front limbs, 1 and 2, are rotated continuously by a spring motor enclosed in the toy and so cause it to rise and fall over. One of the remaining limbs is pliable and allows the figure to fall sideways when it rises". In comparison, Richard Steiff, on 11th December, registered his patent at Giengen am Brenz for "mechanical bears of the type by which clockwork is wound by means of the limbs are so constructed that the limbs connected to the drive shaft can be turned an unlimited number of times in either direction without interfering with the clockwork".

In recognition of their achievements in the first decade of the twentieth century, Margarete and Richard Steiff were personally awarded gold medals at the Brussels World Exhibition, an event at which Dean's Rag Book Co. of England was awarded two golds. At many of the trade and World exhibitions, Steiff often shared a stand with Märklin, the manufacturers of the finest German metal toys. This association extended to some of the toys themselves, with Märklin supplying metal parts and assisting in the design and production of figures, where metal was an important element of the construction.

At this time and until the advent of the First World War, natural and imitation furs were used alongside one another by many producers. Steiff, according to old

COLOUR PLATE 81
Small German bears have often survived in better general condition than larger examples, as they were not so roughly handled. This boot button eyed Steiff, type c.1909, has a very pronounced back hump. In the smaller sizes, foot pads were sometimes not used. Ht. 7in. (17.8cm).   *Author*

catalogues, never used animal skins for their bears, though lambskin was occasionally used for other toys, but companies like Bertha Caspar of Berlin used fur and velvet and Berthold Krauss of Wive und Söhne, who had occupied the same premises for thirty-nine years, advertised in 1910 animals of all descriptions that were made from felt, leather and papier mâché. This firm, with a factory at Rodach bei Coburg, used some of their miniature figures in menageries and Noah's Arks. Many small and realistic bears were sold separately, but there are some examples that were chained in cages or sold for bear pits or bear gardens. A few papier mâché bears were flock covered, which gives a felt-like appearance. Occasionally a bear is found in a wheeled cage as part of a circus train, pieces that are equally popular with toy as bear collectors. Perhaps in answer to a new interest in miniature bears, Steiff's first 6in. (15.2cm) versions appeared in 1909 and were an immediate success, as they were suitable for modest pocket-money buyers.

COLOUR PLATE 82
A German-made pull-along bear in cinnamon coloured mohair. He is mounted on a metal frame, with the early type of iron spoked wheels and has boot button eyes and a short tail. c.1910. 21in. (53.3cm) long.
Courtesy Constance King Antiques

The availability of very small-size mohair creatures made the assembly of bear families attractive to manufacturers, who could costume them with some originality or arrange them in baskets or prams. One enterprising American company claimed their bear family as one of the most popular toys ever produced and sold for only 19¢. Few examples of this successful family can have survived, as the bears were made of cotton over wire armatures.

Some of the small bears were mounted on wood or metal wheels, the most appealing having leather muzzles with drawing chains. Obviously the large riding bears were much more successful as toys, especially those that could be converted from a pullalong to a rocker. Before the First World War, these were available from many makers and in a wide range of qualities, from a thick, tweed-like material to plush, velvet or extravagantly long mohair. Like the conventional bears, their eyes were at first boot buttons but these were gradually superseded by glass animal types. Wheel construction

COLOUR PLATE 83
Two small Steiffs, the darker with a button in ear, take a motor ride in a G. & H. Lines car. Both have boot button eyes and one a brown stitched nose. Ht. of bears 14in. (35.6cm).
Courtesy Constance King Antiques

COLOUR PLATE 84
Teddy Bear coats were the rage in the early 1900s. Every car also carried its mascot. The doll is a German "P.M." and the bear, with his Dulwich College day-boy's boater, is English.   *Author*

gives some help in dating these toys, as iron spoked wheels were almost universally used before 1914. Sometimes for smaller animals, plain wooden wheels were utilized, especially by small firms, eager to produce toys as cheaply as possible. The most expensive riding bears had turning heads and voice boxes activated by a pull string, while from 1913 Steiff introduced a new steering device that was used for better bears. In relation to jointed Teddies, riding and wheeled versions are comparatively cheap and

PLATE 38
"Dear Old Teddy", sitting in a wicker mail-cart. The card, printed in England by Davidson Bros., London and New York. Postmarked March 26, 1910.   *Author*

PLATE 37
"Master Frank Oliver Lowrie Agg, taken at Margate, 10th June, 1909. Aged 3 years and 7 months." His mohair Teddy has large boot button eyes.   *Author*

PLATE 39
The "Vanquished" Teddy shown in this Edwardian postcard appears to be a "Laughing Roosevelt", though his feet are unusually large for a bear of this type. The Roosevelt bears, made by the Columbia Teddy Bear Manufacturers of New York, have white glass teeth set in a wooden jaw. Printed in Germany, the card is postmarked 1910.   *Author*

appeal to toy collectors in general, as many have a deceptively antique appearance.

The pre-war years were a period of constant innovation at Steiff and included the engaging "Bär Dolly", in red white and blue, that was especially produced for the 1912 American Presidential election. This is now one of the most collectable early Steiffs, as is the Pantom Bear, designed by the inventive and artistic Albert Schlopsnies and produced between 1910 and 1918. Relatively few Pantom Bears were made and these were only in the smaller sizes. They are characterised by their retrospective boot button eyes and the fact that they were strung and controlled like marionettes. Puppets of all kinds have always fascinated artists and Schlopsnies, who worked intermittently for the firm over many years, was one of the more progressive influences. Pantom Bear (short for pantomime) was a somewhat doll-like creature with a metal armature and a string-activated voice box. One extremely rare version had a ring through its nose. Pantom was completely in the idiom of a working marionette and he could jump and cavort, scratch, growl and play. The toy must have been an eye-catcher for shop demonstrations and the trade fairs for

COLOUR PLATE 85
Old bears assume great character over the years because of the different ways in which they are handled. This wistful little Steiff, with boot button eyes and felt pads, would have much less charm if one of his ears had not dropped. Ht.10in. (25.4cm).
Courtesy Constance King Antiques

which Steiff always made impressive displays.

Richard Steiff, always receptive to the needs of the vast American market, was anxious that warm, cuddly toys, with the soft appeal of animals, should be most important. In 1913, a Record Teddy was added to the established Record range. This was a progressively designed toy on a wheeled base, but a long way from the cuddly toys that Richard kept demanding. The Record range had first appeared in 1912, with a registered patent for a voice box concealed under the seat of a vehicle with a metal frame and plain, brightly coloured wooden wheels. The largest Record toy was 10in. (25.4cm) high and the bear moved as it was pulled along. Perhaps because in style the Record series seems to belong to a period between the wars, it is not as popular with collectors as the completely traditional Teddies.

There are many novelty pieces from this early period to tempt the collector, from celluloid jointed figures to the Three Bears, cleverly modelled and made of wire jointed bisque. Morrells, an Oxford Street department store, sold "Old Mistress Teddy who lived in a Shoe", an item that would attract world-wide interest if it

PLATE 40
An unmarked Steiff type 1910 bear in golden mohair, with black boot button eyes and a pronounced clipped snout. The black stitched snout is backed with black felt. The pads are replacements. Ht. 15in. (38cm). Sold for £1,725 in 1997.   *Courtesy Christie's South Kensington*

COLOUR PLATE 86
A Staffordshire china plate from the sporting bears series, showing Teddy playing golf.   *Author*

appeared on the market today. Schoenhut's "Teddy's Adventures in Africa", with 53 wooden figures is an equally desirable item, as are any of the topsy-turvy bear dolls and the delightful Travelling Bears, with their suitcases of clothes. For antique bear collectors, these were the golden years, that offer bear cutlery, tea sets, mugs and nursery china, with gloriously coloured scraps and figures, made by inventive printers like Raphael Tuck.

In the secure years just before the 1914-18 War, even the most pessimistic sellers seem to have accepted Teddies as toy box inhabitants that had come to stay. Sears Roebuck and Co., the important American wholesaler, commented in 1912 that Teddy Bears were not a fad but even more popular than ever before: "No toy brought out in recent years will hold the interest of a child as long as the bear, besides giving the most splendid service, as they are almost indestructible." Fine quality German bears were offered by Sears Roebuck, but only in natural cinnamon colour, and in 10in. (25.4cm) to 20in. (50.8cm) sizes. All were provided with glass eyes and "improved" automatic voices that growled when the body was tilted forward. From the line drawing that accompanied the advertisement, it seems

COLOUR PLATE 87
Sets of Teddy Bear china were made in America, Germany and Britain in the Edwardian period. This set is from the "Sporting Bear" series and shows him playing cricket. Marked "Made in England". Ht. of jug 1¾in. (4cm).   *Author*

COLOUR PLATE 88
Commemorative china makers soon realised the potential of the Teddy Bear craze and produced nice quality bone china pieces. Printed with the Redhill coat of arms, the Clifton China bear, which dates to 1910, carries the Registered Design no. 548705. Ht. 3½in. (8.9cm). *Author*

unlikely that the bears were Steiff, as they seem very much plumper, though it is possible that they were produced by Strunz of Nuremberg.

Even by 1914, many of the ideas that had been hailed as revolutionary in the first decade of the teddy were being revived and little that was completely fresh seems to have appeared. The "Electro" bear was suggested as the latest novelty, with "eyes that shine, real electric eyes that sparkle or grow dim as you want them." The original electric-eyed bears did not have this dimming refinement, so this was at least a tentative advance. "By pressing a button on the stomach, the eyes are made to flash." Obviously concerned by complaints about failing batteries that had depressed sales of earlier electric-eyed bears, the "Electro" was supplied with batteries good for 6,000 flashes. In case this was not enough for a particularly energetic child, an extra was provided. Electro was made in cinnamon or grey and measured 20in. (50.8cm). Relatively few examples have survived, partly because the central seam had to be unpicked and re-sewn each time the battery needed changing.

From the years when Teddy first appeared, no firm or country ever owned him completely, so designers were able to develop his structure or alter his personality at will. It was this freedom that inspired such a wealth of innovation, making the bear a completely independent spirit at a time when people were drawing in on themselves and becoming receptive to the nationalism that was to split Europe apart in 1914.

PLATE 41
To save on the cost of expensive mohair, Steiff joined the heads of some of the bears with a seam that runs down the centre of the face. This cinnamon coloured "centre seam" has a pronounced clipped snout and a black stitched nose backed with black felt. Ht. 15in. (38cm). Sold for £1,840 in 1997.
Courtesy Christie's South Kensington

CHAPTER 4
Bear Makers at War

The First World War had an almost instantaneous effect on toy production and even in America, not at first involved in the conflict, smaller and more economically produced Teddies were the order of the day, made of cotton or the cheapest woollen fabrics. Steiff, possibly assisting the war effort, discontinued their use of iron wheels and began to fit wooden ones to their pull and push-along toys. During a war when everything, from garden railings to tin toys, was collected for scrap metal in both Britain and Germany, it is little wonder that Steiff decided to abandon the iron versions that had characterised their products.

American factories obviously continued to use iron wheels until the 1920s, with many small firms making this type of toy in all sizes and qualities. Despite the gradual change of attitude to animals, most of the brown wheeled bears still had a ring through their nose and were pulled along by chains or ropes; a few more expensive models were fitted with metal muzzles. For very small, cheap bears, cotton plush, often a winceyette-type fabric, was used, as it gave a slightly more realistic fluffy effect than colour-printed cotton, such as was used by the Art Fabric Mills. A few interesting bears were introduced during the war years and just before the war there was yet another attempt to introduce a bear doll with two faces that, it was hoped, would appeal to children. In June 1914, Louis S. Schiffer of New York patented a jointed bear with a doll's face on one side of the swivel head that was covered with a blue cap when not required. Though America came late into the war, even their toy production and invention seems to have been stifled in the period and contemporary magazines and catalogues reveal an industry that simply continued to produce well-tried, but unadventurous, designs. There were plenty of ordinary bears available for children but sellers in America were continually complaining about the unreliability of quality supplies.

The situation was very different in Germany, where exports were restricted because of a naval blockade, though, as late as 1916, some toys were still exported to America. Both Bing and Steiff were involved in the war effort and most of their factories

"I've brought you some recruits" smiles the little girl, with her officer bear and flag-waving golliwog. The poster reads "Everybody can help in some way. What will you do? Do it now!" From Raphael Tuck's "We can all help" series, produced in England. The card is postmarked 1915 and reveals the pressure brought upon young men to enlist in the British Army.

Author

diverted into the making of fabric and metal goods for army use. The war years were inevitably disastrous for bear production: bears were comparatively expensive toys, almost completely dependent for their appeal on high quality mohair, the finest being imported from Britain. Even felt, previously obtained by Steiff from the United Felt Co., owned by a relative, was no longer used for toys but needed for the Kaiser's army, where some might well have been worn by Hugo, Paul and Richard Steiff who, like all young German men, were conscripted into the services.

With the German borders closed, a chronic shortage of coal and all raw materials, it is surprising that toy production continued at all and it says much for the tenacity of the Steiff directors that they continued to discuss new ideas and products by letter and succeeded in making some decisions. In 1914, the war in both Britain and Germany was expected to last for a short time, with little effect on civilian life, so patriotic bears and soldier toys were highly popular, as were military dressing-up outfits for children and their dolls and bears. By 1917, things were very different, with both

PLATE 42
Life was hard in Germany during the Great War and few mohair toys could be produced because of the naval blockades. This inexpensive cook, made by a minor German company, has been both patched and mended. Ht. 15in. (38cm).

Courtesy Constance King Antiques

COLOUR PLATE 90
British toy makers were encouraged by the government to produce attractive toys so that the lack of German products would not be noticeable. The Sunlight, Sieve and Co. patriotic naval commander and Red Cross nurse look after Teddy, made by the same Manchester printer. The figures, in unsold condition, were recently discovered in old warehouse stock. The Commander is 15½in. (39.4cm) tall.   *Author*

sides thoroughly sickened by the carnage that modern warfare had unleashed and patriotic jingoism fell strangely silent: soldier dolls were no longer wanted and bears dressed in army uniform struck a chill into families whose young men were lost at the front.

A number of individual Teddies have come to prominence because of their adventures in the "Great War", when they were carried into battle as mascots tucked inside a military tunic or pocket. Others were left with young sweethearts to keep them company or comforted children through dark hours and the fear of Zeppelin attacks. When any bears of this tragic period with a known history appear on the market, they arouse great interest: to collectors, the Teddy Bear is, above all,

COLOUR PLATE 91
Jasper Bowden worked as a free-lance photographer, supplying West Country views to postcard publishers. He died in 1994 in a tiny, run-down cottage with the two things he most loved: his motorbike and his tiny mascot bear, wearing its original mechanic's overalls. The very threadbare little mascot was retrieved from the windowsill of his cottage. The bear is probably English, with boot button eyes, made c.1915 and fragments of his original long mohair are still present under his clothes. Ht. 6in. (15.2cm). *Author*

a companion and he proved himself true to many people in those grim years.

German soft toy makers had created such splendid products before the war that most competition had been stifled but, with the disappearance of Steiff, Strunz and Hermann from the shops, manufacturers in other countries turned their attention to bears. It is unlikely that, without the effect of war, mohair bears would ever have been produced in great quantities in Britain and France, but there was encouragement from government level to prove that German imports were neither needed nor desired. Even before the war, toymakers in France and England were complaining about the flooding of the market with German-made toys and asking for some kind of protection against imports and the hijacking of their ideas. The advent of war presented an opening which many firms were eager to exploit.

Today, the most expensive of the Teddies made in Britain in 1916 are the Harwin

COLOUR PLATE 92
Illustrated in the 1915 Dean's catalogue is "Master Bruno" in the Cuddlemee range.
Courtesy The Dean's Company

Ally Mascot Bears, mohair characters dressed in the military uniforms of the Allies. Harwin and Co. worked from North London and the bears were designed by Dorothy Harwin. The characters include an Australian, a Scot, a British sailor and a Red Cross Nurse. Most toymakers were eager to illustrate the new contribution of women in the 1914-18 War and nurses' uniforms began to be seen more frequently on bears. Fred Taylor, G. W. Harwin's sales manager, had been one of Steiff's most important overseas agents and must have been eager in the war years to promote a readily available toy for his old wholesale customers.

W. H. Smith and Sons, the major British newsagents and stationers, were among the first to promote the new British toys and dolls. A factory was set up at Shelton, Stoke-on-Trent, by the local manager, G. H. Buckmaster. Fully jointed Teddies in all sizes were produced and a range of wheeled toys, including two bears dressed as clowns standing on a wooden platform with cast-iron wheels, which must have equalled anything made in Germany. In East London, Mark Robin established the Britannia Works in 1914 and included in their range of Teddies a Cossack bear wearing Russian uniform. British makers were fortunate, as mohair fabric woven in Yorkshire seems never to have been in short supply, so fine quality toys were achievable, especially as most were still filled with wood wool (excelsior) or sawdust. Though many of these small concerns were begun with high hopes and the owners believed that, after the war, their interests would be safeguarded by a grateful government, they were to be sorely disappointed and many closed within a decade.

"The Bear of Russia, Germany's Crusher" smiled benignly at the world from the pages of Dean's Rag Book Company's 1915-16 catalogue. The company promoted this latest addition to its printed range as a "patriotic line, hygienically stuffed and finished and made entirely in England". This pride in a peculiarly British product remained a feature of Dean's advertising until the 1950s. At the Brussels Exhibition in 1910, where Dean's had won two Gold Medals, a fire destroyed most of the firm's early catalogues, as well as examples of original products. The earliest

PLATE 43
Teddy Bears were already popular as first gifts for baby by 1914. This British made mohair Bruin has a pronounced hump and long, straight arms. He has boot button eyes. *Author*

PLATE 44
Dean's Rag Book Company offered the printed Russian bears in two sizes, both with the flags of the Allies printed on their chests. Actual examples are extremely rare. From a 1914-18 catalogue.

Courtesy Jane Vandell Associates

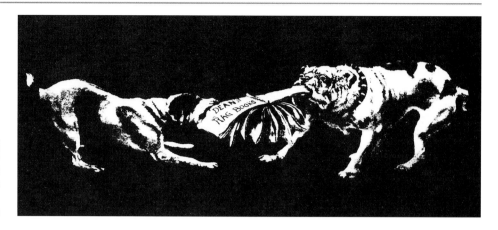

PLATE 45
The famous original Dean's Rag Book Company trademark, used on early products of a firm that became very important once German imports ceased.

Courtesy Jane Vandell Associates

catalogue I have examined dated to 1912-13 when, despite growing anti-German feeling, the cover showed Prince Wilhelm, son of the Crown Prince, reading his rag book and described as "the future Kaiser".

In the 1912-13 catalogue, Mama Bear, Teddy and Sissie are listed among the "1/- Knockabout Toy Sheets". The "6d. Knockabout Toy Sheets" also included a few bears, listed as "Teddy Bear and the Two Little Teddy Bears", the figures being colour printed on a cloth similar to winceyette, which gave a slightly fluffy appearance and was described in the catalogue as "woollen cloth". The trio were of unusual construction, as the main seam ran down the front of the face and the body, allowing for more shaping than was usually possible in toys of the printed type. The rounded effect was created, as in most of Dean's products, by the insertion of a round or oval base that carried the firm's trademark of the fighting bulldog and the smooth-haired terrier. This printed bear had the long arms associated with all early versions of the Teddy, though the general effect was very different.

The Knockabout Toy Sheets were introduced by Samuel Dean shortly after book production had begun and one account of the early period suggests that the figures were at first printed in the rag books themselves, but as to date no examples have been found, this is impossible to prove and certainly Teddies first appeared on the Toy Sheets. Dean's suggested that after assembly the toys should be filled with wood wool or granulated cork that could be obtained free as waste material from glass and china shops, where it was used for packing. The sheets, some plain cotton and others winceyette, were surprisingly cheap and "Mr. Bruin" in the "Bo-Peep Series" must have been within every child's price range, costing just one penny. This model, of a simple two-sided construction, portrayed a realistic wild bear on all fours. A later catalogue suggests that the same model could be used as a pincushion or to teach needlework to children.

Though mohair fabric for bears was available throughout the war in Britain, the raw material being mainly obtained from India, there was no manufacture of this much more expensive item at Dean's, though other printed dolls and toys were sold ready assembled from the 1910-11 season and throughout the war. The Russian Bear, in the large size, measuring 12in. (30.5cm) and selling for one shilling, was made with the usual hygienic stuffing and this bear was not available in the cheaper sheet form.

PLATE 46
The Welsh-speaking bear, who has lived his long life with several generations of a Gower family. Made in England c.1914, he is carried by his original owner. He has the original painted back glass eyes and is straw filled. Ht. 24in. (61cm). *Courtesy Jane Vandell Associates*

I have long hoped to see an example of this curiosity which was advertised alongside such wartime symbols as "The Patriotic Soldier Dolls", but it seems that few have survived. The "Bear of Russia" was a slim, almost human-shaped creature with straight legs and shaped arms – across his chest he carried the flags of the Allies.

Printed bears, long popular in America, were adopted by several textile manufacturers during the war as a cheap line that could be sold through stationers and fancy goods shops. A patriotic range was published by Sunlight, Sieve and Co. of the Crescent Works, Salford, Manchester in 1915. This firm, which closed in 1919, offered wholesale and export products, including flat-printed sailors, soldiers, a nurse and a yellow bear. Sunlight, Sieve and Co. exhibited at the Board of Trade Fair Exhibition and promoted their "extensive range of exclusive designs". A large number of bears must have been made, well printed, but on such flimsy fabric that few would have survived the nursery.

COLOUR PLATE 93
British manufacturers attempted to overcome the shortage of imported toys with bears and dolls that were printed on fabric. Sunlight, Sieve and Co. used an unusually flimsy cotton and few bears have survived, but a quantity of original unused sheets was recently discovered. c.1915.
Courtesy Constance King Antiques

PLATE 47
Despite his small size and plain looks, "Master Teddy" is among the most expensive bears. Made by Chiltern at Chesham, Bucks. in 1915, he has pronounced googlie glass eyes, a black embroidered nose and mouth and a red tongue. Other examples have brown eyes, with sewn-in black pupils. The body is cloth with mohair head, hands and feet. Wearing the original blue trousers with a red patch on the knee and webbing braces, he originally also wore a check shirt with a white collar. The lace-edged coat of this example was added by a child owner. Master Teddy was originally made in five sizes and sold with an oval label with his registered design number and "Master Teddy. Made in England. USA Patent applied for". This example wears its Teddy Tail League badge. The *Daily Mail* used Master Teddy as a character. Ht. 9½in. (24cm). Sold for £2,530 in 1995. *Courtesy Bonham's, Chelsea*

Another Manchester calico printer, Samuel Finburgh and Co. of 63 Granby Row, printed flannelette Teddy Bears from 1909 and augmented these with patriotic figures during the war. The Hammond Manufacturing Co. Ltd. was established by 1915 and worked from Burton on Trent, including bears among a range of toys made to fill the gap left by the loss of German imports. The Teddy Toy Co. was begun in the first year of the war, working from Playhouse Yard, London E.C.1 and using the trademark "Softanlite" on their toys: Vicky, National, Union Jack and Best British were among the popular names, not just for products but for many of the short-lived factories that had hoped to succeed because of the removal of German competition.

The Teddy Toy Company did manage to survive until the Second World War. It was established in the East End of London in 1914 and claimed, during the war, to be the largest British bear manufacturer. Their round labels, reading "Original Softanlite Toys. British Made." reflected their use of kapok as a filling material. Like W. J. Terry, The Teddy Toy Company did not mark its toys with a sewn-on label, and they are almost impossible to recognise without the original swing tickets.

A few bears had been created at the Chiltern Toy Works at Chesham, Buckinghamshire, during the war, notably a costumed version wearing blue felt trousers with a patch on the knee. At first glance, this bear appears to be a home-made production, but carries a label reading "Master Teddy. Made in England. U.S.A. Patent applied for" together with his registration number. Chiltern's Master Teddy was available in five sizes and has a cheeky, widely smiling grin, that defies authority. As an economy measure, the dressed sections of the bear's body are not made of mohair but of cotton fabric. Because Master Teddy is now so rare, he attracts prices far higher than his quality would suggest and those with labels command a further premium.

Chad Valley was also pushed into bear production because of the cessation of German imports during the 1914-18 War. This was a very long established toymaking concern that had originally traded as Johnson Bros. and was founded

PLATE 48
Even children's birthday cards were not without their militaristic content during the war years. This boy, with his rifle, cannon and bandolier, wears a private's cap. His English bear offers a more secure future. Of British manufacture, the card was postmarked 19th September 1918, just two months before the war ended. *Author*

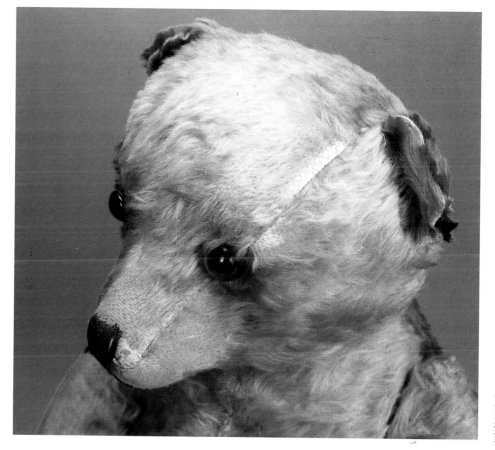

COLOUR PLATE 94
Pre-1920 British-made bears almost invariably have a gentle, kindly expression. *Author*

COLOUR PLATE 95
This Chad Valley "Grunter" is the first type of bear made by the Harborne factory. He has painted back, roughly shaped, glass eyes and was originally a bright yellow, long pile mohair. The nose was defined in felt and stitched over to give a raised effect. He wears the badge of the Allies, Britain and France. His design was a close imitation of German models, though his hump is even more exaggerated. This is the first recorded 1915 Chad Teddy. *Author*

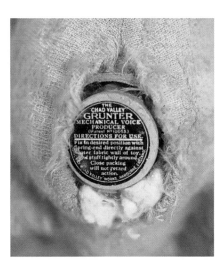

just after the Napoleonic Wars by Anthony Bunn Johnson as a printing and bookbinding concern, working from Lichfield Street in Handsworth. In 1860, Joseph and Alfred set up a similar business on their own in Birmingham and in 1897, Joseph, with his own son Alfred, moved to Harborne, near a small stream called the Chad. Gradually, cardboard and paper games and toys were added to the stationery. Chad, like Steiff, was a steadily evolved family concern that saw an opening for soft toy production on the outbreak of the war.

In 1915, the company included in its first toy patterns a range of Teddy Bears, with a newly patented growler that carried a green label with a patent number for that year. The bear is extremely interesting, as it is the first type made at Chad Valley and is very obviously a close copy of early German designs. He is an example of how

COLOUR PLATE 96
The Chad Valley "Grunter" mechanical voice producer with its 1915 patent. The large form of the growl made it necessary to give the bear a rather pot-bellied shape. *Author*

COLOUR PLATE 97
Farnell stepped up their manufacture of bears during the 1914-18 War to fill the gap left by German imports. This fine white example has the characteristic web-stitched pads and blue glass, painted back eyes. Ht. 17in. (43.2cm). *Courtesy Bernard Beech*

the history of a subject is sometimes extended during the writing of a book, as "Grunter" came into my hands just a few weeks before the manuscript was to be sent to the publisher. Previous research had only proved that Teddies were made in 1920, but this marked example pushed the date back by several years and exhibited a body design and structure that relied heavily on German antecedents. The British government was eager during the war to boost public morale, by ensuring that products previously obtained from Germany should continue to appear in the shops, so they supported both china doll and Teddy Bear manufacture. The 1915 Chad Valley bear, made originally in long golden mohair, has very long, slightly tapering arms, large feet with four embroidered claws and a pronounced hump on his back. He varies from contemporary German designs because of his very fat, Pooh-like stomach, that accommodated the Chad Valley Grunter. The nose stitching was applied over a felt rectangle and the mouth embroidered in a smiling position. The eyes are of glass and of irregular cut, with painted backs. The bear is completely filled with wood wool, contributing to his early appearance. Documentary bears only occasionally appear on the market and are of great importance in the understanding of a toy's development. It is probable that this bear was also made in blue mohair, as a piece was discovered inside the bear, behind its voice-box.

PLATE 49
An unusual double-faced bear, whose head is turned by twisting his tail. One face has glass eyes in black and amber, with a smiling mouth, while the other has boot buttons and a sad, turned-down expression. He has a pronounced hump. Probably French, c.1914. He sold in 1985 for £200. 4¼in. (10.8cm). *Courtesy Phillips London*

Chad's "Home Zoo", published during the war, contained a bear with its cage among the twenty-six animals, each representing a letter of the alphabet. Children cut out the printed animals and cages to assemble a complete zoo scene. Such economically produced toys were acceptable in wartime, when they did not have to compete in the toyshops with beautifully carved or moulded German menageries and arks. While the war led to the establishment and development of more British and French makers, it stultified the international scene, with American trade catalogues revealing a lack of invention, competitive new designs and developments.

In 1920, Chad Valley, because of the increase in business during the war, opened the Wrekin Toy Works in Wellington, Shropshire, with the main emphasis on bears, that were illustrated in their catalogues and reveal a development from the German inspired "Grunter" to a softer look, much more in line with bears made by Farnell in London. In this year, three factories were merged to form the Chad Valley Co. Ltd.

Though in the early years of the war some interesting patriotic bears had emerged, by 1917 there were few new designs for a public that must have wanted an escape from reality rather than reminders of the nationalism that had fed the original enthusiasm for battle. Many well established companies in France and Britain suffered badly because of the absence of engineers and designers; some firms disappeared in these years, while others were affected so badly by the aftermath of war that they ceased trading before 1920.

During, and in the years just after the First World War, children were often confronted with wounded and damaged ex-servicemen and one wonders whether it was just pure coincidence that inspired H. C. Cradock to create Little Teddy as a character that is missing an arm and a leg. Big Teddy and Little Teddy first appeared in 1916 in the famous Josephine books that were charmingly and delicately illustrated by Honor C. Appleton who, in a series of sensitively painted scenes of nursery life, reveals all the toys that a middle-class girl would have owned at the time. It is often thought that artists simply create toy characters, but Appleton drew hers from actual toys. I once possessed Appleton's original copies of the books she illustrated, together with the soft toys that were their inspiration. Quacky Jack, the Japs and the woodentops were all there, together with her notes on colour and many other toys. The central bear characters were absent, and I could only conclude that she must have given them away many years before. I sold the complete archive to a museum but would still like to locate Big Teddy and Little Teddy so that all the characters could be re-united.

Ultimately, the natural desire to succeed, exhibited by so many British toymakers, was doomed. German manufacturers worked on a much larger scale in specially designed factories and with a superb merchandising chain. Their workers were more faithful to the companies than their British counterparts and were willing to

" I wouldn't let any of them have any more see-saws that morning"

COLOUR PLATE 98
Honor Appleton was one of the most prolific children's book illustrators in the first half of the century. Her drawings of Little Ted and Big Ted, who feature in Mrs. Cradock's "Josephine" series are delightful as period pieces.   *Author*

earn less. Though there were trades unions in Germany, they had little effect on the thousands of homeworkers, whose cheap labour was utilized in many areas until the 1930s. British toymakers had also expected some help from the Lloyd George governments and were in desperate straits when protectionism was phased out and the fine German dolls and tin toys again filled the windows of expensive shops. This dislike of anything German, combined with a bitterness towards a government that had applauded their war effort and then abandoned them to foreign competition, screams out from the pages of British and French toy trade journals and advertisements in the years immediately after the war, until the factories again resigned themselves to a secondary position.

PLATE 50
Anne Maria Holmes bought the large bear, made in Austria c.1914, because he reminded her of the bear her Viennese soldier father gave her as a child. She was never allowed to play with the toy, as her father died on the Russian Front. Her collection of bears reminds her of Vienna when she is living in Britain.
Courtesy Jane Vandell Associates

CHAPTER 5
Cocktails and Flappers

After the bitterness and despair of war, young people in the 1920s were eager to enjoy life again and rushed into a headlong pursuit of new pleasures and ideas. Because the old order was dead, together with blind patriotism and belief in governments, there was a brittle heedlessness among those who had suffered and a new spirit of adventure among the young. Their children were allowed much greater freedom of expression – with the old certainties lost, perhaps the next generation would avoid disaster by being allowed to travel, read widely and experiment with every new device – one little girl was even taught to fly.

Toy manufacturers were among the first ambassadors of peace. Anxious to put their factories back into production, they were re-opening their warehouses in Europe and America and travelling the world to seek new orders. Because of devaluation and the grim state of German industry, many small firms were wiped out, though the giants survived. American makers had probably gained rather than suffered as a result of the war but had shown little adventurousness, probably because of the lack of competition and knowledge of fresh products that they had seen annually before the war at the great trade fairs. In general, firms such as Ideal had continued to produce their traditional bears, simply filling the vacuum left in America once German imports had dried up.

Financially, the German toy industry had already reached its zenith between 1895 and 1915 and toy exports doubled between 1900 and 1913. The anti-German feeling engendered by the conflict, together with the difficulties in obtaining raw materials, had a tremendous effect and by 1920 exports were reduced by about 20%. German manufacturers had always relied mainly on the British and American markets that, in the boom period, had taken 55% of German output. The unusual

PLATE 51
A softer, more cuddlesome Teddy was evolving by 1920, to suit children who were encouraged to express their affection more openly. The long pile mohair bear is German, though not made by Steiff.   *Author*

FACING PAGE: COLOUR PLATE 99
An early 1920s Teddy Wedding, celebrated in a Norman church. Both bears are English and unmarked, though the bear on the right is probably an early Chad Valley. "Baby" has pink felt pads. c.1925. Ht. of larger bear 20in. (50.8cm).   *Courtesy Constance King Antiques*

COLOUR PLATE 100

The standing mohair bear with a long, shaved snout and large ears, has backed glass eyes and is kapok filled; his nose is re-stitched. He was probably made by Gebrüder Bing c.1924. Ht. 23in. (58.4cm). The seated 1930s bear, also made in Germany, has large, widely spaced ears and is straw filled. He has a shaved snout and replacement felt pads. Ht. 24in. (61cm). They sold for £1,977 and £920 in 1995.   *Courtesy Bonham's, Chelsea*

popularity of soft toys was propitious for manufacturers, both in Europe and Britain. Before 1900, most toys were designed and constructed by men, but with so many workers who never returned from the war, the industry came to rely to a much greater extent on women's labour. Soft toys could be manufactured wherever there was a sewing machine and were ideally suited to a homeworker system. Even wheeled riding bears could be sewn by outworkers and then mounted on a metal base at a small factory.

Great firms, like Steiff and Bing, relied to some extent on the industry of outworkers and, with times hard and a disinclination on the part of factory owners to invest in new machinery, the public affection for soft toys, such as bears, must have been a boon to an industry strapped for cash. The devaluation of the mark, a general strike, a shortage of coal and raw materials and a high level of unemployment all contributed to a very difficult home market for toys. The *Deutsche Spielwaren Zeitung* in 1920 claimed that only the richest of parents could buy good toys for their children and urged makers and buyers that it was their patriotic duty to save the German toy trade.

Mohair was, inevitably, the most expensive soft toy-making fabric and supplies to firms like Steiff and Schuco were only adequate for the export trade. Smaller factories fared worse and were often forced to use inferior fabrics or economise by only making the head and visible parts of a dressed bear out of fur. Just before the 1914 war, there were at least forty-four makers of quality bears in Germany, while there must have been hundreds of small factories, making very cheap items for local sale. Some of the larger concerns produced fine bears, that were often direct copies of Steiff designs, which is why completely unmarked Teddies are always such a problem to attribute.

Two of the world's most famous bears, Winnie the Pooh and Rupert, dominated Britain in the 1920s. Writers must have turned with relief after the war to the creation of light-hearted children's stories, through which they could fashion an innocent and stain-free world. Pooh Bear and Rupert represent completely different facets of childhood, yet both have an underlying morality combined with basic ingenuity and an

FACING PAGE: COLOUR PLATE 101

An extremely rare, long golden mohair with brown and black eyes, made by Eduard Crämer c.1920. The firm was established in Schalkau, Thuringia, in 1896 and was among the first German firms to make Teddies. The company also produced mechanical bears. This version has a short, cut muzzle and inner ears, a brown stitched nose and claws. The red felt open mouth was something of an innovation for the period and its presence is often used to identify unmarked bears. The bear has long limbs and spoon-shaped paws and feet. His unusually large size contributed to his high value. Ht. 28in. (71.1cm). Sold for £4,830 in 1997.

Courtesy Christie's South Kensington

ability to survive under difficult circumstances. A. A. Milne, in his stories and poems, created a placid and reasoned watercoloured landscape through which Christopher Robin and his whimsical animal friends are moved with delicate sensitivity. The great problems of the day for a little boy, who always runs "Hoppity, hoppity", concern avoiding the lines between paving stones, in order to outwit the bears who wait at street corners. In the poems for his little son, Milne talks of the stairs and nursery chairs that are the places and magic carpets of a child's imagination and carries the reader back to a wholesome world where little boys still said prayers on their knees at night and always had sand between their toes, in a perpetual summer existence.

Rupert, in comparison, is tough and resourceful, always willing to pilot an aeroplane or to take charge of an expedition to the Blue Mountains before returning, in time for tea, to his comfortable mum and dad in their modest cottage. Rupert, half boy, half bear, is a thoroughly progressive hero, who adapts to suit the interests of succeeding generations of children and, though he seems to belong to the present, he is, in fact, four years older than Winnie the Pooh.

Alan Alexander Milne introduced a Teddy Bear in *When we were very young*, a book of poems published in 1924. This bear was short and fat, hardly surprising as his main exercise was falling off an ottoman and lying on his back. After fretting over his excessive fat, Mr. Edward Bear meets the fat King Edward and becomes proud of his own adiposity. E. H. Shepard, who illustrated the poems, drew a bear that is believed to have been inspired by his own son's bear, "Growler". Milne himself was thirty-eight and a survivor of the Great War when Pooh took over his life. Already a successful playwright and a regular contributor to the satirical magazine *Punch*, he began to write the stories to amuse his wife Daphne and his little son. The playwright's eye for timing and crisp dialogue underlies all the adventures, which seem to demand to be read aloud. His wife, some ten years his junior, later remembered how they laughed and played as Milne dictated the animal stories, which were intertwined with her own reports of the day in the nursery and their delight and wonder at the sayings and engaging behaviour of the beautiful fair-haired child they had created.

Christopher Robin had received a Farnell bear, purchased at Harrods by his mother, for his first birthday in 1920. Like many children, he identified completely with the toy, talking to it and claiming that the bear had uttered impolite comments that he could not make himself. He called the bear Pooh after a swan he talked to when the family stayed at Arundel in Sussex, while Winnie was a famous black bear he loved to visit at London Zoo.

The Milne stories about Christopher Robin, Pooh, Piglet, Rabbit, Eeyore the donkey, Owl and Kanga use the animals to represent facets of human character that could not frighten or alarm children. It is the gentle humour, combined with E. H. Shepard's inimitable drawings, that have attracted children and adults across the world. Pooh Bear was part of Christopher Robin's own personality – "Wherever I am there's

COLOUR PLATE 102
By the mid-1920s, construction techniques were no longer hidden and even bears were externally jointed. This Christmas card pulls out to reveal six scenes: "I've lost/ my little Teddy Bear/ I cannot find him anywhere/ He wears no suits/ No socks or boots/ He really is a Teddy Bare". A "Pocket Novelty Card. British Manufacture throughout".
Author

PLATE 52

A large 1920s English bear made by Farnell with the typical "webbed" pad stitching. The pronounced snout is clipped and the large feet are card-lined. In golden mohair. Ht. 26in. (66cm). Sold for £2,415 in 1997. *Courtesy Christie's South Kensington*

always Pooh, there's always Pooh and Me" – so the stories, read in early childhood, cement a bond between child and Teddy Bear that is remembered throughout life. Almost every British adult knows something of Pooh, making him a symbol of our childhood beliefs, triumphs and mistakes, a combined fall-guy and muse.

In his first days, before such unpleasant and un-Pooh-like concepts as merchandising, the bear only existed in the poems that recreate the atmosphere of Ashdown Forest, where the Milnes retreated from Chelsea at weekends and where there were plenty of hollow trees in which boys and bears could hide. *When we were very young* was published by Methuen in 1924, in a first printing of 5,140, with a special edition of 110 on hand-made paper. Within two months, 43,843 copies of subsequent printings had been sold, as well as the rights to produce other, related merchandise. In 1926, *Winnie the Pooh*, in a first edition of 32,000, appeared, with *Now we are six* in 1927 in a first edition of 50,000. *The House at Pooh Corner*, the last of the series, appeared in 1928 in a printing of 75,000, a truly astonishing number for the period. It was inevitable that the series should end at this time, as Christopher Robin was ready for Preparatory School and was already becoming embarrassed by a fame that was to last throughout his life.

PLATE 53
"It's a very funny thing", said Bear "But there seem
to be two animals now… Would you mind coming
with me, Piglet, in case they turn out to be Hostile
Animals?" Signed with the initials of Ernest Howard
Shepard (1879-1976). Pen and ink. Unframed. Size
8½in. x 6½in. (21.6cm x 16.5cm). An original
illustration for "Hunting the Woozle" in *Winnie the
Pooh*, published 1926. Sold for a record £80,500
against a pre-sale estimate of £10,000-15,000.

Courtesy Christie's South Kensington

Christopher Robin, Pooh and their friends live in a forgotten world of nannies,
maids and walks in the park and it is this quality of innocence and tranquillity that still
holds appeal in a fast and noisy world. In the early '30s, the stories were read on the
radio in *Children's Hour* and this took the characters into the lives of many children
who would not have owned the books. In 1934, Chad Valley manufactured a Pooh
Bear with some of his friends, though The Teddy Toy Company of London, with a
board game and a range of soft toys, had predated the Chad editions by some four
years. The first recorded toy manufacture was not English but American, as Stephen
Slessinger Inc. had obtained sole copyright for the toys, which were produced, in this
instance, by Woolnough. The original advertisement claimed that Winnie the Pooh had
picked out Woolnough to make him "perfect in form" for the thousands who had read
about him. The line drawing shows a bear with characteristic short legs and long arms,
made in plush fabric. American children were familiar with Pooh as all the Milne
books had appeared in America, where they were published by E. P. Dutton and Co.

Today not only the early editions of the stories and poems, but also the songs, are
avidly collected. *Teddy Bear and Other Songs*, with verses by Milne and the music by
H. Fraser-Simpson, was published in 1926 with a dedication to Princess Elizabeth,
with *Songs from Now We are Six* appearing in 1927. Milne was quick to accept the
fact that the success of the stories rested on the lively but sensitive drawings of
Ernest Shepard and, very unusually, he was given a percentage of the royalties. In
December 1927 a special exhibition of the drawings was held at King Street,
Covent Garden and from this earliest period, they were already appealing to
connoisseurs. Perhaps it was hardly surprising, as Winnie the Pooh was already in a

PLATE 54
"It makes him very proud to be a little cloud", drawing by E. H. Shepard for A. A. Milne.

Courtesy Jane Vandell Associates

PLATE 55
"Do you see, Piglet? Look at their tracks! Three, as it were, Woozles, and one, as it was, Wizzle. Another Woozle has joined them!" Pen and black ink unframed original drawing by Ernest Howard Shepard for "Hunting the Woozle". Published in *Winnie the Pooh* by A. A. Milne. 3½in. x 5in. (8.9cm x 12.7cm). Sold for a very high £59,800, against a pre-sale estimate of £8,000-12,000.
Courtesy Christie's South Kensington

fifth edition. In 1928, *More Very Young Songs*, using the same composer and illustrator, appeared, as well as *The House at Pooh Corner*.

Any original drawings by Shepard for the series are now highly prized, with that of Christopher Robin dragging Pooh down the stairs from *Winnie the Pooh* (1926) selling in 1991 for £18,700. The last of the series, *The Hums of Pooh*, was published in 1929, when, with the flair for timing that had characterised the dialogue in all the books, Milne accepted that Christopher Robin was no longer an infant and left him and his toys in their innocent and enchanted world. To have updated the stories would have destroyed their perfection, which lovers of Pooh still guard jealously.

PLATE 56
Christopher Robin and Pooh, drawn by E. H. Shepard. When Pooh's arms became stuck aloft because he held on to a balloon for so long.
Courtesy Jane Vandell Associates

PLATE 57
Stories about the Abominable Snowman have always attracted speculation. This rare white fur "Yeti" bear was made by Farnell in the 1920s, without ears, to commemorate the first sighting of the Snowman. Ht. 19½in. (49.5cm). Sold for £460 in 1995.
Courtesy Bonham's, Chelsea

Since their creation, Milne's stories have attracted the interest of psychiatrists and educationalists, who struggle to understand the universal appeal of stories set in such a lost world. It is obviously strange that these tales appeal as much to adults as children and many confess to fully appreciating them only when they read them aloud to their own children. Perhaps this was inevitable, as the stories were written as much for the amusement of his wife as for their baby son and their whimsicality is very much that of grown-ups playing. A. A. Milne was to write that Christopher Robin told him very coldly that Pooh did not like the poems *When We were very Young* and many years later he was to claim that the stories had very little to do with his nursery life, from which his father held himself remote. It was inevitable that any person, made so famous by a character that he could only have resembled for a few years, would have become embarrassed and weary of the pretty child who sat always on his shoulder.

Though Christopher Robin the man grew thoroughly bored with the stories, children across the world have grown up with Pooh card games, nursery wallpaper, china and even clothes. The early American version of Pooh was a satisfactory

COLOUR PLATE 103
One of the "acts" from the "Animated Nursery", showing the typical toys owned by children in the 1920s. Made by Mathews Animated Dolls. T. Mathews and Co. Leicester. Figures 4in. (10.2cm) tall. *Author*

interpretation of the character, though many later toys have cheapened the concept and converted the bear into a fur cartoon. The official Walt Disney Pooh, made in the 1960s, though appealing as a bear cub, had little connection with Milne's creation and wore an offensive sweater with his name embroidered across the front. Since the mid-1970s there has been a flood of merchandise, though currently there are some attractive interpretations by doll and bear artists, who are able to make much more expensive figures than could be manufactured as children's toys.

Just as the later, or even pop-up versions of the books are never as satisfactory, so have attempts to manufacture the original soft toys failed, because new production methods negate their simplicity. Agnes Brush, under licence from Stephen Slessinger in the USA, made the most successful versions, as she used traditional fabrics in natural tones, that are in sympathy with the originals, now at the Donnal Centre in New York Public Library. The Farnell bear, once owned by Christopher Robin, can also be seen at the Library, though of course the original Pooh, owned by Shepard's son, seems to be lost. Shepard gave many of his original drawings to the Victoria and Albert Museum in London, aware that, from the very first, they were of interest to scholars and collectors. Though Pooh looks completely unlike a traditional Teddy Bear, his character, thoughts and sayings permeate every bear image, and subsequent writers and illustrators are bemused by his elusive, whimsical presence.

COLOUR PLATE 104
"Fond Birthday Greetings", with a 1920s German-made plush bear. Some manufacturers continued to use atavistic boot button eyes until the late '20s, especially for pull-along bears. The card is marked "British Manufacture".
Author

No. 46.—Rupert safely Home.

COLOUR PLATE 105
Rupert, drawn by Mary Tourtel, is delivered safely home to Mum and Dad by the balloons. In the early drawings, Rupert has a rather furry face and a more realistic outline. From *The Adventures of Rupert, The Little Lost Bear*, published by Thomas Nelson, 1921. This copy is inscribed "Darling Christine from Grandma, Christmas '21".
Author

Like Pooh, that other great character of the 1920s, Rupert Bear, also appeared with an entourage of animal friends, though these were completely anthropomorphic and almost invariably walked on their hind legs. Rupert forms a complete contrast to Pooh and belongs to contemporary life, rather than a time when nurseries were ruled over by nannies. He was created by Mary Tourtel, whose husband was a night editor on the *Daily Express* and provided the text for the stories. The newspaper was eager to find a rival to the *Daily Mail*'s "Teddy Tail" and the newly created Rupert first appeared on 8th November, 1920. Tourtel had

PLATE 58
The New Adventures of Rupert, Daily Express, 1936. Printed in red and black. The first *Daily Express* Rupert Annual. With slightly damaged dust jacket and one illustration hand-coloured. Sold for an unusually high £990 in December 1994.
Courtesy of Dominic Winter Book Auctions, Swindon

written and illustrated several children's books of animal stories in pictures and verse, an ideal formula for a daily comic strip.

In the first stories, Rupert's two principal friends are Jacko the monkey and Golli and their adventures are a mixture of toy box and fairy tales, combined with inventions of contemporary life, represented by road vehicles, airships and parachutes. Rupert hovers alluringly on the borderline between boy and bear – he has human hands and feet, but a bear's head – under his check trousers and red sweater there lurks a boy's, rather than an animal's body. His pedigree is firmly established by Mary Tourtel in the first *Adventures of Rupert the Little Lost Bear*, when a balloon carries Rupert back to a conventional Teddy Bear believing it to be his father. Confronted by a Teddy Bear, Rupert's face loses its look of joy. "I think there's some mistake" he said "My Daddy's not a toy."

Soon Rupert was joined by the friends with whom he is now mainly associated, Algy, Pong Ping, Edward Trunk, Podgy Pig, Bill Badger and Wise Old Goat. In the early representations, Rupert is a sturdy fellow with a more animal-like face, but by the mid-1930s, after Alfred Bestall had taken over the illustrations, he was thinner and his clothes were simplified into block shapes, rather than Tourtel's more anatomical rendering. The stories have survived because Rupert has been adapted for each generation and though the central characters do not change, children are always able to identify with the narrative. Since 1965, *The Adventures of Rupert* have been illustrated by a team of artists, who follow all the basic conventions established in the 1920s.

Surprisingly, Rupert did not appear as a commercial soft toy until the 1960s, when he was made by Burbank Toys. Because of his dressed body, he made an excellent toy which was economical to produce. Pedigree also made a foam-filled version, with stretch fabric clothes and a white nylon fur head. A real effort was made by Merrythought to create a more convincing model and a mohair version is made for their International Collectors Series, together with Bill Badger. The most highly collectable of all the Rupert merchandise is the series of ceramic figures produced by Beswick but discontinued in 1986, which immediately made the price escalate for the complete set in the collectors' market.

Rupert, because of the old Rupert League and a new specialist collectors' club, established in 1985, has a world-wide following of buyers of early annuals, puppets and rubber toys, as well as more recent items. For generations of children, Rupert was a friend and companion. My bear named Rupert accompanied me on canoe journeys up the Amazon, to dolls' funerals, for rides in a pedal car and on exciting broomstick adventures with witches. Because I was an only child, I talked incessantly to Rupert, Pong Ping and all the other Nutwood characters, though to me, as to many others, Rupert was more of a child companion than an animal, with a face that held much more appeal than that of any little boy. To me, Christopher

COLOUR PLATE 106
A 1921 edition of *The Adventures of Rupert, The Little Lost Bear*. Because the books contain simple, outline drawings, they were ideal for colouring and painting. Mary Tourtel preferred Rupert in a blue sweater and grey scarf.   *Author*

PLATE 59
A variety of 1920s bears sold in 1985. Left to right:
An English rough plush bear, with a solid straw-filled body. 17in. (43.2cm) £121.
A brown fabric German-made bear on wheels, 11½in. (29.2cm) long. £231.
A large, plush fabric bear with a straw-filled body and wide-apart ears. 24½in. (62.2cm). £209.
A small German fabric bear with a hump back. 8½in. (21.6cm) £209.
A Steiff button in ear woollen fabric bear on wheels. 15in. (38.1cm) £330.
A baby bear in a knitted suit, 13in. (33cm) £286. *Courtesy Sotheby's Billingshurst*

Robin and his friends belonged to a fairy tale, Alice in Wonderland time, whereas Rupert was a contemporary. It is this aspect of the character that keeps him alive today. Like many children, I read the stories in the annuals rather than the newspaper strip and can fully appreciate the allure of the bright covers and fast-moving stories, with their excruciating verse and mundane prose.

For the majority of collectors, the annuals are the mainstay, though to have any value they must be in pristine condition, as so many were produced. The earliest are in a small format and were uncoloured, much as the news-strip originals. Unfortunately for book collectors, they were ideal for colouring and painting, so a large number have been ruined by the enthusiasm of their young owners. Rupert merchandising reached its peak in the 1970s and the current strength of the limited edition market will no doubt encourage artist makers to create a more satisfactory image than that which has appeared purely as a toy. Rupert is extremely difficult to re-create because of his crossed animal/boy identity and in general he has been most successful when modelled in rubber, as in the Bendy Toys versions, rather than in plush with conventional plastic animal eyes.

Both Rupert and Pooh appeared at a time when adults were turning in relief away from war and its hardship and looking for light and amusement. For those who took refuge in the past, there was Pooh, for those who looked to a better,

PLATE 60
Made in the 1920s, this yellow plush bear has wide-apart ears, brown and black glass eyes and is excelsior filled. Ht. 17in. (43cm). Sold for £1,380 in 1997. *Courtesy Sotheby's London*

COLOUR PLATE 107
An unusual pink mohair bear with an elongated body, made in
England in the mid-1920s, when coloured bears of all kinds were
popular. He has small ears, brown glass eyes and a straw-filled
body. Ht. 24in. (61cm). Sold for £460 in 1995
Courtesy Bonham's, Chelsea

COLOUR PLATE 108
An unusual black and cream shaggy mohair, probably made in
England. The mohair is backed on to black fabric. He has
painted back glass eyes, a black, horizontally stitched nose, large
ears, brown cloth pads and is kapok filled. c.1925. Ht. 24in.
(61cm) Sold for £575 in 1995.   *Courtesy Bonham's, Chelsea*

brighter future there was Rupert – two bears who still absorb children and offer
collectors specialist fields.

Though the literary characters dominated the 1920s, many toy factories were eager
to get back to work and produce standard bears of comparable quality to those of the
pre-war years. There was no shortage of plush or mohair, except in Germany, so on
both sides of the Atlantic, makers were busy updating and improving their designs. An
interesting feature of the 1920s was the sudden increase in the range of fabrics and
materials available to toymakers. Felt and mohair were the principal media before the
Great War but the availability of new fillers, eyes and voice boxes all encouraged a spate
of inventiveness. In 1920, the London based Teddy Soft Toy Company patented its
"Softanlite" kapok-filled bears, which were soon copied by other makers, such as W. J.
Terry, while imitation leathercloth, patented by Dux of London, offered an alternative
to felt or fabric for paws and feet. Artificial silk plush, in a beguiling range of strong
colours, must have inspired many firms to produce fashionable Teddies, though it was
the British United Toy Manufacturing Co. that claimed to have first introduced this
fabric to the home soft toy industry. Plain gold mohair was obviously much too
traditional for the dancing '20s and bright colours, as well as a new shaggy material
were used. "Shagylox" bears were manufactured in 1925 by W. H. Jones in London,
while in 1926, Chad Valley made a rainbow coloured bear with a ruff and hat.

In the war years, Chad had concentrated on German look-alike Teddies, but also produced soft Art Velveteen bears in three sizes. These very early toys were unmarked but, by 1921, Teddy Bears were made in six qualities and thirteen sizes. The more expensive contained growlers and brass sleigh bells were fitted to the 8, 10, 11 and 12in. (20, 25.4, 28 and 30.5cm) sizes of all versions. A 1921 catalogue described Chad Valley Soft Toys as "The most life-like toys ever produced. Made throughout from British materials". The largest bear was 28in. (71cm) high and available in Best Long Golden Fur, Long White, Upright Golden, Long Beaver Brown, and Thick Nigger Brown Woolly Fur. Included in the "Pull-Along" wheel frame toys was a grizzly bear in nigger brown woolly fur. Like Steiff, Chad was using shaped metal wheels at a comparatively early date. These pull-alongs were only made at this time in an 8½in. (21.6cm) height, but were fairly expensive at 14 shillings each. The Chad bears in the 1921 range have wide-apart, large ears and eyes that are small and set closely together.

One curious feature of this period in Britain was the growing number of intellectual and artistic ladies of a philanthropic disposition, who gathered in small groups in towns and villages to establish creative toy workshops, usually employing local people to manufacture their avant-garde designs. Soft toys and dolls were the most popular creations, as no heavy or expensive machinery was needed. Some of the groups met in village halls or in the outbuildings of large houses and worked with any materials that were readily available. During the 1914-18 War, when toys were difficult to find, the local cooperatives and philanthropic manufacturers provided a useful source of playthings, but most of the groups had ceased production by the mid-twenties.

A typical small factory of the period was the East London Federation Toy Factory, founded in Bow by Sylvia Pankhurst, the famous suffragette leader. The products were designed by artists from Chelsea, though their early bears are not documented. By 1924, Teddy Bears in eleven sizes were in production and fine quality plush was used. This business, unlike most of the other artistic enterprises, lasted until the 1950s, working under the trade name "Ealontoys", first registered in 1926.

These small firms were highly praised during the war, with such slogans as "Another British Victory" or "War, War, War on the German trade", and it is a great pity that their work was unmarked. Occasionally old newspaper and magazine articles feature some of these craft groups, such as the one in Kelvedon, in Essex.

By 1929, most bear-making companies were utilizing various types of artificial silk plush fabrics, as they were cheaper and sometimes easier to sew, especially into miniatures. Chiltern in Britain made their first artificial silk plush bear, "Silky Teddy" in that year, in competition with Farnell's "Silkalite" versions. Because art silk plush was so easy to handle, it inspired many clown, Pierrot and jester outfits, that complemented the use of these figures in paintings, prints and furnishings. Images of Pierrots and clowns haunted designers in the twenties, who seemed to

COLOUR PLATE 109
Postmarked 1925, the French Christmas card shows a group of typical nursery toys of the period. The brown short plush bear appears, due to the long body, to be of French manufacture. *Author*

COLOUR PLATE 110
The 1920s saw great interest in coloured and dressed Teddies. The larger bear, possibly American, has the upper body in the form of a red mohair, bell hop type jacket. He is made of mohair and has the larger head and fatter body associated with the late '20s and early '30s. Ht. 18in. (45.7cm).
The smaller golden mohair is by the American Ideal Toy Co. He has boot button eyes, large, well apart ears and a prominent hump. c.1910. Ht. 12in. (30.5cm). Sold for £690 and £632 in 1997.

Courtesy Christie's South Kensington

PLATE 61
The "Acrobato" bear, made by
Schuco in Germany c.1920, but
now without the original trapeze
on which he performed. The
bear has a golden mohair head,
linen pads and wears a black and
white cloth suit with a red felt
jacket. The body has a metal
armature. Ht. 9½in. (24.1cm).
Sold for £437 in 1997.
Courtesy Christie's South Kensington

be escaping from reality behind masks and fancy dress. The toymakers were simply following fashion when they created Teddy clowns and Pierrots, in their parti-coloured outfits, sometimes decorated with pompoms and lace. Many of these were intended not so much as children's toys but as mascots, with some firms, such as the Zoo Toy Company of East London, specialising in this adult field.

Though mechanical invention in the 1920s is dominated by Schuco, specialising in novelties, other firms made amusing clockwork figures, such as a bear twirling an umbrella, Teddies mounted on bikes or the velveteen versions of the "Gee Line", made in New York City by Gund. Flocked tinplate was ideal for the manufacture of clockwork bears, as it provided a suitable texture without the problems of attaching a separate fabric bear to a metal scooter or bicycle.

By 1920, few companies were still using atavistic boot button eyes – in Britain, painted-back glass versions were popular, as well as blue and brown glass eyes with dark pupils. Blinka rolling eyes for Teddy Bears were used in 1921 by a Finsbury Park factory, while sleeping composition eyes were used by American makers by 1923. Any bears of this period with novelty eyes are of great interest, as comparatively few were produced and the survival rate must have been low.

PLATE 62
Plain wooden wheels characterise many of the bears made in the 1920s. Metal was in short supply in Europe during the Great War and its use in toys remained unfashionable afterwards, as the move was towards greater simplicity. This button in ear brown mohair Steiff has a pull-cord growl. The wheels are joined by metal rods. 23in. (58.4cm) long. Pull-alongs do not usually attract very high prices, making the £1,840 achieved in 1997 quite remarkable.
Courtesy Christie's South Kensington

By the mid-1920s, all of the more expensive traditional bears, together with push- and pull-alongs, the big rocking and riding versions were again available. As some firms continued to use spoked metal wheels into the 1930s, it is not easy to date some of these toys, though all the more progressive firms were moving to the general use of shaped, smooth metal wheels with tyres, that were both safer and quieter.

PLATE 63
Many of the nursery toys made in the 1920s look surprisingly old-fashioned, as sometimes metal wheels were still used and general body designs had changed little. The small 6¼in. (15.9cm) soft toy wild bear has a straw-filled body and is made of short bristle plush. The large pull-along is art silk plush, with a Steiff button in ear and a ring pulled growler. Ht. 17½in. (44.5cm). Sold for £143 and £264 in 1985.
Courtesy Sotheby's Billinghurst

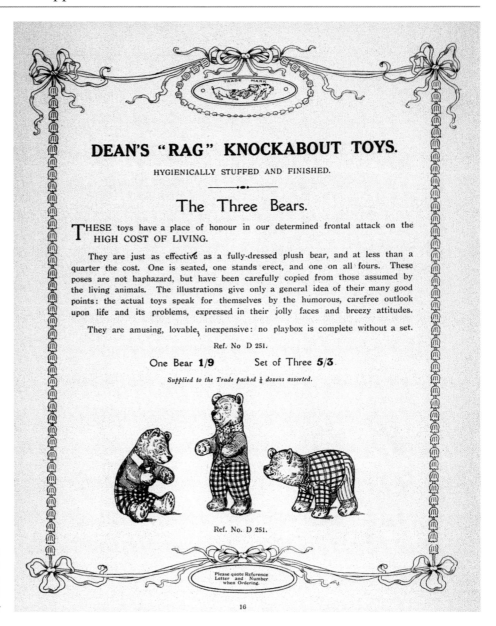

British toymakers who had survived the war and, despite adversity, managed to extend their range, were naturally self-congratulatory. Dean's, in their twentieth annual catalogue, spoke with pride of the way production had been maintained and claimed that among soft toys, their products held a position of "unchallenged superiority". Fortunately for Dean's, their toys relied on cheap cotton that had not been in short supply. Dean's claimed that their animal models were frequently imitated but "never equalled".

The new models carried an "A1" label, only brought into use "when a grade of excellence was achieved which fully justified its adoption". This new A1 label was triangular and was used on dolls as well as plush animals. Special designs were introduced, particularly the new "Evripose" construction that was used in bears. This invention was described as the one touch of nature needed to perfect them. "Bendy Bears are in the same relation to their primitive forerunner as man to the man-like apes." One of the most charming features of advertising and copywriting of the period is the odd mixture of wonderfully dated humour, juxtaposed with

COLOUR PLATE 112
"Bearing the Flag". Two golden plush Teddies with sewn-on foot labels "Dean's Rag Book Company, London, England". Both have pronounced humps on their backs and felt pads. The heads are curiously and very recognizably shaped. Ht. 16 and 18in. (40.6 and 45.7cm).
Courtesy Constance King Antiques

claims that would give a modern trading standards officer nightmares.

Dean's A1 toys available in 1923 included the Three Bears, still selling at the same price as before the war. The sitting model was 8½in. (21.6cm) high and they were not available, as were many of the toys, in flat printed sheets for home assembly. A range of plush toys was also offered, though a comment in the introduction to the catalogue suggests that they were a recent innovation, probably dating to 1921. The 1923 range, it was claimed, showed improvements in both design and materials and,

PLATE 64
"Old Floppy" was bought for Brenda Foster in Shepherds Bush for Christmas 1927. "He was so battered when my son was born that I re-covered him like a chair! When I became a collector, I kept looking at him and wondering if Old Ted was still there underneath. So one day I got my nerve up and stripped it off and there he was. A lovely original Teddy. It was lovely to see him again in the flesh after thirty years. I can't imagine why I gave him a new skin."
Courtesy Jane Vandell Associates

COLOUR PLATE 113
With his long arms and large ears, this English mohair Teddy was purchased in Bristol in the 1930s. It is unmarked and has large, rounded feet. Ht. 26in. (66cm).

Courtesy Constance King Antiques

judging from the illustrations, the bears were certainly well-made toys. The A1 range was filled with wood wool and fully jointed. These were chubby creatures with long fur and the round faces associated with British designers. The smallest size was 11in. (28cm) and this was available in both first and second quality plush. The best were fitted with growlers, while the cheaper range had only squeakers. The largest bear in the top quality range was 25in. (63.5cm) tall, but in the cheaper range only 19in. (48.3cm).

The "A1 Bendy Bears" were all kapok filled and fitted with the patent "Evripose" joints. Collectors are often led to believe that all kapok filled bears were made after 1930, but it can be seen that Dean's was using kapok alongside cork or wood wool from just after the First World War. Straw or sawdust filling cannot then be taken as any more than an indication of the date of manufacture. The Bendy Bears were extolled as:

"A novel combination of soft cuddly stuffing and the wonderful Evripose system of jointing. The movement of the limbs of these bears is no longer rigidly confined to the circular motion of the ordinary cotter-pin joint. Body, arms and legs have all the flexibility and movement of a live bear, positionable and changeable at will to meet every fancy of the youngsters. The patent Evripose jointing gives a still greater future to A1 Toys in general, soft stuffed Bendy Bears being perhaps one of the finest examples of the possibilities of the invention."

These Bendy Bears were only made from the finest quality plush and were all fitted with growlers. Once again, they were plump, well-fed animals, with a gentle, country aunt expression. Presumably many of these interesting bears, which could assume any position, are in collections today but are unrecognised, as few enthusiasts would twist an old bear's limbs for fear of incurring damage.

By 1925, Dean's Rag Book Company had set up a new showroom for their ever-growing range of products at 29 King Street, Covent Garden. The increasingly large demand for their soft plush toys was obviously a little unexpected and, in 1924, they had been unable to fulfil the orders. Despite the importance attached to the newer ranges, the Three Bears were still available. In order to bring them right up to date, they were mounted on scooters, the current craze among children in that year. "Each model in the 'Wheeld-on' series is mounted on a strong iron frame, fitted with running wheels and trailing cord. 'Scootakids' and 'Scootazoo' figures are attached to a patent collapsible scooter by means of spring clips, which allow it to be partially detached and folded together." Fortunately, the printed bears adapted fairly happily to their new mounts and their costumes and stance were unchanged.

The A1 grade of plush bears was, in 1925, still filled with wood wool. They were made in fourteen sizes, ranging from 11½in. (29.2cm) to 16in. (40.6cm). The second grade A1 bears were made of cheaper plush and fitted with squeakers rather than growlers. The

COLOUR PLATE 114
An English birthday card, c.1930, shows how the design of bears was gradually changing, with thicker, shorter arms and bodies, though the heads are still fairly narrow. *Author*

PLATE 65
Dean's Rag Book Company "Wheeld-on" printed bears with "Scootazoo" figures attached to a patent collapsible scooter by means of spring clips, allowing it to be partially detached and folded. *Courtesy Jane Vandell Associates*

COLOUR PLATE 115
Hump-backs were still used on many American and English bears in the late '20s and '30s. Probably by Terry of London, he has long, tapering arms and a hard filled body. Ht. 26in. (66cm).
Courtesy Bernard Beech

A1 Bendy Bears continued to be fitted with Evripose joints, a system which, it was claimed, "Reproduces in its main essentials the plan on which living bodies are constructed, having a skeleton, a soft inner covering to represent the fleshy and muscular tissues and an outer integument or skin. The utmost freedom of movement enables the limbs to be set and changed at will" and the bears could be arranged in a variety of poses, such as carrying baskets, so they were particularly suited for arrangement in groups in shop windows. The largest sizes were 16½in. (42cm) and 19in. (48.3cm) and these were fitted with growlers. The four smaller sizes had squeakers.

In the same year, Dean's introduced a completely new style bear, "Bendigo the Australian Bear". He was described as a rival to the Teddy with the advantage of British origin, design and manufacture. "Apart from these sentimental considerations, Bendigo is every bit as pleasing and cuddlesome as Teddy, is

COLOUR PLATE 116
Wearing his Grenadier Guards uniform, the off-duty bear was made by Dean's c.1925. He has brown felt discs behind his painted back eyes and is fully jointed, with velveteen pads. The foot label reads "Made in England by Dean's Rag Book Co. Ltd." He stands by a 1901 American shooting game. Ht. 17in. (43.2cm).

Courtesy Constance King Antiques

Evripose jointed and is moderate in price." Bendigo is not mentioned in the 1927 catalogue and it seems likely that he remained in production for just one year. He was shorter-nosed than the Bendy Bears and was made only in grey with a white front. He measured 14in. (35.6cm) and was fitted with a squeak. Presumably he was too adventurous for public taste and was soon forgotten.

Certain changes in production methods had taken place at Dean's by 1926 and all the 1st Grade of A1 Teddy Bears were now stuffed with kapok instead of the cheaper wood wool that had been used for the complete range. There was, from 1926, a greater difference between the 1st and 2nd grades and the second continued to be filled with the old style stuffing, apart from the smallest, whose size made kapok more satisfactory. A1 Bears in the kapok filled range measured 11½-25in (29.2-63.5cm). Up to 14in. (35.6cm), they were fitted with a squeak only. All the bears in the 2nd Grade were fitted with squeakers and these measured 9-16in. (23-40.6cm), measurements being taken to the top of the head, excluding the ears.

In 1927, with their offices still at the Elephant and Castle, Dean's commented on

PLATE 66
Pat Birkett, photographed in 1983 with her favourite Teddy, an unusual externally jointed French type bristle mohair, whose mouth, with a protruding tongue, could be opened and closed by means of a pull-string. "He always makes me laugh" commented the owner.

Courtesy Jane Vandell Associates

their own products in the most unashamedly glowing terms: "Talented writers and stern critics have penned columns of kind words about these modest playthings; profound and weighty Reviews have published these opinions: grave and reverend voices, as well as silvery and melodious, have sung their praises." The company went on to claim that the durable quality and careful finish of all items had remained their first care. Though the A1 Plush range was of more recent growth than the traditional products, there were many other new additions and the range of bears was particularly mentioned, a line that was obviously becoming a much more important element of production – "in quality, finish and price, these bears are unequalled".

The A1 range, now described as having "long fur", was for the first time available in 1927 in a selection of colours – gold, rose pink or saxe blue – and all of course carried the sewn-on Dean's label on their feet. They were sold to the trade either singly or by the quarter dozen and were packed in assorted colours, unless a shopkeeper requested one in particular. The 2nd Grade A1 bears were still filled with wood wool and fitted with squeakers and these were only sold in the traditional gold colour. Both 1st and 2nd Grade bears had the rather solemn faces and long arms that might well be associated with an earlier period. Around their necks were a ribbon and bell as well as the A1 label.

It seems that the great boom in bear production that had encouraged such a fast expansion had diminished to some extent and though the 1928 catalogue was one of the largest produced by the company, the range of bears was not extended and the old favourites, the printed Three Bears (illustrated every year from 1920), are omitted. The selection of A1 bears remained the same and the 1st Grade range was still made in a variety of colours. It is noticeable that other heavily promoted lines, such as the Bendy range, had all been discontinued and, by the late 1920s, it was only the A1 Plush range that was made.

The complete reorganisation of production took place because of the severe economic depression, resulting in the General Strike, which Britain was suffering. When family economies have to be made, toys are always the losers, which is why the state of the trade is such a reliable barometer. Despite all the novelties, such as the "Scootazoo" figures, it is obvious that the firm was suffering from one of the periodic down-turns that still

PLATE 67
A 1920s Jopi Teddy with a musical movement. The cub has a pronounced clipped snout and a beige, horizontally stitched nose. The musical movement is the concertina squeeze type. "Jopi" was a 1922 registered trademark of Josef Pitrmann of Nuremberg. The long mohair, sometimes with a tipped effect, characterises the bears, that are often unmarked. Ht.16in. (40.6cm). Sold for £1,265 in 1997. *Courtesy Christie's South Kensington*

make the toy industry particularly hazardous.

Among the dozens of small bear manufacturers whose work was unmarked, the history of a few has survived. Established in 1890, W. J. Terry was one of the oldest London-based manufacturers of soft toys. Like several German firms, skin and fur-covered animals were produced, as well as more conventional felt and plush toys. Terry became famous in the toy trade because it manufactured "I am Caesar", King Edward's dog. Though the company is often mentioned in contemporary advertisements, the date when Teddy Bear manufacture began is not known, though it is probably around 1912. Collectors often dub bears with long, tubular bodies, pronounced humps and painted back glass eyes as "Terry", but it is at present almost impossible to authenticate any bears made by this firm, as no marked early examples have been found. During the First World War, a type of webbed claw, rather like that used by Farnell, was introduced, followed in 1921 by the use

COLOUR PLATE 118
A straw-filled 1920s mohair with card backed feet and painted back eyes, made in Germany, probably by Schuco. With remains of tag hangers on chest. Ht 18in. (45.7cm).
Courtesy Constance King Antiques

of kapok as a filling material. Perhaps the most irritating feature of Terry's is that such an old firm, with trade documentation, produced thousands of bears which are completely unrecognizable. Terry continued to produce average quality bears until the late 1930s, when the factory closed. The firm was typical of dozens of soft toy factories that operated in North and East London between the wars, but rarely marked their work in any way, presumably because their cheaper products were being sold in competition with leading makers like Steiff.

Despite the difficulties British manufacturers suffered once they were in direct competition with the Germans, they were, as a body, surprisingly magnanimous. In 1921, the *Toy Trader* asked its readers whether German firms should be allowed to advertise in its pages and strangely, despite wartime memories, the resounding answer was "yes". The toy industry was obviously eager to resume all its old trading patterns and international friendships.

Times were very hard for German manufacturers by 1923, with the currency continually devalued by runaway inflation and over five million unemployed. Savings became worthless overnight, while bank notes lost all their value between printing and delivery. One of the results of the hyper-inflation was the gradual disappearance of the old wholesalers from the German market. Most were simply swallowed up and bankrupted when they were unable to pay their suppliers. Their loss is the modern collector's gain, as more firms were forced to market themselves individually and there was a great increase in publicity material and catalogues.

The financial debacle in the years after the 1914-18 War was to poison relationships between countries and firms for decades, as there was great bitterness at the way foreign merchants exploited the manufacturers and set up their own buying concerns in the old toymaking centres such as Sonneberg, in this way cutting out the middlemen who had previously earned a good living from the work of local makers. Purely from the viewpoint of the collector, this change had real benefits, as the makers themselves were forced to illustrate catalogues and they more frequently travelled to trade fairs to exhibit their own wares, rather than sending a local merchant with a group of items from different sources. A great deal of information is available from such contemporary sources, especially as photographs were steadily replacing line drawings in all catalogues and advertisements, which makes it possible to recognise and identify individual bears.

It is impossible to fault the designs of the German makers in the twenties, who were not going to risk their continued survival by creating toys without universal appeal. American and British children at this time were as likely to own a German bear as one made in their own country and the trade papers were filled with exciting novelties, made particularly by that firm of inimitable wit and novelty, Schuco, founded in Nuremberg in 1912.

Schuco-dressed bears and monkeys, with heads that turned by moving the tail, were on sale in America by 1923. Obviously any anti-German feeling had subsided in the USA, as they were praised in the toy trade press as "perfected by German craftsmen". The buyer was told to ask the bears a question, so they could cock their heads "in the cutest sort of knowing way and nod yes or shake their heads no". These Teddies, with "knowing black eyes", were made of fine golden brown plush and were sold in 11in. (28cm) and 13in. (33cm) sizes and had made their first appearance at the 1921 Leipzig fair. There was also a 5in. (12.7cm) cub with spectacles, jointed limbs and a head that could turn in any direction. The body was made of unbreakable metal covered with soft golden brown plush.

The 1926 German catalogues claimed that the Schuco animals had conquered the international toy market, as they were ingenious, yet relied on simple, easy to handle mechanisms made of first class materials. The German manufacturers were eager to assure buyers that the fabrics and materials they used were equal to those utilized before 1914, as some very shoddy goods had left the country during the devaluation period.

"Piccolo" bears and monkeys of a small 3½in. (9cm) size were promoted as new in 1926. They enclosed a scent bottle for use in ladies' handbags and could be pinned to a lapel or used "for squirt ball as joke" (sic). This bear is now usually sold

COLOUR PLATE 119
Schuco made many small, jointed Piccolos, with a typical seam down the centre of the head. This is made of bristle plush, has glass eyes and is jointed at the shoulders and thighs. The plush is faded, but it was originally green. Ht. 5in. (12.7cm).
Author

COLOUR PLATE 120
Schuco bears conceal all sorts of useful items, from spirit bottles to penknives. This faded gold Teddy is a compact, c.1930. Ht. 4½in. (11.4cm).

Courtesy Constance King Antiques

by dealers as a scent atomiser, though it was originally intended as a type of water pistol, the liquid shooting out of a small metal tube in the bear's nose, to startle anyone examining it on the lapel. All the Schuco toys were protected by international patents. Some of the Piccolo bears contained bottles with cork stoppers and there were special sets of three in display boxes with see-through gelatine tops. One illustration shows a bear with glasses, a drinking bear and a knitting monkey.

Schuco was particularly proud of the nodding head mechanism, produced by sliding the tail up or down, right or left. "In true imitation of nature, Schuco raises and lowers its head, looks to right and left and round about and therefore Schuco is claimed to be a living toy preferred not only by children but even by ladies." Over one million Schuco "yes, no" bears in long pile gold or white mohair had been sold in a single year. The mechanisms were proveably superb, as every single example I have handled, even up to a later 30in. (76.2cm) size, has still worked perfectly.

"Sparkling Eyes" was another 1926 novelty and could be fitted to most Schuco products, as could spectacles. The bears of smaller and medium sizes had press voices but the larger versions had automatic growlers. Their large wheeled toy bears had "draw voices", with a cord or string. Schuco refer to the wheeled bears as "Roller animals" and a few were given the patented head movements. One piece that is now very hard to find is the hanging bear, made for use in a baby's pram or cradle. The gold tumbling bears, reminiscent of Steiff, were made only in a small 5in. (12cm) size and could not be overwound.

Schuco was founded by an ex-employee of Gebrüder Bing and this probably accounts for the similarity of the mechanical bears made by the two companies. Heinrich Müller joined with Heinrich Schreyer and the firm initially traded as Schreyer and Son, producing wheeled bears in 1913. In 1921, after changes in the partnership, "Schuco" was used as the trademark. Some of the Schuco catalogues and advertising material is contradictory and the Piccolo series was hailed as new in the late 1920s, despite having been made since 1924.

Schuco Piccolos are found in astonishing variety and in a number of sizes. Most commonly discovered is the standard scent bottle, revealed when the bear's head is removed. Larger versions were made to hold a small bottle of spirits, though it is possible that these were made as special advertising items. In another Piccolo, the bear opens from the top to the bottom of the stomach to reveal a compact, with a mirror on one side and a lipstick in the other, all made of a cheap, brassed material. Except where sparkling eyes were fitted, the Piccolos have tiny, black metal, bead-like eyes and stitched features. Manicure sets in leather lined containers were another line intended for the adult

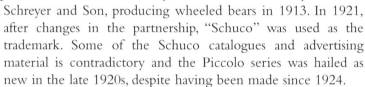

COLOUR PLATE 121
A miniature 1930s Schuco bear, with orange glass eyes and jointed legs. Tiny bears of this type are popular, as they make charming inhabitants for model schools or doll's houses. Ht. 3¼in. (8.3cm). *Author*

COLOUR PLATE 122
Schuco made their yes/no Teddies from the early 1920s. This example in cream mohair has painted back glass eyes, a pronounced clipped snout and is fully jointed. He has a key-wound musical movement, while the tail operates the yes/no head. He wears the original Schuco spectacles. The musical movement adds greatly to the value, as standard yes/nos are not uncommon. Sold for £4,025 in 1997.   *Courtesy Christie's South Kensington*

COLOUR PLATE 123
The Schuco compact bear opens to reveal the mirror and powder sections, with a lipstick holder in the head. Ht. 4½in. (11.4cm).
Courtesy Constance King Antiques

rather than the infant market, as were torches and sets of dice.

Piccolos come in a wide variety of colours, from dark green, gold, lilac and pink to red and black and can easily form a collecting field in their own right. They remained on sale in the toy shops for many years and were largely ignored by toy collectors even in the 1970s, when huge baker's trays of mixed bears and monkeys in all types and sizes were sold at Phillips in London. The toys were obviously ex-shop or factory stock and were auctioned forty or more in a single lot for prices around £30. To my eternal regret, I did not buy any, considering them too bright and modern. Today, even the simplest cost over £100, with unusual colours, such as the red, white and blue patriotic version being at a considerable premium.

Schuco's Tumbling Bear, dressed in felt, has the black metal eyes used on Piccolos and the same rather rough, prickly plush. The firm was still manufacturing until 1970, which accounts for the number of novelty pieces that are available. Their mechanical bears stand firmly on the borderline between tin and soft toys and appeal to both groups of collectors. Metal tumbling versions made of lighter, lithographed metal are liked by the tin toy collectors, and form amusing additions to a Teddy Bear display. Novelty wind-up bears were made by many German factories, but they are usually unmarked. One comes with a twirling umbrella, while

COLOUR PLATE 124
Schuco produced miniatures in several bright shades, those in unusual colours, such as purple, being most collectable. c.1930. Ht. 3½in. (8.9cm).
Courtesy Constance King Antiques

PLATE 69
A German-made tumbling bear with boot button eyes made around 1920. The arms wind to operate the clockwork mechanism, causing the bear to somersault. One leg remains in a fixed position. A similar mechanism was invented by Décamps. Ht. 10in. (25.4cm). Together with a 1930s Dean's Mickey Mouse. Sold for £352 in 1987. *Courtesy Sotheby's Billingshurst*

another plays with a beach ball. Especially popular with American children were the so-called bell toys, where a bell is mounted on a wheeled base and rings when the toy moves along – several toys of this type incorporate the figure of a bear.

Fur covered bears continued to be made well into the 1930s, though they are so atavistic that late pieces are almost impossible to distinguish without some evidence, such as the original box, the fabric of an old bow or late types of eyes. In 1925, at the Decorative Arts Exhibition, Gaston et Décamps, among their display of automata, showed a scene including a white polar bear, who poured himself a cup of chocolate and appeared to drink it. I have sold several Décamps-type bears, including one that I would have considered to date from 1900, were it not for the decidedly 1930s paper covering the original box, suggesting that identical designs remained in production over a long period.

COLOUR PLATE 125
A late 1920s Schuco that opens to reveal a manicure set. Ht. 3½in. (8.9cm).
Courtesy Constance King Antiques

COLOUR PLATE 126
A German-made carved wooden bear, which turns over on a bar when the string is pulled. A whole variety of novelty pieces of this type was made in South Germany and the Swiss Alps and were popular tourist gifts from the ski resorts of the '20s and '30s. *Courtesy Constance King Antiques*

Wooden toys, because of the renewed interest in crafts and folk art in the 1920s and '30s, captured the attention of many progressive adults and intellectuals, who were eager to promote reform. Art in the Nursery became a highly fashionable concept and stylised figures and animals were created by small firms in most countries: Caran d'Ache in Switzerland, Dryad in England and Steiff in Germany all included jointed wooden bears among their animal ranges. The figures were considered to be the height of good taste and were constructed of fine natural materials and decorated with stylish painting. In Britain, various small factories were set up, utilizing local skills to make expensive toys of the type which sold in elegant shops in the Kensington area and the Burlington Arcade. Despite the creative energy expended in these short-lived enterprises, their products are not now highly regarded, though individual items can be of interest as period pieces, particularly if stylised. Waltershausen trade catalogues show several ranges of such animals which must have been sold in commercial numbers but they are now difficult to find, presumably because the wood split or the joints separated. Among the larger wooden toys made between the wars was the Teddy Shoo-Fly (a seat fitted between two flat outlines of bears), which must be one of the most durable items.

The name Gebrüder Süssenguth would be almost completely unknown to arctophiles, were it not for one gloriously inventive and progressive creation, Peter, a somewhat dog-like Teddy. Christian and Franz began production in 1894 and

COLOUR PLATE 127
The bright yellow version of "Peter" is rare. This example has flirting black glass eyes, a moving tongue and moulded teeth and mouth. He carries his original chest label "Peter. Ges. Gesch. Nr. 895257". He was sold in June 1997, together with the Süssenguth catalogue of bears, dolls and novelties. c.1925. Ht. 14in. (35.6cm). Sold for £3,220. *Courtesy Sotheby's London*

COLOUR PLATE 128
"Peter" bear, made by Gebrüder Süssenguth, showing the detail of the moulded teeth and tongue. He has glass flirting eyes. The doll is a googlie by Armand Marseille. The bear has his original ribbon and neck tag and, like many other Peter bears, is boxed.
Courtesy Constance King Antiques

founded the factory as a dolls' parts manufacturer in Neustadt near Coburg in Thuringia. From the 1890s, they were registering patents for carton-type shapes covered with fabric or leather. Their famous Peter, though he has the body of a Teddy, has several interesting additions, such as rolling glass eyes, a shaped composition head under the fur covering and a moving tongue of a hard material. A large number of unsold Peter Bears were discovered in the 1970s, when I was buying them for around £35. At the time, many collectors felt Peter was not a Teddy Bear and they often remained on sale for a long time. As it became obvious that the toy was rare, prices escalated and Peter is now very expensive, with examples difficult to find. All bears of this type are in excellent condition and carry a breast tag edged with metal reading "Peter/ Ges. Gesch./ Nr. 895257". The registration number indicates the mid-1920s as the date of his manufacture, as does

COLOUR PLATE 129
A Swiss carved wooden bear cub "At Prayer". By the 1930s it was fashionable to use much lighter, unstained wood and allow chisel marks to show on the surface. Ht. 4in. (10.2cm).
Courtesy Constance King Antiques

COLOUR PLATE 130
A small, typically French bear of coarse mohair, with black glass eyes and a horizontally stitched nose. The wire jointing was used by several manufacturers in the 1920s, when the safety of children was of minimal concern. He was given to the owner recently because he had never had a bear as a child. Ht. 9½in. (24.1cm). *Courtesy Andrew Edwards*

his wood wool filling. The most commonly found Peter Bears with composition teeth are brown, but grey and apricot versions were also discovered, along with a few larger examples in pink. Peter's history since the mid-1970s has illustrated how a lightly regarded toy can soar to fame and fortune once its rarity is acknowledged. When the grey-boxed Peter originally appeared, it seemed to be on sale everywhere and I remember one collector, whose husband had purchased the bear as a Christmas present, returning it to me, as it had so little appeal to her.

Despite the problems of running a firm when the managing directors were serving in the army, Steiff, by dint of cheaper fabrics and the introduction of new, more economical toys, had managed to keep the family firm going through the war years. While many other German factories failed, Steiff, largely because of solid American orders, had re-organised trading so successfully that, by 1927, Richard Steiff was prepared to admit that most of their money problems were over. Much of this achievement was due to his clever marketing and keen eye for the novelties and innovations that kept the American toy trade alive.

Richard emigrated to America in 1923 and threw all his enthusiasm into promoting Steiff products by impressive displays in department stores and warehouses. Previously, Steiff had concentrated on beautifully constructed, German designed toys but Richard was alive to the fact that Americans liked brighter colours, novelty fabrics, very long pile mohair and soft, cuddly filling for toys that

COLOUR PLATE 131
Because an unsold stock of Peter bears was discovered, those in collections are usually in mint condition. The grey version is more unusual, though the tipped brown bear often appeals more to collectors. Both are boxed and with their labels. *Courtesy Constance King Antiques*

were expected to be really gentle and appealing to the touch. Though wood wool had been an excellent filling for the slim, almost doll-like bears that had been made before the war, it was of little use for the bodies of hug-me toys and kapok was gradually substituted.

In an effort to offer a range of good toys in 1920 Steiff created some cleverly jointed wooden animals and wheeled toys and produced bears in very economical short plush, or even paper plush or wood fibre. Again in an effort to minimise costs, the factory began a conveyor belt method of manufacturing and by 1922 the firm was again expanding its factory buildings. Mohair costs were extremely high in the early twenties but by dint of careful buying and economies in production methods, Steiff was again able to offer all the sizes of bears contained in the pre-war catalogues. Presumably Richard Steiff, seeing the factory at home well organised and ready to take over the international market again, felt that his skills would be best used in America.

He was immediately struck by the noise, colour and vibrancy of the New York toy trade. Everything had to be new and exciting, as novelty lasted for only a few weeks or months. This was a hazardous and potentially expensive world to explore, as fortunes could be made or lost in a space of time that would have made Margarete Steiff, with her ingrained German prudence, shudder. Flashing eyed Teddies that barked like dogs were not for Steiff and even in this period, when novelty was deliberately pursued, the firm's products retained a large element of caution that sometimes inhibited their most progressive designers, such as the Prussian-born Albert Schlopsnies.

COLOUR PLATE 132
Despite his spaniel-like re-backed ears, this late 1920s English bear, with his cord jacket, gave pleasure to hundreds of children who visited the Burrows Toy Museum in Bath, which closed in the mid-1980s.

Courtesy Constance King Antiques

COLOUR PLATE 133
"Teddy Clown", made in 1928 by Steiff, is one of the most appealing bears. This dual plush with brown tipped cream mohair is an especially fine example. He has brown and black glass eyes, is fully jointed and has cream felt pads. He wears the original cream and red ruff and cream felt hat. He has the Steiff button in ear. "Teddyclon" was first shown at the Leipzig Trade Fair in 1926. Ht. 10in. (25.4cm). He sold for £9,200 in 1997.

Courtesy Christie's South Kensington

From 1925-30, when Steiff celebrated its 50th anniversary, the American influence and input from Richard Steiff is easy to see in the introduction of bright new colours, more extravagant mohair and a new willingness to costume bears. To appeal to young American girls, zip fastening animal purses, velvet lined, appeared in 1927, including one featuring a bear. Two years earlier, some small 4in. (10.2cm) mascot bears had been offered to cyclists, as they could be fitted to the handlebars with small clips. A few of these Tali Bären also carried a flag and must have been irresistible to younger children as well as the teenagers for whom they were intended.

It was Richard too who inspired brightly coloured bears in pink, yellow and tipped mohair and, an introduction of 1925, "Teddy Bu" (Teddy Boy), with a smart coloured waistcoat. Teddy Clown, with a ruff around his neck, was also patented in 1926 and is now among the most expensive collectable pieces. In response to the American demand for a cuddly toy, Teddy Clown was kapok filled and contained a press-type voice box. The original range seems to have been made of brown-

PLATE 69
Made c.1925, this bear has large glass eyes with painted backs. The long, shaggy pile is tipped with a darker colour. He has long arms with narrow paws, a brown stitched nose and carries an embossed Steiff button. A similar bear, but with fabric, rather than the felt pads shown here, sold for £55,000 at Sotheby's in 1989.

Courtesy Jane Vandell Associates

tipped mohair and wore fabric frills around the neck and a felt conical hat decorated with pompoms. Teddy Clown was produced in a range of sizes from miniatures of 9in. (23cm) up to window and display pieces of 45in. (114cm). He was also made in plain gold mohair and in pink. Steiff are said to have produced 30,000 Teddy Clowns between 1926-28. Originally a round paper label printed "Teddy Clown Steiff original" hung from the front of the bear, though it is very rare to find this still in place. The bear was fitted with brown glass eyes and is considered among the most appealing creatures of the period.

With some 1,800 employees at the German factory, as well as hundreds of outworkers, Steiff dominated the international bear market by 1930. Improvements were regularly introduced to the standard ranges and in 1929 the riding bears were fitted with more advanced steering mechanisms and fashionable metal disc wheels with rubber tyres. When found today, some of these riding animals look surprisingly old-fashioned, despite their Art Deco wheels, and reflect Steiff's traditional manufacturing methods.

Again in response to American taste, a more infantile form of bear cub appeared in 1928. This little bear was designed with wired ears, which could be set at different angles, to increase the toy's appeal. Petsy was of great importance in the general development of Teddy Bears, as it established a completely new, much rounder form that, it was thought, would hold more appeal for children. Petsy's wired ears were larger than on previous designs and the bear was often given blue eyes, rather than the basic brown, the blue eyes being referred to by collectors as "Petsy googlie eyes". Another distinctive feature of the much sought-after Petsy is a seam that runs down the centre of the head. The bear was originally designed with a red, vertically stitched nose, that looked appealing with the blue eyes – to match the nose, red stitching was also used for the claws on the paws and feet. Unlike earlier Steiffs, this bear was sold with a coloured ribbon around its neck. Petsy, made only until 1930, heralded a completely different approach to bears and introduced the bear cub or baby, rather than the adult form. In this way, bears were conforming to the move among dollmakers, away from tall adult bodies to chunky toddlers and babies.

Because Petsy was only made originally from 1927-30, prices for examples in good condition are very high. As a novelty item, small versions of Petsy were mounted on wheeled metal bases in the "Record" range and he was also sold as a glove puppet. The tipped effect was given to the long mohair by lightly dipping the ends of the pile in dark dye. It was thought that this treatment gave the animal a much more realistic appearance.

Teddy-Baby was a logical design progression from Petsy and was patented in 1929. Sold in dark brown and gold, Teddy-Baby had a much rounder face that could be adapted for different expressions. This bear, with its many variations, continued in production until the late 1950s. It has very large rounded feet and a clipped muzzle that gives its characteristic appearance. In response to Richard Steiff's demand that the bears should have smiling faces, Teddy-Baby often has an open mouth, occasionally with rather fierce felt teeth. Because the bear cub was made over such a long period, it is found in many colours and grades of fabric. Sometimes Teddy-Baby has a bow of ribbon, others have a blue or red collar with a brass bell hanging beside the round Steiff label.

PLATE 70
Made by the Knickerbocker Toy Company c.1920, this black mohair American bear has painted back glass eyes and velveteen pads. He is fully jointed and straw filled. The nose has been re-embroidered. Ht. 18in. (45.7cm). Sold for £276 in 1995.
Courtesy Bonham's, Chelsea

While Teddy-Baby was one of the most successful Steiff products, his design also marks a change in attitude to toy production which antique collectors must regret. Early reporters, writing about Steiff's bears, frequently commented on how the integrity and dignity of the animal was always preserved. While Teddy might sit at a desk, drive his motor or perform in a circus, he is essentially an animal. Teddy-Baby crossed this line when the bear was dressed in baby shoes and pink frocks or trousers and fitted with a frilled bib for feeding time. Though the product is, to our eyes, less tasteful, it does reflect the brash period of its inception, when novelty and entertainment value were paramount.

Teddy Bear makers in America had a much more prosperous time in the years of the Flapper, with their boudoir dolls and mascots, than those in Europe, and the designs seem more in tune with the light-hearted, but abrasive, spirit of the age. Bubbles, cocktail glasses and cigarette holders seem to symbolise a period when having fun became a religion and every child's toy had to have some in-built novelty.

Whistling Teddies, patented by the Globe Teddy Bear Co. of Brooklyn, were certainly novelties. When shaking hands with the bear, a voice-box in the forepaw was activated and the bear appeared to whistle. The Globe Teddy Bear Co., described in 1921 as the largest Teddy Bear manufacturer in the world, was established in 1908. They produced brown, white and cinnamon bears in long and short pile plush. Morris Michtom's Ideal Toy Corporation, generally manufacturing rather staid bears, was forced to introduce movement to their range and produced Walking Teddy Bears in 16-24in. (40.6-61cm) sizes, also made of long or short pile plush. Collectors tend to differentiate American bears by the use of plush rather than mohair, though some American makers did use the much more expensive fabric.

"The more you hug them, the more they squeal!" screamed one Teddy Bear poster for a particularly loud squeeze box mechanism. There were Teddy pull toys, with bears sitting in engines, Teddy Acrobats and even Teddy soldiers with guns. Though these would not have sold in Europe at the time, the American love of shooting meant that bears with guns were regarded as amusing rather than menacing.

Because new eye mechanisms were so popular in dolls, the bear makers soon felt the need to compete and sleeping eyes, made of composition, were on sale in America by 1923. The public was still showing concern about filling materials and manufacturers were providing details of the stuffing they used in all their promotional material. Many firms used cork, though wood wool remained in use for the cheapest bears on either side of the Atlantic. Some firms attempted to make very large bears in the most economical way and forced reputable makers to state that "These bears have not been stretched out in order to get greater length".

Pudgy Baby Bears, Swiss music-box Bruins in green plush, Woof-Woof bears, tumblers and acrobats were all turned out by enterprising factories, particularly in New York and Chicago, alongside the traditional riding and pull-along toys. The Sensation of 1929 was the new tri-colour Teddies, a combination of pink, white and blue in medium pile plush. With their white heads and parti-coloured bodies, they wore clowns' hats and cloth ball buttons down their front, a reference to the Pierrots, so popular at the time. Another firm produced a blue and white clown, while the Montgomery Ward wholesalers catalogue showed a gold and light green plush bear with the usual cap and ruffle, identifiable because the finger and toenails were outlined with embroidery. A barking clown bear must have been zany enough to appeal to the most jaded buyer, who had perhaps turned down a Pudgy Baby Bear wearing a bib and dummy and felt shoes with pompoms, exhibiting some of the most distasteful aspects of Teddy design, as it hovered uneasily between human and animal and must have confused any child owner.

As parents grew less fearful of the serious childhood diseases, due to improvements in prevention and medicine, they became more concerned about everyday infections and were anxious to shield children from unnecessary dangers. Many Victorian toys, though visually exciting, were inherently dangerous – the child could gas herself by linking her toy stove incorrectly to the gas main, he could set himself on fire with methylated spirits or poison himself by sucking lead soldiers. All these horrors loomed large in the memory of parents of the twenties and thirties and they demanded much safer toys. Chad Valley was eager to jump on the safety bandwagon and even warned parents of the dangers inherent in the products of other manufacturers. In 1929, Chad issued a "very important announcement regarding the absorbent textile toys produced in unhealthy slum factories or homes that might convey infectious diseases to children of tender age who fondle them closely". In contrast, it was claimed, Chad Valley toys were produced in a country factory under ideally clean conditions and from hygienically pure materials. The factory claimed that "no outworkers were ever employed by the Chad Valley Company, who submit that guarantees of alleged purity from toymakers whose goods are partly produced by homeworkers under conditions outside their control and afterwards mixed with their own factory made articles, may only create a feeling of false security and should be disregarded".

Much of the Chad Valley advertising material was aimed at their German rivals, who had traditionally relied on the input of homeworkers and Chad was eager to accentuate the superiority of their label of Hygiene, obtained after inspections by the Public Analyst in 1923. This certificate also declared that all the dyes used by Chad were free of all injurious substances. Chad Valley had gained from the cessation of German imports during the 1914-18 War and had extended both its ranges and factories. In 1920, the Wrekin Toy Works In Wellington, Shropshire, was opened and from this time the firm was registered as the Chad Valley Company Ltd. Soon other firms, such as Peacocks of London, makers of fine dissected puzzles, and Isaacs of Birmingham, makers of Isa bouncing toys, were absorbed into the Shropshire empire.

By 1929, Chad was offering a wide range of bears, though the largest was a size 13, measuring 29½in. (75cm). The bears were all soft kapok filled and made of gold or tangerine plush in long or short pile. The smallest, size 1, bear was 8½in. (21.6cm). The 14-20in. (35.6-50.8cm) Chad bears were produced in coloured art silk and had the characteristic broad black embroidered noses and a bow of ribbon at the neck. The art silk bears, in pink, blue or white, were all fitted with growlers.

Another introduction of 1929 was "Cubby Bear. The Real Baby Bear. Very soft beaver or fawn fur plush". Cubby Bear in art silk was made in the colour combination of gold, pink and blue with white. The bear was only produced in a sitting design and measured 9½, 11½ and 13½in. (24, 29 and 34cm). He was obviously created as an answer to Steiff's Petsy, introduced in the previous year. These bear cubs set an agenda for the 1930s and were created for children who were perceived to be demanding an increasingly soft and cuddly type of Teddy Bear in brighter colours. Art Silk plush, introduced as Silkalite by Farnell, offered manufacturers a vast range of colours, which were used to create tri-coloured or rainbow effects. In 1929, Chiltern introduced "Silky Teddy", their first Art Silk plush bear and expanded their production with a new factory at South Tottenham.

In general, the late 1920s was a period of expansion for most of the firms which had survived the war, especially those who were willing to develop progressive designs for a generation of more opinionated and outwardly self-confident children.

COLOUR PLATE 142
Probably made in America, this short plush bear, acquired in the '30s, has the wide-apart ears and long, hard stuffed body with a back hump typical of such toys as the earlier "Teddy Good". Ht. 26in. (66cm).
Courtesy Jane Vandell Associates

CHAPTER 6
The League
of Bear Cubs

Childhood was still a period of innocence within a protected nursery environment for most middle-class children in the 1930s. The single parent family was regarded as a tragedy, rather than the commonplace feature it is today and amusement was obtained from books, games, puzzles and toy theatres rather than films or television. Teddy Bears were such an accepted feature of infancy by this time that manufacturers were constantly changing designs and introducing variants, in order to keep ahead of their competitors. For the collector, this is the last period of truly antique Teddies, as those made after the Second World War fall more into the realm of collectables and there is now a wide divergence of price.

Clubs and associations of all kinds attracted young people, with the Scouts and Guides, Christian groups and the Fascist youth organisations all fostering a love of the outdoor life and physical exercise. Even bear-related clubs flourished in Britain in the 1920s and '30s, especially the Rupert League and the Bobby Bear Club, whose membership reached a surprising 400,000 in 1932. Bobby Bear first appeared in the comic *Playtime* and proved so popular that his stories began to appear as an annual in 1922. He was drawn as a newspaper cartoon by Wilfred Houghton but, following in the footsteps of other loved cartoon characters, he sold particularly well as an annual that lasted until the 1950s, when television characters began to hold more immediacy. Children in the pre-war years enjoyed the whole process of joining clubs and receiving the newsletters and badges that confirmed

FACING PAGE: COLOUR PLATE 143
Farnell's musical bear, introduced in the late 1930s, was the ultimate nursery toy of the period, made in soft pastel colours in artificial silk, it has blue painted back eyes. This example is labelled on the foot "Harringtons Baby Goods. Made in England". It also has the Farnell's Alpha Toys embroidered label. Another example carried a Harrods label, as the toys were specially supplied to several shops. Ht. 12in. (30.5cm). *Courtesy Constance King Antiques*

PLATE 71
Bears became much rounder in form by the 1930s and the torsos were hard filled so they did not lose their shape so easily. Forms of external jointing were used for cheaper bears in most countries. This mohair, with a slightly upturned nose, was probably made in England. He is straw filled. Ht. 11½in. (29.2cm).

Courtesy Constance King Antiques

their identity as members of a special group. The Rupert League ended in 1935, so any metal badges or club publications are now collectable, as are the Bobby Bear Annuals and other related merchandise.

From this period, interesting toys ceased to be the province of the middle classes and were made to appeal to all sectors of the market. Manufacturers needed mass sales for survival, resulting in a very gradual downgrading of quality. Comic strip and animation characters were available to children of all sections of society and those created by Disney in particular crossed frontiers, so their related merchandise could be sold around the world. Though some inventive, and now very collectable, toys were created, this gradual globalisation of design ultimately took too much individuality from manufacturers and, from the antique collector's angle, was to result in a more characterless industry.

Traditional mohair bears, made by Steiff, Hermann or Chad Valley, still led the field in the more expensive section of the market, with their products selling from exclusive shops. Designs of top-class mohair and alpaca plush animals changed only slightly between 1920 and 1940 and without labels or provenance, some examples are difficult to date precisely. The more cub-like form of bear, introduced by leading makers in the 1920s, was widely imitated, as was the fashion for providing

COLOUR PLATE 144
A 1930s Rupert League badge. The club began in 1932, founded by Stanley Marshall, editor of the *Express* children's page, who later became "Uncle Bill". The enamel badges were sent for three 1d. stamps and are marked "Roden. London". Today, many reproductions are made. *Author*

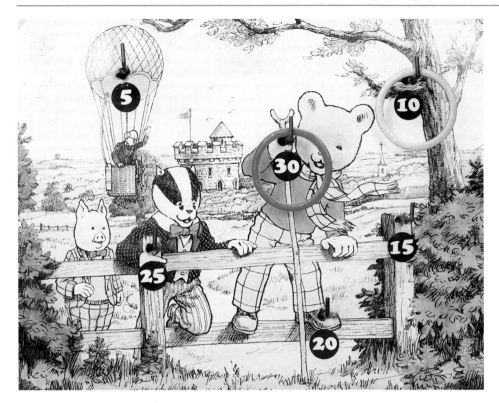

COLOUR PLATE 145
Rupert's image appeared on a wide range of merchandise. This wooden-backed game, with its card quoits, also served as an attractive nursery picture. c.1938. 11in. x 14½in. (28cm x 36.8cm).
Courtesy Constance King Antiques

baby bears with feeding bibs and bottles for milk. To save on manufacturing costs, more soft toys in the cheaper ranges were made with sewn-on clothes or with cotton fabric bodies, with the head and paws made of mohair. This was the era of the baby Bear, with variants produced in almost every country. To celebrate their 50th anniversary, Steiff began retailing Teddy Baby in 1930, a soft, roly-poly, young animal, that begged for cuddles and hugs.

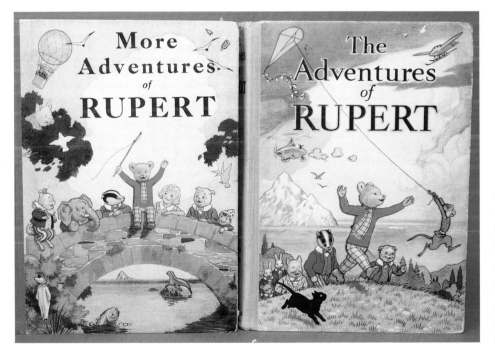

COLOUR PLATE 146
More Adventures of Rupert, published in 1937 and *The Adventures of Rupert*, published in 1939, illustrated by Alfred Bestall (1892-1986) with their colourful covers that delighted children. Though now highly collectable, the early annuals have to be in excellent condition to achieve good prices. *Author*

PLATE 72

Made by Merrythought in Ironbridge, Shropshire, this group of mainly 1930s bears is illustrative of the early productions. They were sold in 1995. Left to right:

A "Bingie" guardsman with a Merrythought button in ear and a foot label "Merrythought Hygienic Toys. Made in England". Ht. 26in. (66cm). £402.

Of dark brown wool, with a Merrythought ear button and a foot label, filled with kapok and straw. Ht. 18in. (45.7cm). £483.

The gold mohair "Bingie", made in a seated position and with blonde inner ears, jointed only at neck and shoulders. Ht. 13in. (33cm). £276.

Sitting on top of the bureau, "Cheeky" is much later and dates to the 1950s, with orange plastic eyes, a velvet snout and the characteristic bells in the large ears. The front paws are brown felt. Ht. 13in. (33cm). £414.

Sitting in front of the book is a 1940s gold mohair with a foot label for "Merrythought, Ironbridge, Shrops. Made in England". He is fully jointed and has brown felt pads. Ht. 15in. (38cm). £253.

"The Magic of Merrythought" by John Axe, together with a 1986 limited edition, no. 37 of 1,000. Ht 16in. (40.6cm). £253.

Courtesy Bonham's, Chelsea

Despite German ascendancy in the international bear market, a few brave business people were willing to set themselves up in competition and bear collecting is dominated at this period by the many innovative characters introduced by Merrythought. These good quality bears have their ancestral roots firmly established in Ironbridge, Shropshire in 1930. The bears produced by the firm were made of an especially fine mohair, that was not popular with the furnishing trade in the 1920s because of cheaper synthetic products. The Yorkshire mill owners, W. G. Holmes and G. H. Laxton, aware of the declining market, engaged ex-employees of Chad Valley and J. K. Farnell as directors of a toymaking factory in Ironbridge. The company was also fortunate in persuading another Chad Valley employee, Florence Atwood, who had worked under Nora Wellings, to become designer of the new Merrythought range in 1931.

The first Teddy produced by Merrythought was the Magnet Bear, made in a choice of gold or coloured good quality mohair: a chunky fellow, with large ears and the shorter, thicker limbs that were fashionable, Magnet was made in four sizes from 12½ to 24in. (31.8 to 61cm). A cheaper version was made of British Art silk plush in romantic-sounding colours that were inspired by the 1931 selection of Paris dress designers, such as Copper Glow, Jade, Iris and Myosotis. Fortunately for collectors of today, Merrythought always marked their products with a sewn-on embroidered label – "Merrythought. Made in England". After the first years of production, the words "Hygienic Toys" were added.

In competition with German makers and British firms such as Chad, the Ironbridge company made unjointed bear cubs from 1931. "Tumpy", with a white front and ear lining, was made of soft woolly plush and was described as feather light and soft. "Bingie", with a winsome appearance, who appeared alongside him, also had white inner ears, but was modelled in a sitting position and made from tipped white curly plush. The first range measured from 9–14in. (23–35.6cm). While most of the firm's animal and doll designs were very progressive, the standard bears were always atavistic and this obviously adds to their appeal for collectors.

PLATE 73
"Teddy Pratt" was given to his owner by Dr. Arthur Pratt of Grimsby on the only occasion she met the gentleman. He is an English-made toy, with painted back eyes and large, cub-like ears. He now serves as guardian of the whiskey bottle. *Courtesy Jessie Harley*

COLOUR PLATE 147
The ultimate for the fashionable nursery of the '30s, a hard stuffed pouffe with a leathercloth base. Width 15in. (38cm).
Courtesy Constance King Antiques

163

PLATE 74

"Bobby Bruin" by Merrythought, in dark golden mohair. The ears are set well apart and the jointed arms have an unusual bend at the elbow. The unjointed legs are cut in one with the body, a style that was later to become popular. With Merrythought label on right foot pad. c.1936. Ht. 16in. (40.6cm). Sold for £805 in 1997.

Courtesy Christie's South Kensington

These early products were made from mohair woven at the Yorkshire mill and were meticulously finished by hand, one average animal taking an hour to stuff. Even by 1939, only two hundred people were employed and the firm was never able to meet demand, as every toy produced was slightly different and always intended for discriminating buyers.

By 1933, the general popularity of costumed bears encouraged Merrythought to dress Bingie in sailor, guardsman and Highlander outfits, though the standard model was still made, the firm claiming that he held that "Babyishness that so appeals to children". The costumes were well made and detailed, quite unlike some bears, where fabric costumes were simply a means of cutting down on the use of expensive mohair. Bingie, in a small size, was also made as a pram toy, to be hung off a ring on elastic. A new bear for 1933 was "Chubby", with a white nose, paws and feet, made of downy fawn and brown alpaca. "Bobbie Bruin" was fitted with patented "movie joints" and was promoted as a golden brown mohair bear designed from nature. He was fitted with metal rods in his legs so

PLATE 75

Merrythought is now one of the oldest established toy-making firms. This 1930s bear has a button in ear marked "Merrythought, Hygienic Toys, Made in England". The nose is horizontally stitched and he is filled with kapok and straw. He has been re-padded and the original foot label has been sewn back. Ht. 20in. (50.8cm). Sold for £460 in 1995. *Courtesy Bonham's, Chelsea*

he could be posed easily on his flat, cardboard-backed feet. These traditional bears, in addition to the sewn-on foot labels, carried a wishbone-shaped tag reading "Merrythought Hygienic Toys". By the late 1930s, some mohair bears also carried a pewter button. In the nineteenth century, wishbones were known as merrythoughts in Britain and thought to carry a wish, giving the image happy associations.

Florence Atwood continued to design Merrythought toys until 1949 and was obviously highly receptive to changes of taste and the 1930's love of caricature and novelty. Her strangest bear was heavily inspired by Mickey Mouse, but was registered and patented as Teddy Doofings. The name of the toy was virtually the only thing that linked it to any other bear and most people would fail to recognise it as one of the species. One interesting advance was eyes that shut and opened and fingers that moved. "Such playability has never before been incorporated in a single toy." Teddy Doofings does not seem to have sold as well as the Dutch Teddies, with characteristic baggy trousers, that were featured in 1938, or perhaps he was simply too complex to make in quantity.

Few early Merrythought riding bears are now discovered, but they were in production from 1937. The metalwork was lacquered and the "Grizzly Bear" stood on metal wheels with rubber tyres. Standing from 13–31½in. (33–80cm) tall, the grizzly was a splendid pull-along, though necessarily expensive at the time. Many of these large Merrythought and Chad Valley toys were sold only through the most exclusive toy shops and department stores and the numbers made were always limited, though they can sometimes be glimpsed in old photographs of fashionable nurseries or in children's wards in hospitals. Though Merrythought products were often ignored by bear collectors because of their comparatively late beginnings, they are now included in the most prestigious auctions and exhibitions but antique interest is centred mainly on the pre-1940 ranges, with the later bears appealing to a more general collectors market.

Curiously, fictional Teddy Bears are almost invariably masculine in gender, but one exception of the 1930s was Mary Plain, who always wears her red and white striped shorts. The first volume of Gwynaed Rae's books, *Mostly Mary*, was published in 1930 and had been inspired by the antics of a real bear cub, which lived in the bear pits in Berne and was watched by Rae when she was recovering from an illness. Mary Plain's grandmother was Big Wool and there was an unpleasant bear named Harrods. The books appeared regularly and in 1942 *Mary Plain in Wartime* was published. The original bear had an inset muzzle and part coloured ears and was a typical product of her period. Because of the burgeoning bear market, the books are now popular with collectors, though they have never developed the cult following of Rupert or Pooh.

PLATE 76
Gwynaed Rae wrote a series of books about "Mary Plain", the lady bear, seen here at Rottingdean. The first book, *Mostly Mary*, was published in 1930. Contrasting muzzles are a feature of some bears of the '20s and '30s. *Courtesy Jane Vandell Associates*

Fernand Martin and Décamps had created exciting and unusual mechanical bears long before the entry of mohair Teddies to the market, but for some reason, French manufacturers have never established themselves as leaders in a field always dominated in Europe by the Germans and the British. The only Paris maker whose work is appreciated by collectors is M. Pintel Fils et Cie, whose bears were marked with a brass-plated button, embossed with a pair of hugging bears, a trademark that was first registered in 1913 and is found on the bear's chest. Unusually, the firm continued to use boot button eyes until the 1930s, though most surviving examples are found with the characteristic glass eyes with painted backs, that have usually rubbed clear. Pintel bears are economical in appearance and are frequently constructed of short, bristle mohair. When new the bears, with their long, thin bodies, were attractive because of their rich colour, but their appearance has often suffered badly over the years and they do not appeal greatly to the international market.

Like the earlier French bear-makers, who had concentrated on movement, Marcel Pintel first created a mechanical figure in the

PLATE 77
Made by Chiltern in the peach-pink coloured art silk plush that was so popular in the 1930s, the bear has painted back glass eyes, a pronounced shaved snout and the card-lined foot pads used by many English firms. Ht. 14in. (35.6cm). Sold for £483 in 1997. *Courtesy Christie's South Kensington*

COLOUR PLATE 149
Soft toys of all kinds rode on scooters and tricycles in the 1930s. This externally jointed French bear with glass eyes is marked "Unis France" and rides a wood and metal tricycle. Ht. 8½in. (21.6cm).
Courtesy Constance King Antiques

form of a bear clown. With the loss of imported German soft toys during the 1914–18 War, the French toy industry gradually gained strength and Pintel developed a wider range, including mohair Teddies, that were in production by 1920. All the known Pintel Teddies were filled with wood wool and have vertically stitched noses, long, straight arms and large feet.

COLOUR PLATE 150
Few Japanese-made bears are of such nice quality as this clockwork clown in a parti-coloured yellow and blue felt suit. He has wooden hands and metal feet and the Japanese tag remains around his neck. Other bears in the series played violins. Ht. 5in. (12.7cm). *Author*

COLOUR PLATE 151
Bell toys of this type remained popular until the Second World War. These art silk plush, unjointed Teddies stand back-to-back and carry the original silk hearts on their necks. Ht. 8in. (20.3cm). *Courtesy Constance King Antiques*

Because of the general interest in cub-like bears in the 1920s and '30s, Pintel designed an appealing range, with set-in muzzles of contrasting mohair and the large heads associated with young animals. The new range was filled with kapok, for the essential, soft, take-to-bed look and was made of a long, soft mohair. This infant look was further exaggerated in the work of Article de Luxe Fabrication Artisanale, known as Alfa, whose first bears appeared in 1936. These are fully dressed bears, with the "Alfa" mark printed on their feet. Pre-war examples were made of mohair and are similar in concept to the baby bears made by other European firms, though these have a special character with their open mouths, that give the faces a cheerful, smiling look.

Thiennot was another French company that began operating because of the cessation of German imports and was established in 1919. Emile Thiennot, who had worked for Marcel Pintel, used the trademark "Le Jouet Champenois". Even French collectors have difficulty in identifying Thiennot products, as they were not marked. As in all countries, there were some small manufacturers of bears who did not mark their work in any permanent way, but their products are identifiably French because of the primitive jointing systems and the cheap fabrics from which they were made. The most idiosyncratic of all French bears was "Prosper", a character that first appeared in 1933 in *Le Matin* and was created by Alain Saint-Ogan. The white bear appeared in a series of adventures in a daily cartoon strip and has thin arms and legs, a long nose and an exceedingly bad-tempered attitude to the world. In one toy version, he has a papier mâché head and a bristle mohair body. He always has a chain fixed to a ring in his nose, to prove how his life was adversely affected by man.

Prosper was a highly individualistic creation, both in cartoon and soft toy format, and French manufacturers appear to have distanced themselves deliberately from old German designs – even today many commercial bears made in France have a distinctive style of their own. American and British toymakers were much less individualistic and copied and casually adapted German ideas to suit the demands of young buyers.

Early in the 1930s there were many imitators of Steiff in America. Teddy Baby of 1929 must have inspired the "Fat Pudgy Baby Animals" that Montgomery Ward advertised the following year. The bear had "Just finished his dinner and with his bib still on he is placidly nursing his pacifier. His fat little tummy is just so big that he can hardly balance on his hind legs." This bear was made of long plush in a variety of solid bright colours. He had glass eyes, an embroidered nose and mouth and wore bright felt shoes with pompoms. "A Regular Little Clown" was another line, influenced by Steiff's Teddy Clown. The Montgomery Ward bear was made of gold silky plush on one side and light blue on the other. He had a swivel neck and wore a clown's hat and neck ruffle. "Little Clown" was made in 16½ and 18½in (42 and 46.4cm) sizes and contained a squeak-type voice box.

Alongside the novelty pieces of the 1930s, many old favourites regularly appeared for the Christmas market. Squeeze bears with Swiss musical movements in the torso were brought up to date in brightly coloured plush of brilliant green and blue, while rubber bear-shaped hot water bottles were made up in gift boxes with soap and toilet items. Even the Three Bears were improved upon and made a delightful Christmas present, complete with table and chairs, three porridge bowls, spoons and a red and white country bear style checked table-cloth.

COLOUR PLATE 152
"The Three Bears" story is recounted in a series of transfer prints on a boxed 1930s set of toy china, made in Staffordshire, England. The fashionable Art Deco style of the pottery contrasts rather strangely with the traditional prints. Box 17in. x 13in. (43.2cm x 33cm).
Courtesy Constance King Antiques

COLOUR PLATE 153
The most famous and innovative bear of the 1930s was the American-made "Feedme", introduced by the Commonwealth Toy and Novelty Co., which was first used to promote Barnum's Animal Crackers. The child pulled a ring at the back of the neck and the mouth opened wide to devour candy or even toast. A zip fastening in the bear's back was then opened to remove the food. Made of plush mohair, they originally wore "Feedme" bibs and carried a lunchbox of animal crackers. High chairs were also available to seat the Teddies. Ht. 18in. (45.7cm).

Courtesy Constance King Antiques

To attract American customers, several makers in New York and Chicago began using soft, long-piled alpaca for the more traditional bears, though these old nursery favourites were being pushed hard by the hundreds of novelty items, such as the memorably named "Musical Shag", with his very woolly yellow feet, hands and face. This curious bear wore a sweater and cap and contained a Swiss music box. His red tongue hung out greedily.

Most curious of all the oddities created by the inventive New York toymakers in the late 1930s was the eating bear marketed as "Feedme". Made by the Commonwealth Toy and Novelty Co. the bear "devoured" real food. M. Greenfield, then president of the company, claimed that the toy was attracting widespread interest and was to be used by the National Biscuit Co, in the promotion of Animal Crackers in 1937. "Feedme" is a cartoon-like animal with a wide mouth. When the child pulled on a ring at the back of the neck, the bear's mouth opened and animal crackers, candy, rolls or even toast could be placed inside. A zip fastener on the bear's back made it simple to remove the food. They were made of plush mohair and stood 18in. (45.7cm) high. Some were sold complete with a baby-type high chair for feeding time and all wore coloured bibs and carried a lunch box filled with Animal Crackers. The Commonwealth Toy and Novelty Co. was founded by M. Greenfield in New York in 1934 and still produces unusual bears in West 23rd. Street, though "Feedme" was the most famous and strangest of all its products. Presumably a 14in. (35.6cm) version sold in 1941 was also made by the company, as it had a metal-lined throat and stomach and the jaws were forced open when the head was tilted back.

In England, even Deans's Rag Book Company, notorious in its early years for labour-intensive designs, often in comparatively short production runs, had by 1930 become more economical. Dean's cheaper products had often been sold through corner shops and 1d. Bazaar-type outlets and these were suffering badly in Britain because of the General Strike and the long years of depression. The 1928 catalogue had been the largest produced by the company but the range of Teddy Bears had not been extended and those old favourites, the Three Bears, illustrated every year from 1920, were omitted. The selection of A1 Teddy Bears remained the same and

COLOUR PLATE 154
Miniature mohair bears are sometimes discovered in old doll's houses, This early 1930s, German, short-legged bear lived for many years in a doll's house in the Burrows Toy Museum in Bath, now closed for some years.
Courtesy Constance King Antiques

PLATE 78
Most Chiltern bears are relatively unexciting, but this "Winter Skater" has great appeal. It is unmarked and the arms are wired to hold them away from the body, to carry the mohair muff. The art silk plush sweater is pink and white, with a large white collar. c.1937. Ht. 16in. (4.6cm). Sold for £575 in 1995.
Courtesy Bonham's, Chelsea

PLATE 79
A rare Lineol polar bear, c.1938. Lineol and Elastolin were competitors in the area of realistic composition figures.

Courtesy David Hawkins

the finest grade items were still made in a variety of colours, but it is noticeable that other heavily promoted lines, such as the "Bendy" range had been discontinued and by 1930 only the A1 Plush range was still in production.

Several tentative efforts were made throughout the years to introduce adventurous variants on basic Teddies but none had any lasting success, though, of course, they are now desirable collectors' items because of their rarity. The Polar Bear, for instance, made in 1933, would be a wonderful addition to any collection, as he was so completely realistic. The Polar Bear was launched in conjunction with the introduction of a completely new line of Dean's toys:

> "Bears are universally popular as playthings and here is a Polar Bear produced in a specially woven plush and constructed in a manner that leaves nothing to be desired. Just note the original design employed for the claws which are quite soft and harmless and at the same time realistic. Not only a fine toy but a really useful item for use as a window attraction."

This splendid bear stood 21in. (53.3cm) high and was fitted with a growler. Though his unusual stance and turned head now make him immediately recognizable, he failed to become highly popular and was discontinued.

Another equally short-lived animal was "Edward Bear", introduced in 1937, in honour of the new King Edward VIII. He was completely unlike his human namesake, the former Price of Wales, and was plump and cuddly, with fat arms and legs. "Edward" was described as a "New version of the Teddy Bear and one which should please those who are looking for something different. This toy, which is sure

COLOUR PLATE 155
Schuco miniatures of all kinds were sold throughout the 1930s. Ht. 3¼in. (8.3cm).

Courtesy Constance King Antiques

COLOUR PLATE 156
Some traditionally made Teddies are difficult to date unless their history is known. This large English-made bear was purchased new in 1936. He is unmarked. Ht. 28in. (71cm).

Courtesy Constance King Antiques

of a warm welcome, is produced in long curly plush and is beautifully finished." From his appearance, most collectors would date Edward to the 1950s rather than the '30s, as he is very much more a soft, child's bear cub. He was made only in three sizes, 20, 24 and 28in. (51, 61 and 71cm) but marked another stage in the evolution of the Teddy Bear from the rather lean figures of the early years to those plump creatures, all fur and cuddles, that characterised later toy production. With the abdication of Edward VIII in 1937, "Edward Bear" proved an embarrassment to his manufacturers and disappeared from the catalogues, though he no doubt reappeared in another guise.

During the 1930s, Dean's was gradually shifting its operations from the old Elephant and Castle site to its new address at 61, High Path, Merton, SW19, a brand new factory, built on the site of Lord Nelson's old farm. It seems that the move was a very slow affair and it was only completed after the old factory was damaged in the London bombing of the 1940s.

PLATE 80
A Farnell type English golden mohair bear, with amber and black glass eyes, a clipped snout and black stitched detail. He has the rexine pads that identify the models of the later 1930s. Ht. 19in. (48.3cm). Sold for £460 in 1997.　　*Courtesy Christie's South Kensington*

PLATE 81

For the first time ever, a bear took a photo call at No. 10 Downing Street – just a day in the life of a busy Teddy who had his own engagement book. Bears owned by famous people always attract great interest. "Humphrey", a sheepskin with leather paws, was the childhood companion of the ex-Prime Minister Margaret Thatcher, who christened him. Being a true patriot, Humphrey has a "Made in England" label on his back. He has amber eyes and brown pads and was bought around 1930. Though he lived at 10 Downing Street in the 1980s, he was frequently away from home attending charity events. Ht. 22in. (56cm).

Courtesy Jane Vandell Associates

COLOUR PLATE 157

A page from a 1930s Chad Valley catalogue, showing the cub-like bears that were becoming fashionable in Europe and America.

Courtesy Jane Vandell Associates

COLOUR PLATE 158
With his large, somewhat wedge-shaped head, this mohair bear was made by Dean's in the 1930s. He has glass eyes and a vertically stitched nose. Ht. 18in. (45.7cm). *Courtesy Constance King Antiques*

The majority of Dean's pre-war Teddies were traditional, though a new, cheap range was completely unjointed and made in gold, pink or blue mohair plush. A new jointed gold mohair bear was introduced in 1937 but, in contrast to the progressive Edward, this new model was in decidedly antique style, with long arms and large feet. A new "Silkeen Teddy" was another 1937 introduction, which was fully jointed and kapok filled and was made of art-silk plush in coral, saxe, buttercup, jade and tango, ranging in size from 12–18in. (30.5–45.7cm). He appeared in the catalogue alongside popular favourites, such as Popeye, Henry and Lupino Lane.

Though Teddy Bears were very important to Dean's they were, as at Steiff, just one element in a large soft toy production range and it is obvious, in the years leading up to the Second World War, that bears were not as important as they had been in the 1920s. Their place had been usurped by cartoon characters and bright novelty toys, that must have accorded more with the spirit of the period, with its fabrics in stark, solid colours and furniture with sharp angles. For a while, it must have seemed that Teddy Bears were too old fashioned, too traditional, to appeal to the children of the 1930s, with their fairy cycles, scooters and pedal cars.

The rapid expansion of Chad Valley during the 1930s meant that separate factories and catalogues were used to segregate soft toy and games production. The seal of purity was still a very important element in promotional advertising and this, by 1938, took the form of a long, book-mark shaped seal that was fixed to the soft toys. Many of the bears by this time were of a much simpler shape, obviously designed for the cheaper section of the home market and made of kapok-filled art silk plush in shades of gold, green, brown, pink and blue. Fortunately, the traditional bears in de luxe quality were still produced in sizes up to 18in. (45.7cm). Thick amber coloured plush with "erect pile" was made, as were quality Teddies in golden curly mohair plush or short mohair. While most types of Chad bears were of

PLATE 82
Sitting comfortably at home in 10 Downing Street, Humphrey, in his proletarian blue dungarees, is joined by Mrs. Teddy, another British bear who was also owned by Baroness Thatcher when she was a child. *Courtesy Jane Vandell Associates*

COLOUR PLATE 159
Made of bristle mohair, the laughing bear, with composition teeth and a red felt tongue, is straw filled and has glass eyes. From the time of the Laughing Roosevelt Bear, various manufacturers have made open-mouthed bears with teeth. This version dates to around 1930 and is probably American. Ht. 24in. (61cm).   *Courtesy Bernard Beech*

average size, a few in curly mohair measured 28in. (71cm).

Cubby Bear had proved to be very successful and was joined in 1938 by Baby Bruin, made of soft wool plush, and by Sonny Bear. The latter was promoted as "Cubby Bear's fat little brother and going to be the pet of the family… the children will love his quaint little puzzled expression". Cubby was made of closely woven biscuit coloured plush in sizes up to 15in. (38cm).

In recognition of Chad Valley's success in the manufacture of top quality toys, the firm was granted a Royal Warrant of Appointment as Toymakers to Her Majesty the Queen in 1938, an honour that, judging from the catalogue of that year, was well deserved. Chad, more than any other British soft toy maker, concentrated on the bear market and its products are becoming increasingly appreciated by collectors. Though they are mainly associated with somewhat atavistic designs, in the late 1930s they joined other toymakers in the production of dressed bear families and even a range of koala bears in alpaca and wool plush. In the Bear Family Group, mother and daughter wear gingham, while father and "Master Sam" wear plain trousers. A larger "Bobby Bear" was fully jointed and wore felt trousers.

In an early example of "collectors' toys" for children, a concept that became very popular in the 1980s, Chad offered a family group that could be purchased separately and assembled into a "Bears' Tea Party". The small bears, all under 4in. (10.2cm), were made of close-woven plush and dressed in felt and print clothes. They were accompanied by a square-topped table with a central pillar and three

Colour Plate 160
Open-mouthed bears have appeared throughout the century but are never completely satisfactory. This English version, with a felt lined mouth, dates to the late 1930s. He has glass eyes. Ht. 26in. (66cm).
Courtesy Constance King Antiques

chairs, all finished in cellulose. Almost any soft toy at this time was costumed as an economy measure, and dogs, rabbits and lambs were all turned out in felt and gingham. One particularly recognisable bear, made of nigger-brown alpaca and biscuit wool plush, has curious dark pompoms on his stomach, with dark ears and parti-coloured arms. The fully jointed toy was described as "something really new". Curiously, it was called "Honey Bear", but looks something of a cross between a bear and a panda.

Children of the 1930s who lived in secure homes must have enjoyed a period when the the whole concept of a perfect infancy was most fully realised. Few mothers were out at work, streets and roads were not too dangerous for children to ride their scooters and bicycles and there were few television sets to lure children away from books and play. Even the toy manufacturers seem to have become more aware of a child's basic need to receive and give affection. Chad Valley introduced "Bedtime Toys" which, they claimed, evolved from careful study of every feature necessary to please an infant. "Bo-Bo Bear", with a pink body and white paws and

Plate 83
"Petzi", a 1930s German-made bear, originally belonged to Walter Steinkogler's aunt, who gave it to his former girl friend. "When we split up, I said she could go, but I was keeping the bear! While lecturing in England, Petzi has supervised all my tutorials." He now lives in Austria.
Courtesy Jane Vandell Associates

COLOUR PLATE 161
Learning to count and tell the
time, a late 1930s, English-made
bear, wearing a sailor suit, in front
of a Glevum Toys abacus. Ht.
30in. (76cm).

Courtesy Constance King Antiques

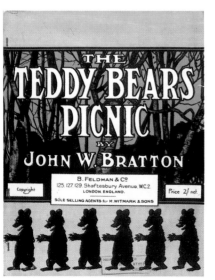

head, was filled in a special way to create a pillow-like effect and make the bear
delightfully soft and cuddlesome. The eyes and features were made from soft
materials, "eliminating all fear of harm to the tiniest kiddie" and satisfying every
child's love of bright things.

"Cuddlechums" was a similar soft and cuddly range and was claimed to be free
from anything which might harm the smallest child. "Do the kiddies want
something to cuddle and love – here they are." Despite all the care and affection
that was lavished on children in the 1930s, just a few years later, the same adults
who were so indulgent and considerate of their own young were subjecting infants
in other countries to some of the most horrific conditions ever known to civilian
populations. Perhaps some foreboding of war inspired the comforting and amusing
novelties of the late '30s, the same toys that children clutched in air raid shelters
and garden dug-outs.

Toy-makers were always influenced by the products of other firms which they
encountered at the international trade fairs, and many of Chad Valley's products in
the '30s, such as the miniature schools, bulldogs, elephants, tango-dancing toys and

COLOUR PLATE 162
Originally called *The Teddy Bear Two Step*, the re-named *Teddy Bears' Picnic* became a hit with
children in the 1930s when words were added to the tune and the distinctive sheet music cover
was designed.

Author

PLATE 84
Brenda Herdman's Teddy with his family, just before leaving for India in 1937. He was bought in Hong Kong in 1932 and terrified his new owner, when she saw his big, dark shape at the end of her bed on Christmas morning. In the photograph, it is her doll that she holds affectionately. *Courtesy Brenda Herdman*

PLATE 85
Though this 2ft. (61cm) high golden Teddy, with his pink plush paws, at first frightened his child owner, "He has remained a life-long friend and my own children were not allowed to play roughly with him. He is seen with me in my garden in Scotland. He sometimes wears a woolly cardigan against the British cold. As he was raised in Hong Kong, he probably feels it badly." *Courtesy Brenda Herdman*

some of the wheeled bears, are reminiscent of Steiff in Germany. Like Steiff, Chad Valley was interested in mascot bears, those ultimate security symbols, intended for adults as well as children. The range of miniatures was recommended either as toys or "ornaments for the lounge". The "Wee-Kin" mascot series was claimed to hold an irresistible appeal, which made them suitable not just as toys but also as carnival and party novelties. "Fuzzy Bear" was the latest adult mascot, with spectacularly long fur and a neat felt waistcoat. Dean's Rag Book Company had also shown some interest in the adult miniatures in the 1920s and commented on ladies who were adopting little girls' playthings as mascots, boudoir ornaments or dance companions. In Europe and America, motors and cycles were frequently decorated with a costumed bear, giving the toy and novelty makers an ever expanding market.

COLOUR PLATE 163
Clockwork walking bears with fabric coats covering their metal structures have remained popular throughout the century and have to be dated by the type of plush used and the material of the collars or muzzles, as they are almost invariably unmarked. Made in Germany, this 1930s bear has a leathercloth muzzle and an art silk coat. Length 6½in. (16.5cm). *Courtesy Beryl Gapp, Bath*

COLOUR PLATE 164
A late Schuco Piccolo, the thicker body and larger head giving a more cub-like form. Ht. 4in. (102cm).

Courtesy Constance King Antiques

Possibly as a glance backwards at the animal origin of the Teddy, a bear with printed pads was designed by Steiff in 1930. Dicky Bear was made of white or blond mohair, was fully jointed and made more realistic by the rather curious printed paw and foot pads with all the toes carefully defined. Again in response to Richard Steiff's advice that the Teddies should look happy, the mouths were upward-stitched in a broadly smiling position. In general, Dicky was promoted as a cheaper type of bear and was only made in the smaller sizes, up to 17in. (43.2cm). They formed an excellent contrast to Teddy-Baby, yet remained within the Steiff traditional ranges. "Dicky" was marketed from 1930-36 but is now often difficult to identify, as the characteristic printed pads have often been replaced.

Steiff's "Circus Bear" is a typical '30s product, with a contrasting muzzle and the thick, cub-like body, so popular at a time when baby dolls had also superseded more adult-shaped forms. The circus bear, first made in 1935, was fitted with a neck movement that had first been patented in 1931. He could move his head from side to side and his legs could be positioned so he could stand, crawl or sit. These bears must have proved expensive to make, because of the metal armature with snap joints that was adapted for different types of soft toys.

PLATE 86
"Dicky Bear" in golden mohair made by Steiff, c.1930. He has glass eyes and a cream clipped-cut plush muzzle and a black, horizontally stitched nose and mouth, with the remains of a painted smile. He has colour-printed velvet pads. Ht. 13in. (33cm). Sold for £747 in 1997.

Courtesy Christie's South Kensington

In general, the 1930s was not an especially adventurous period for Steiff in relation to bears, as much more energy was expended on cartoon characters, dogs and, in 1938, the Teddy Bear's closest relative in the toy box, the Panda. A few amusing bears, particularly a kelly-like Roly-Bär, with an open mouth and made of mohair plush, appeared in 1937, while a baby bear, lying on its back and mounted on wheels, though reminiscent of an earlier period, was made more attractive by the addition of bells on his front paws.

The late 1930s, because of the rise of the National Socialists, was extremely difficult for all the German toy-makers. George Borgfeldt in New York, one of the most important merchandisers of bears, was soon affected by the Nazi's ban on Jewish businesses, while imports, particularly of fine quality English mohair, were also barred. The final blow came in 1939, when Richard Steiff died in Michigan. Because of the German government's heavy-handed control and manipulation of industry to suit its own ideology, valued employees had to be sacked and the old export houses, always run by German Jews, were taken over or put out of business. Gradually, the whole country became geared towards war and the frivolous little bears which had capered on Steiff's displays in the big department stores and trade fairs across Europe and America became a thing of the past. For the reputation of Steiff, this virtual cessation of production was fortuitous – Steiff Teddies do not combine with Nazi uniforms and aggression – so it was as well that Teddy Steiff bowed out of the spotlight in this ugly period.

To many collectors of bears, the Teddy himself should not have survived the war. The brainchild of Richard Steiff, with its inspiration in old Germany, untouched by two horrific wars, bears have an essential dignity and innocence that evokes sun-filled Edwardian afternoons, nursery tea and company that seemed to enjoy life so much that there was endless time for play and frivolity. Society itself changed irrevocably after 1940 and it is the modern longing for the benign certainties of pre-war days that attracts us to that ultimate Edwardian, the Teddy Bear.

PLATE 87
"Hero", a 1930s bear, who lost a leg and an eye somewhere in the 1940s but was put back on his feet by Pat Thompson, seen holding him. Provided with a wooden leg and an eye patch, he was again able to face the world.

Courtesy Pat and Ken Thompson

PLATE 88
Manufacturers updated bears in the early 1930s by using contrasting, brightly coloured plush – in some instances, three colours were used together. The two-coloured Teddy go-karts in the company of a German mohair with rexine pads, presumably a close copy of Steiff's "Dicky", introduced in 1930.

Courtesy Jane Vandell Associates

181

CHAPTER 7
War and Aftermath

Commercial and political upheavals, population movements, rationing and currency restrictions all combined to make the 1940s a difficult and almost completely unadventurous period for toymakers in Europe. A few backroom-type manufacturers struggled to make small ranges of toys from cheap or readily available materials, but there was little significant change in basic design. Wounded servicemen, convalescing in hospitals, were encouraged to make soft toys, though the only material available to the occupational therapists was a type of bonded fabric known as American cloth. In Britain, even felt was in short supply. Though unpleasant to handle, the American cloth bears were immediately attractive because of their bright colours, but few have survived because the material cracked so quickly. Other ex-servicemen made wooden pull-along animals on wheels, usually cut with a fretsaw, though again they usually relied on colour rather than artistry for their appeal.

As the only infant in a family of adults, I was often the recipient of curiously constructed wooden and soft toys and remember objecting strongly to a pink pull-along bear with the type of brightly painted back-cloth I knew elephants should wear. Until the early 1950s, there were few attractive toys in British shops and virtually no mohair bears. My own bear, made by Chad Valley, was a 1938 model and persuaded out of a shopkeeper who had put aside a group of pre-war toys, presumably out of nostalgia for the type of stock she used to sell. My other toys were sometimes inherited from cousins in the services, or were home-made. Occasionally the adults

PLATE 89
The author aged six with Rupert/Teddy Villers, a Chad Valley. "I remember scowling when a cousin took the snapshot because my bear was never carried like a doll – he was my companion adventurer." *Author*

OPPOSITE COLOUR PLATE 165
Clemens made their very first bear in 1948 in Kirchardt/Baden in West Germany. Having lost their factory in Alsace because of the War, Hans Clemens opened a gift shop in Mannheim, where bears made from old German army blankets were sold. They were made by Hans and his sister. Today, Clemens specialise in the collectors' market. *Courtesy Clemens Spieltiere*

183

on leave were able to find a few toys in Petticoat Lane in London, though these were usually pre-war stock and there were never any bears to discover when I rummaged hopefully in their kitbags. Despite the general shortage of toys, it is doubtful whether infants felt deprived, as our basic needs for soft toys to sleep with and handle were well satisfied by home-made knitted or fabric rabbits, golliwogs and bears. Older children must have suffered more, as they were without the metal wheeled toys, construction sets and luxury mascot-type soft toys that they were used to seeing in the shops. In response to the shortage of toys during the war, Yootha Rose, who was later to found the Rottingdean Toy Museum with Lesley Dakin, began to produce her artistic and innovative toys, setting trends that were fully developed in the 1960s. Once good, commercially made toys began to re-appear on the market, most of the home-made toys of the 1940s were discarded by parents, giving any surviving examples added interest to toy historians and collectors of folk items.

One commercially made bear that many babies owned in the 1940s was the gas mask carrier. These occasionally appear on the market, though the original maker is unknown. They were intended to contain the Mickey Mouse inspired rubber gas masks that were issued to children and which were to be carried around at all times. Despite the efforts of the War Ministry to make these appliances less frightening,

COLOUR PLATE 168
Gas mask cases were made of scrap barrage-balloon fabric throughout the war. This was commercially made by a London firm, which used a variety of toys, including rabbits, to decorate the fronts. It was probably intended for a girl, as babies and toddlers were supplied with "Mickey Mouse" gas masks with tongues. 8in. (20.3cm). It sold for £1,150 in May 1997.
Courtesy Christies South Kensington

they must have been extremely unpleasant to wear in the practice sessions that were held in schools. Toy manufacturers soon took advantage of the situation and designed bags, made from silver barrage-balloon material, with bears and rabbits sewn to the fronts, that were substituted for the square cardboard boxes supplied by the government. The mohair dressed rabbits, bears and cats all had glass eyes and long whiskers. Mohair was presumably not too difficult to find in the early years of the war in the small quantities needed for heads and paws. Like many of the home-made toys of the period, few gas mask carriers have survived, in relation to the number produced, probably because parents were eager to expunge all traces of the hard years from the lives of the young.

Just as in the nineteenth century bears had been constructed from animal fur, this material again became popular in wartime as rabbit and sheepskins were readily available. Some extremely curious bears evolved at this time and some are virtually patchworks of different coloured furs. At fairs and markets around the country, soft rabbit skin bears in white or grey were sold as mascots and were made in small back street factories. Because rabbit skin is so fragile, few of these primitive bears have survived, though they were attractive when new. Sheep and lambskins were much stronger and some firms specialised in these during the Second World War.

Lambswool bears had been made much earlier, especially in Australia and America, though commercial production is not recorded until the 1930s, when they

COLOUR PLATE 169
A large headed, round-bodied British-made bear with rexine pads, dating to the late 1940s. He has plastic eyes, a stitched nose and is filled with wood wool and kapok. His fur is art silk rayon plush. The shape reflects the popularity of round, well-fed animals that suggest a time of plenty. Ht. 18in. (45.7cm). *Courtesy Constance King Antiques*

COLOUR PLATE 170
Swedish manufacturers, particularly Merimex, used lambskin with great skill to create bears that closely resemble those of mohair fabric. Swedish, c.1950. Ht. 18in.
Courtesy Constance King Antiques

were advertised in the American press. Some were fitted with musical boxes and were kapok filled. As though the natural skin was made by a process designed exclusively for the manufacturing company, the advertisement claimed that the wool would not pull out. Margaret Thatcher's Teddy Bear, Humphrey, is made of long natural sheepskin and is soft and yielding to handle but others were dyed yellow or brown, such as those produced in the 1940s by the Swedish firm Merimex. Despite the abundance of sheep in Scotland and Wales, commercial production of these bears was centred in New Zealand and Australia, though Schenker, making mainly sheepskin toys, was established in Austria in 1952. As Teddy Bears have become collectable, more small companies have introduced sheepskin bears to their ranges and some examples can now be found in most countries.

The disadvantage of the material is the difficulty of tailoring the sections, as the skin is too thick to allow for precise shaping, and consequently most bears of this type are extremely basic in design and rely on their soft, pillow-like feel for their success as toys. Undeterred by the problems, one American firm recommended lambs fleece bears as they could be "treated like a real live pet and washed in water".

Occasionally exclusive furriers have created luxury bears for the adult collectors' market and in the '70s and '80s it was not unusual to find mink Teddies with

COLOUR PLATE 171
Muzzled and chained bears that carry a pole are usually Berlin souvenirs. This dark brown clockwork version was purchased in the occupied zone of Germany in the late 1940s to be sent home to a small child. Ht. 9in. (23cm). *Courtesy Constance King Antiques*

PLATE 90
Chiltern was one of the leading British bear makers of the 1950s, when the "Ting-a-Ling" was made. This cub has a golden mohair coat, a clipped plush muzzle and a ting-a-ling growler. Ht. 13in. (33cm). Sold for £299 in 1997.
Courtesy Christie's South Kensington

jewelled eyes and fine silk ribbons. They were a relatively short-lived fashion, as the anti-fur trade lobby made the use of animal fur for this type of market unacceptable.

While in Europe bear manufacture virtually ceased during the war, the American trade was largely unaffected and most of the '30s designs continued to be available. Though mohair was difficult to obtain in sufficient quantity, the plush mills were able to produce enough attractive fabric to satisfy home demand. Even so, bear design was not progressive, presumably because the makers did not get inspiration from other products, which used to be encountered at the international fairs.

Bear cubs and anthropomorphic baby bears continued to be popular, as were "snoozing bears", a more appealing name for the nightdress case animals. Swiss musical boxes were still available for American Teddies, though one of the more interesting was a Mama and Baby Bear. Mama rocked the cub in her arms while a lullaby played. A touch of reality was added as mother wore a dressing-gown. Feed Me bears, first used for advertising purposes, were offered in American toyshops, complete with their bibs. Much more economical in design were the fluffy animals in very bright colours that were unjointed and much fatter than most cub versions – the most expensive of this range were fitted with flirting eyes.

One bear that does reflect the constant changes in lifestyle engendered by the war

COLOUR PLATE 172
Made of art-silk rayon plush, this type of bear was made in Britain from around 1939-55. Collectors sometimes refer to them as "Woolworth's" bears, as a number are recorded as having been purchased there. The bodies are always very round and the voice boxes still work. Ht. 25in. (63.5cm).
Courtesy Constance King Antiques

was the Autograph Bear, made of pure white fabric, suitable for friends to sign. The Teddy was intended to keep on his body a permanent record of friends and family, though at 36in. (91cm) he must have proved too large to carry to many functions. He was obviously intended as a college companion and the bear shown in the firm's advertisement carried a signature "Yale '42".

American bears of the '20s and '30s had been characterised by their long, thin bodies with little suggestion of the humps of German and English bears. One very unusual feature of bears made by one of the best known manufacturers, the Knickerbocker Toy Co., was a metal nose that seemed to have been used only around 1930. Though long established as toymakers, Knickerbocker-labelled bears usually date after 1930 and all have somewhat triangular heads with large, widely spaced ears. Many bears made by Knickerbocker were cinnamon coloured, possibly because brown grizzly bears were familiar to American children.

Gund Manufacturing Company was founded in 1889 and was making bears in New York by 1906. Early products seem to have been unmarked and Gund only becomes interesting in the development of bears after 1927, when they produced the "Gee Line" jumping animals. The firm took off in the 1940s because of the lack of European competition and, in 1948, they adopted a new trademark of a rabbit faced "G" and began to produce toys under licence from Disney. Though their 1940s bears were made of cheap cotton plush, a few, such as their version of Winnie the Pooh and the googlie-eyed bears, are of some interest.

Chad Valley, despite many problems, continued to manufacture a limited range of toys during the war, though, in general, output was limited to government contracts, with the wooden toymaking factories producing instrument cases and electrical work. The printing works was adapted without much difficulty to producing charts and the sewn toys had to take second place to a wide range of utility marked children's clothing. By a special arrangement with the government, one factory, staffed by the most elderly workers, made some toys and games, notably a clown bear, marketed in 1945. Most British tinplate production was earmarked for the war machine and, until 1948, all metal toys were made of aluminium.

COLOUR PLATE 174
Comparatively late bears are valuable if they are unusual and have the addition of a maker's label.
This Lefray bear dates to the 1950s and has a very unusual body construction with thick, short
legs. He is labelled "Lefray. Hygienic Toys. Made in England". He has orange plastic eyes and the
ears are lined with brown velvet. He has cloth pads and is jointed at the neck and shoulders. His
filling is a mixture of wood wool and kapok. He sold in 1995 for £3,680. Ht. 21in. (53.3cm).

Courtesy Bonham's, Chelsea

COLOUR PLATE 175
"Panda, Bear and Bible", the author's own toys. "The three were given to me together in the dark days of war, when children still said their prayers at night." The Bible is inscribed "Presented by her Mother at the age of six months". She later commented that she wanted me to play a lot, but I would need a basic awareness of right and wrong from the earliest years. The two soft toys have always lived together and were constant bedtime companions. The toys were made in the late 1930s but were unsold until the 1940s. The Chad Valley bear is 16in. (40.6cm).   *Author*

COLOUR PLATE 176
Toys rarely survive in "unsold" condition but this Chad Valley still carries the card neck label as well as the square fabric foot label. He has the characteristic vertically stitched nose and the "Queen Mother" label. c.1958. Ht. 26in. (66cm).

Courtesy Constance King Antiques

Unlike the First World War, virtually no interesting patriotic bears or unusual printed examples were made in Britain or France. This was the first total war, with an effective U-boat campaign halting exports and imports of all but the most essential products and with constant bombing causing complete disruption of civilian life. In the early years of the century, firms such as Chad Valley were able to benefit from the Great War and expand production, using mainly female labour, but in this instance women were also conscripted, causing labour shortages in weaving mills and toymaking factories. The Zoo Toy Company, in East London, was forced radically to limit production. In an attempt to organise the toy industry more satisfactorily, the British Toy and Hobby Manufacturers Association was founded in 1944, the year that also saw the death of Henry Farnell.

Non-essential manufactures, such as toys and fancy goods, came low on the priority list of European governments in the years after the war and firms were

PLATE 91
Chad Valley produced good quality, well constructed bears that usually carry their square fabric label under one foot. This example is made of short plush mohair, has glass eyes and a vertically stitched black nose. His pads are dark brown velveteen. c.1950. Ht. 22in. (56cm).

Courtesy Jane Vandell Associates

COLOUR PLATE 177
Made by Gebrüder Märklin, this German clockwork scooter bear is a rare example of a toy that was produced for export only in the years immediately following the War. It is marked "U.S. Zone Germany" and "Gebr. M. FEWO". He has glass eyes and is made of art silk plush. Similar bears were marketed by Fehn & Co. of Dörfles. They also appear in Siku catalogues. Ht. 6in. (15.2cm).   *Author*

slow to reorganise. Shortages of basic materials, bombed factories and loss of employees all contributed to a period of almost unrelieved gloom. While fascism had been defeated, the cost had been high and it was a decade before the toy factories were again running smoothly. When dolls and jointed bears did appear in the shops, they were expensive and in very short supply. Few stores, even in Paris or London, were able to show big displays of soft toys as, once the factories started up again, the emphasis was necessarily on exports, particularly to America. Because of the shortage of playthings for the home market, many of the women's magazines included patterns for knitted Teddy Bears and soft toys, with craft firms, such as Dryad, selling felt patterns and instructions. Teddy Bears were at their lowest ebb in the 1940s and early '50s as the mohair versions demanded expensive fabrics and relatively skilled workers.

Because women had been conscripted, the toy factories lost many of their workers, who were not eager to return to mundane and repetitive work after a period in the services. The 1914-18 War had not cut so deeply into toy production, as the British Empire was still largely self-sufficient and had continued to rule the seas. Things were completely different in the '40s because of U-boat attacks and the

COLOUR PLATE 178
A number of bears made in the 1950s, because of rough play use and their old-fashioned basic design, suggest a much earlier date than that of their purchase. Bought c.1950 when he was new, this bear has the bent arms and long nose of an earlier period. Ht. 18in. (45.7cm).

Courtesy Constance King Antiques

COLOUR PLATE 179
The use of plastic noses was becoming increasingly popular by the 1950s and bears were more often thought of as·female. Ht. 17in. (43.2cm).
Courtesy Constance King Antiques

bombing of towns and cities. This was the first war in which British civilians, as well as servicemen, were in the front line and many of the romantic bear stories associated with the Great War were absent from the Second. A few soldiers, such as Colonel Henderson, carried their mascot bears and there was a vogue for such good luck symbols in the Royal Air Force, particularly in Bomber Command, but in general the Second World War did not engender much poetry as it was too fast and mechanical. Eventually some of the scientific advances of the time were to influence toy manufacture but, by 1950, things were still bleak in a Europe that was also suffering from partition and new regimes. A few managed, despite the odds, to re-start old businesses, such as Karl and Else Althans, who came from a Sonneberg soft toy manufacturing family but escaped when the Soviets occupied East Germany. With great determination, Karl and his new wife began life afresh and started to make bears in a farmhouse and sell them in local markets and towns. Gradually the business and the space they occupied grew and over one hundred workers were employed by 1950, working under the trade name "Albico". Because

COLOUR PLATE 180
A 1950s British-made bear with rexine pads. He has brown plastic eyes and the hard, round body associated with the period. Ht 26in. (66cm).

Courtesy Constance King Antiques

toys were in such short supply, the public was happy to pay high prices for bears that would have attracted little interest in the pre-war years and this lack of selectiveness aided some of the new makers and helped them overcome difficulties.

Wendy Boston was among a few adventurous people in Britain who began making toys at home for local children, while larger companies were in expansionist mood – Chiltern was training staff at the new Pontypool factory and Merrythought in 1946 was re-starting bear production in Ironbridge and, in the following year, manufactured a new "Cradle Bingie", with a squeeze-box "Tummykins" introduced in 1948.

Pedigree Soft Toys, registered in 1931, was part of the Triang Toys empire, founded in 1919 when three sons of Joseph Lines broke off from their father's older establishment and set up on the Old Kent Road in London. The firm grew at a surprising rate and began producing soft toys in 1937 from their Merton works. The war soon limited production but by 1946 Triang was again in an expansionist mood and Pedigree soft toy factories were opened in New Zealand and Belfast in Northern Ireland, though in 1955 most of the soft toy production for Great Britain was moved to Belfast. Pedigree bears of the early '50s have a sewn-in label reading "Made in England", which makes them easy to date. The Teddies always have fairly

COLOUR PLATE 181
Probably made by Chiltern, c.1959, this nylon fabric bear has plastic eyes and is filled with kapok for a soft and cuddly look.

Courtesy Constance King Antiques

COLOUR PLATE 182
A square-nosed plush bear with very short arms and a heavy, rounded body that was purchased in the late '40s in Woolworth's. The flat ears are typical of those used on bears sold by the shop from the late '30s onward. Ht. 23in. (58.4cm).
Courtesy Constance King Antiques

short arms and the '50s Pedigrees have prominent ears. A few were made with a musical movement. In the larger mohair sizes, the bears can look quite impressive, though in comparison with the numbers produced, there are not as many on the market as might be expected. The early Pedigree bears have oval foot pads but by 1960 they had become much rounder, in line with other competitors who were creating a more squat, cub-like animal.

When Queen Elizabeth II was crowned in 1953, the toy and gift trade enjoyed its first bonanza since the war – every mascot-type toy that could carry a patriotic, royalist slogan was decorated with a badge and there were red, white and blue bears, made of the cheapest fabrics, to serve as souvenirs. Even in 1953, there were still shortages of materials, so most of the coronation toys, with their red, white and blue labels, were of the flimsiest type and few have survived. Because good quality mohair bears were so expensive, they were offered as prizes at Coronation street parties, or raffled. One splendid large chap wore a crown and velvet cape and sat at the head of the table at a country house party near my home and was the prize for the best junior fancy dress. Though I coveted the bear and would have given him a loving, if untidy, home among my puppets, theatres and paint boxes, I was sadly disappointed when he was claimed by "Roy Rogers", who arrived with a real

COLOUR PLATE 183
Many bears endure great suffering because of the enthusiasm of their infant owners, who drown, flatten and even de-fluff their best friends. This war-time bear was fitted with replacement eyes. Ht. 11in. (28cm).
Courtesy Constance King Antiques

horse. Small toy shops often found that the large, expensive bears that they used as impressive window displays remained unsold, so they made a virtue out of necessity by raffling them on Christmas Eve.

Because of their lack of innovation, Irish-made bears have never held much appeal for collectors, as they are too bland and derivative. Perhaps because the Irish soft toy industry was not affected by the Second World War, the country having declared itself neutral, the manufacturers seem to have concentrated more on traditional patterns rather than embarking on adventurous new designs. Most of the marked bears which originated in the Republic of Eire carry English language labels, though some are found in Gaelic. Of all the makers working in the Irish Republic, Tara Toys, a government subsidised rural industry, is the best known, though the bears are very difficult to identify when they have lost their sewn-on labels. The only innovative design, for a bear with a mouth that can be opened and closed with a lever, was produced by Tara in the late 1950s. The government appointed board of Gaeltarra Eireann illustrates the difficulty of manufacturing toys without the individual spark of an entrepreneur or a very progressive designer and though the bears must have been much loved by their child owners, they do not as yet command high prices on the collectors' market.

Polish, Czechoslovakian and East German industry, like that in Ireland, suffered from a lack of inventive drive, probably because the state had too great an influence. Many of the bears were acceptable as basic toys despite being made in economical, if somewhat tired, styles.

In 1949, the British toy trade received a welcome boost from the birth of a polar bear cub, named Brumas, at the London Zoo. Dean's first post-war catalogue appeared in that year and a soft toy version of the mother with the cub was included. While hardly in the form of a Teddy, Brumas, who was also made by Chad Valley in 1954, has always been collected by arctophiles. Dean's seems to have become willing to create more adventurous toys than in the pre-war years and was alive to new ideas and materials.

Rubber has been used periodically for bear production throughout the century, though comparatively few toys have survived because of the inherent fragility of the substance. Its most common use in the '20s and '30s had been for bear-shaped hot water bottles, though very few appear in collections as they were thrown away once they began to leak. Bear squeak toys for babies are another perennial and sometimes carry patent marks and design numbers which make them possible to date. Unless rubber toys are kept in cool, moist conditions they soon harden, discolour

PLATE 92
The original swing card label on this bear adds greatly to its attraction for collectors, while the polar bear and her cub are also in superb condition. The label, with a child and a rabbit, reads "Dean's Hygienic Toys. Made in England by Dean's Rag Book Co. Ltd. 61, High Path, Merton, London, SW19", with the fighting dogs logo. The polar bears were popular because of the birth of the cub, Brumas, to Ivy at London Zoo in 1949. There was a newspaper competition to find a name for the cub: Brumas was selected. Ivy is white mohair and has a leather nose, Brumas is white wool with peach felt pads. Ht. 19in. (48.3cm). Sold for £575 in 1995. *Courtesy Bonham's, Chelsea*

COLOUR PLATE 184
Sylvia Wilgoss, who designed for Dean's from the 1950s to the '70s, was inspired by the bears at London Zoo and created a figure from a complex mixture of rubber and mohair. This version is labelled "Made in England by Dean's Co. Ltd. London" and has a black rubber nose and painted back glass eyes with rubber rims. His realistic rubber paws have hardened with age. Ht. 21in. (53.3cm). He sold in March 1995 for £1,035.

Courtesy Bonham's, Chelsea

and crumble, spoiling their appearance as collectable toys.

A few manufacturers in the '40s and '50s utilized rubber for the noses and feet of bears but again relatively few examples exist, because eventually the material disfigured the bear's appearance. In the mid-50s, Dean's introduced a very distinctive black acrylic plush bear, with realistically moulded rubber feet and paws. This bear, despite the frequent damage and distortion of the rubber, is now very popular with collectors, as it was innovative and appealing. The bear also gains prestige because it was designed by a known artist, Sylvia Wilgoss. This bear must have been expensive and time-consuming to produce, as the eyes were set in the rubber sockets of the face mask and the muzzle, in white plush, was inset. Because of so many fitting problems and processes, the bear, which was made in three sizes, must have given the manufacturer many difficulties but its realism and natural pose make it one of the most endearing of the bear cubs of the period. The designer intended the animals to walk on all-fours and the polar bear version is sometimes found, like her monkeys, with the original collars and leads. All the '50s Dean's bears still carry the old Dean's Rag Book Company fabric labels and, when new, also carried round card labels with the fighting dogs logo and the much softer image of a child sleeping with her rabbit.

The Sylvia Wilgoss bears are the only really progressive '50s English bears, as so many firms were still suffering from the aftermath of war, with its limited range of mechanisms and fabrics. Dean's worked to serve the lower ranges of the market, with unjointed baby bears in various colours, glove puppets and the colourful dressed Teddies that had been originally designed in the 1930s by Richard Ellet. When soft toy production moved to Rye in 1956, a completely different range emerged, though the rubber-faced bear remains the most memorable.

"Cheeky", made by Merrythought, is the most long-lived of their soft toy family. Created in 1957, with especially safe "locked-in eyes", he was originally made of mohair or art silk plush. "Cheeky" hovers between a cartoon-type character and a bear cub, and he has such lasting appeal that he still delights modern children, though he is now made of synthetic plush or mohair. He has huge flop ears containing bells, a massively high, broad forehead and a wide smiling mouth set within a contrasting muzzle. He was designed by Jean Barber. "Cheeky" was made in several shades of art silk plush in the 1950s and was also sold dressed, the clothes forming the body. Many variations of "Cheeky" have been made over the years but are not easy to date precisely. After the war, Merrythought used sewn-on cloth labels that were printed instead of the embroidered versions. In 1957, the wording on the printed labels was changed and the words "Hygienic Toys" were omitted.

The design of "Cheeky" was obviously adapted from the character bear "Punkin Head" that was made by Merrythought in 1949 for a Canadian department store. "Punkin Head" has differently positioned and rather smaller ears than "Cheeky" and his particular distinction was a white mohair inset on the crown of the head. Early "Punkin Head" bears carry the "Hygienic Toys" label. Merrythought's "Mr.

PLATE 93
Gina Campbell with her father's mascot bear, "Mr Whoppit". Donald Campbell's Teddy that was found floating on Lake Coniston after his fatal record-breaking attempt in the speedboat *Bluebird*. Gina is photographed with Mike Standring on the *Agfa Bluebird* in 1984. Mr. Whoppit, made by Merrythought in 1956-57, was later auctioned.

Courtesy of Agfa Gevaert

PLATE 94
"Sooty on a tricycle", with his sewn-in "Chiltern Hygienic Toys. Made in England" label. Made in orange plush with black ears. He has orange plastic eyes and a black plastic nose with pink plush hands and feet. He sits on a red tricycle. Made in the 1950s. Ht. 11ins. Sold for £276 in 1995.

Courtesy Bonham's, Chelsea

Whoppit" became a particularly famous little bear, when an example owned by Donald Campbell floated to the surface of Coniston Water after the horrific failure of his attempt to break the water speed record in 1967. Whoppit, with a brown plush body and red felt coat, was made between 1956-57 and was one of three characters from "Robin", which featured in *Hulton's National Weekly*. Many of the cartoon-type bears made in the '50s have little resemblance to their ancestors and Whoppit is no exception. With his two-piece, long, fat body and short, stunted legs, he could well be a muff or hot water bottle cover. Donald Campbell always carried Mr. Whoppit with him as a mascot and this special little bear carried a *Bluebird* motif on his jacket, after the names of the cars and boats the family used for their record-breaking attempts.

Because it was a relatively small family firm, Merrythought was able to introduce new and innovative designs without the prolonged preparatory research that is too often necessary today. The 1950s was one of the firm's most innovative periods, with its designs more exciting and progressive than Steiff, presumably because the home market was starved of quality toys and eager for its products.

The Teddy Bear sensation of 1952 was the glove puppet, Sooty, who appeared on television with his friend Sweep, both manipulated by Harry Corbett. Soon Sooty, with his black ears, appeared as a comic strip and on related merchandise, such as toy china. Puppets of this type had been manufactured for many years and were sold particularly by magicians' and variety artistes' suppliers. Because of the fashion for puppetry in schools, soft toy versions began to appear in the shops and it was one of these bright yellow bears that caught Harry Corbett's eye on Blackpool Pier, where it lay among a variety of other cheap toys. By blackening the glove puppet's ears with soot, immediate character and a name were provided.

COLOUR PLATE 185
A large-headed cub-type Teddy made in Britain in the
1950s. Ht. 14in. (35.6cm).

Courtesy Constance King Antiques

Corbett conceived Sooty as a lovable, but naughty, little boy bear of about five years old, somewhat younger than Rupert. Sooty is pert and mischievous and gets away with a variety of naughty pranks. Young children immediately identified with the bad little bear and envied his pranks and repartee. The first commercially produced Sooty puppet was made by Chad Valley in 1952 but, as virtually identical toys continued to be made into the '80s, they are not sufficiently rare to be of financial interest to collectors. Many carry the Chad Valley sewn-in label and these are obviously preferred, as imitations soon appeared on the market. Chad also made Sooty in a jointed form in synthetic, rather cheap, plush and these are now popular, especially with the Japanese, suggesting that their price will rise substantially.

Bears changed both their form and texture in the 1950s with the gradual introduction of synthetic fibres, with vinyl often being used for faces and paws. Various polyester fibres, which create a type of wadding, make an excellent filling material, that is light and washable. When the bear itself was made of nylon or orlon, it was possible to machine wash the toy. This advance meant that any separately applied parts, such as the eyes, had to be securely locked in place and the colours used for the toy were necessarily fast. Though washable bears were hygienically a great advance, the synthetic materials, with the accompanying safety

COLOUR PLATE 185
Inspired by the William Tell story, this cartoon type bear is marked "British Made". The puzzle has a metal case and glass cover. c.1950. 2½in. (6.4cm) square. *Courtesy Constance King Antiques*

COLOUR PLATE 187
The fat, seated bear is a Chad Valley of the 1950s with a printed foot label and safe, child-proof plastic eyes. The smaller bear dates from the same period, but was a much cheaper product.

Courtesy Constance King Antiques

regulations that were also more rigidly enforced, stifled inventiveness and forced commercial bears to become progressively more bland. Perhaps the complete designs of Teddies should have been altered to adapt to the new materials, but instead the conventional shape was slightly flattened and the limbs thickened. By 1960, completely unjointed bears, often in several colours, were most common, as they were cheap to manufacture, but they held little individual character and very few were treasured by their small owners.

Unfortunately, many synthetic toys were dangerously inflammable and from the late '50s in Britain, rules for safeguarding children's toys were more rigorously enforced. Wendy Boston, working from Crickhowell in Wales from 1945, invented safety screw-locked plastic eyes made in three parts, that were used on the washable nylon bears in which the firm specialised. The synthetic Teddies were made to the simplest designs and even the ears were cut in one with the head. These were completely modern toys, that relied for their appeal on the soft pile of the fur and their pillow-like shape. They carry a sewn-on label, erroneously reading "Wendy Boston. Made in England. Wash in lukewarm water". A few of the bears recommend Persil for washing. At least the Boston toys were appealing but many firms, who imitated her simple designs, made bears from very cheap plush, so that

COLOUR PLATE 188
Margaret Tarrant captured the new security of nursery life in her illustrations for the *1947 Story Book*, published by Collins. The bear was called "Cub" and he tells his story to the child who lies in bed. He was originally a Canadian bear who fell asleep and woke up as a Teddy in Britain. *Author*

COLOUR PLATE 189
Nursery bears have added appeal when they retain the decorations or costumes supplied by their child owners. The jointed British bear shows the rough mends that were necessitated by play. Ht. 14in. (35.6cm).

Courtesy Constance King Antiques

they exhibit the worst features of soft toy production. By 1964, Wendy Boston Playsafe Toys Ltd. was a substantial manufactory, producing a quarter of Britain's soft toys for export. After takeovers, the factory, which had grown from the home-made soft toys Wendy had created during the war, was closed in 1976.

Cheap nylon plush was used much more inventively by Japanese toymakers in the 1950s and '60s and their toys are now avidly collected. Though a few bears were made in Japan before the Second World War, they are difficult to distinguish from the many cheap European products that were their competitors. In a great surge of inventiveness after the the war, an ingenious range of battery-operated mechanical figures was designed. The basic structures were made of metal but, with a skilful use of costume and caricature, a complete bear garden of amusing figures flowed from the factories:

The battery-operated bears balance on large feet or sit on a metal trunk or chair and sew, knit, play instruments, drink or dance. Teddy the Artist, with rolling eyes, is one of the cleverest battery toys of the period, as he draws nine different animal pictures. There were accordion players, clowns, dentists and even blacksmiths, all with cartoon-like Teddy Bear heads. Several of the toys poured water but this soon corroded the action and damaged the bears. Even inoperative battery toys of this type have some value, though obviously only a toy that is in full working order and boxed will command the top price.

Japanese battery bears were manufactured by a number of companies, though this

COLOUR PLATE 190
A boxed musical bear in mint condition, the box marked "Blue Ribbon Playthings", made for export c.1951. Key-wound, it plays the *Teddy Bears' Picnic*. Ht. 16in. (40.6cm).

Courtesy Constance King Antiques

part of the market is driven more by complexity of movement and originality rather than attribution. Many of the 1950s and early '60s bears have colourful and well designed boxes that add considerably to the toy's appeal. They were not only sold from toyshops but also the cheapest market stalls, such as those on the Whitechapel Road, where they always attracted crowds of adults, who seemed to respond to their ingenuity much more than children. Because so many were purchased by adults, they have survived in surprising numbers, especially when their comparative fragility is considered.

American Teddy Bear designers had moved towards a stouter-looking animal in the years immediately after the 1914–18 War. Some of the Ideal bears dating to the early '20s might be taken for later European examples, as the arms are much shortened and the bodies thicker. Many American bears were made of short bristle mohair and there was an even wider range of qualities than in Europe, with some of the finest Ideal bears comparing well with Steiff.

Ideal's most famous individual bear was "Smokey", especially commissioned and licensed by the U.S. Forest Fire Prevention Campaign in 1953. "Smokey" was interesting, as the firm used soft moulded vinyl for his somewhat doll-like face, with its snub nose, and his moulded vinyl paws and feet. Early versions of the bear carry the printed fabric label "It's Ideal". It is said that the name "Smokey" was chosen because the bear that Roosevelt had refused to shoot in 1902 had been singed by a forest fire, though the more likely explanation is that he was named

PLATE 95
A curly mohair 1950s Steiff, known as "Jethroe". He has brown glass eyes and a brown, horizontally embroidered nose and mouth. He is straw filled, with gold felt pads. Ht. 20½in. (52cm). Sold for £920 in 1995. Photographed with a 1920s cinnamon coloured Steiff, with brown backed glass eyes. Ht. 16in. (40.6cm). Sold for £598 in 1995. *Courtesy Bonham's, Chelsea*

after Smokey Joe Martin, a well-known assistant fire chief of New York City. The bear became so popular that in 1952, Congress passed the Smokey Bear Act, allowing the Forest Service to licence Smokey, so the royalties could be used to prevent fires. Ideal helped with the forest fire campaign, by giving every child who was bought a Smokey an application form to become a Junior Forest Ranger. Smokey Bear had originated in 1942, when there was concern about a possible Japanese invasion of the California coast, that might result in widespread forest fires.

The Ideal Smokey carried a blue plastic shovel to fight forest fires and wore a silver Smokey belt buckle and the Smokey ranger's cowboy type hat. In 1954, Ideal's second version of the bear was issued with a body completely made of brown plush and without the realistic vinyl paws. The Smokey Bear campaign was given additional appeal as it became interlinked with the sad story of a real bear cub which was rescued from a forest fire in New Mexico in 1950. The bear, burned and pining for its mother, refused to eat but improved rapidly when it was taken home and, in a family environment, fed on honey and baby food. Soon the bear was sent to the zoo in Washington and was used as a publicity attraction, visited by thousands of children who were delighted to buy toy Smokeys and become committed to the slogan: "Only you can prevent forest fires". Ideal's advertisement

PLATE 96
The appearance of bears is often altered by the re-stitching of noses and the replacement of pads. This group of three dates from the 1940s, though they are all unmarked. The larger bear resembles the late 1930s Chad Valley. Ht. of largest bear 22in. (56cm).

Courtesy Jane Vandell Associates

PLATE 97
A Durso of Belgium hard plaster bear, based on an older Elastolin design.   *Courtesy David Hawkins*

COLOUR PLATE 191
In the years immediately after the war, there was a great rush to the seaside and holiday camps. Many of the bears that have survived look surprisingly old, though the short arms and straight legs of this bear, bought by its one-time owner on a trip to the seaside in 1949, support the date. Ht. 15in. (38cm).

Courtesy Constance King Antiques

for Smokey in 1954 proclaimed "Nationally famous Smokey Bear - now the famous symbol of forest fire prevention is a cuddly toy - acts as a reminder to be careful. Smokey is a plaything for children, a mascot for adults - it's Ideal." In a third version of Smokey, made in the 1950s, he has a plush instead of a vinyl face and is much more in the nature of a conventional Teddy Bear.

American children led the world in the 1950s with their casual dress, extrovert behaviour and, above all, Rock and Roll. From the age of ten or eleven, childhood was over and that new species, the Teenager, emerged. Special records, clothes, magazines and books fed the new group with ideas and entertainment but also, eventually, shortened childhood, so that toy manufacturers were forced into satisfying an ever smaller age range. When Elvis ruled our hearts and our bedrooms were decorated with posters and photographs of James Dean, there was little time for the soft mascot toys that young people in the early part of the century had found so much fun. As most toys were still economical, they were not sufficiently attractive to be purchased as mascots or companions and the toys of childhood were soon packed away in cupboards, only occasionally to be handled or cleaned.

Many firms in Germany were unable to recover after the War, not simply because important staff had been lost but also because of the difficulty in obtaining materials. Schuco, always great innovators, were again market leaders in the field of novelty toys and in 1954 introduced "Janus", the two-headed bear with a somewhat golliwog-like expression. Their roller-skating bear and a Dancing Bear soon followed. It was remarkable that Schuco had managed to survive the War in any form, as one of the partners had been forced to flee Germany because he was Jewish and the factory was also bombed several times. In 1947, Schuco Toy Co. Inc. was established in America, with all the import rights for the toys. This new structure must have helped considerably, as a second generation of their typically inventive little bears appeared. Unfortunately, the firm fell prey to the spate of takeovers in the 1970s and finally disappeared when it became part of the Dunbee-Combex-Marx Group. Fortunately their bears continue to exist to some extent, as the Schuco trademark was sold to another German firm and replica miniature bears are now made by Karl Bär, who uses original Schuco patterns and equipment, bought from the receivers in 1977.

As the Allied troops moved across Germany, they seized many items, from works of art to children's toys, that could be justified to themselves as souvenirs. Steiff had ceased toy production during the last years of the War and become a munitions factory, though fortunately the firm's archive had been stored safely around the town of Giengen and, miraculously, has survived intact to the present time, together with samples of all the toys made over the whole period of production.

It is this archive that enables Steiff to identify and date old products and that has underpinned the tremendous popularity of its work with collectors. Though there are other old established firms, none has such a detailed archive or museum as fine as that at Giengen, where the chronology of the many toys can be studied. While the interest of wealthy collectors is mainly centred on the pre-war Steiffs, as these become progressively more expensive, much greater interest is being shown in the later work, especially that of the 1950s.

By 1946, the Steiff factory was back in business and offering a limited range, made exclusively for the American occupiers of the country. Once production had started, the economic situation gradually eased and other fabric and wooden toys, mainly for export, were added to the list. Because Germany needed foreign currency so desperately in order to rebuild its infrastructure, the civilian population could not at first obtain toys and it was only in 1947 that normal trading began again, though it was not possible to obtain good quality mohair until 1948, when Steiff toys were shown at a Hanover Export Fair.

A Teddy-hungry post-war public was desperate to obtain the products of the famous German firm and even prepared to accept the curious feel of the economic paper plush animals. There were many supply problems during the late '40s, as the

COLOUR PLATE 192
"Janus", with a golliwog type head on one side and a Teddy on the other. He was made by Schuco in 1954 and has metal bead eyes, a metal mouth and a celluloid tongue. He always has straight legs and is jointed at the shoulders and hips. The head is turned by means of a knob at the base of the spine. Ht. 3½in. (9cm).   *Courtesy Bernard Beech*

PLATE 98
A pair of miniature "Teddy Babies" by Steiff, made c.1950. One in dark brown mohair with a velvet cut contrasting muzzle, the other in pale golden mohair, also with a velvet contrasting muzzle and matching foot pads. Ht. 3½in. (8.9cm). Sold for £299 and £437 in 1997.

Courtesy Christie's South Kensington

firm was periodically unable to obtain parts, such as voice boxes, but even so a few more expensive bears, such as the riding animals, were produced.

Even in the early '50s, Steiff had to concentrate mainly on foreign currency earning orders and the toys were always available to British and American service people. In 1950, the great toy trade fair, no longer viable in Leipzig, as it was in the Russian zone, moved to Nuremberg, where it has remained to the present. Steiff staged an impressive display at the entrance to the fair, re-affirming their importance as the premier maker of soft toys.

Aware of the importance of American orders and of the necessity to pander to the occupiers, who still controlled much business, the Steiff company staged a special event for the 100th anniversary of President Roosevelt's birth, in October 1958. This was a tremendous and successfully staged publicity event and attracted international attention. Teddy Bears and Roosevelt became linked together for all time in the imagination of the public and the festival must also have contributed to better relations between German civilians and the American occupiers, already improved by a huge Teddy Bears Festival which included an amusing Teddy Bear ballet.

Designers had become so constrained by the war and its aftermath that there was an overwhelming need for change and innovation in the 1950s. With labour costs steadily rising, manufacturers were also aware that simpler, more economical designs had to be introduced. The cub-type models, introduced by all soft toy makers in the '20s and 30's, were still popular, as the public demanded somewhat squat soft toys that were more in the nature of cuddly bedfellows than playtime companions. In this, the makers were also reflecting the way in which children were beginning to grow up more quickly and were leaving toys behind them at a progressively earlier age. Bears and other soft toys consequently became more exclusively connected with the first years of childhood and aimed less at the eight

COLOUR PLATE 193
By 1950, even German-made bears had assumed a well-fed, tranquil look. This tipped lady has contrasting plush lined ears that match her nose. Probably made by Hermann in Sonneberg, her long nose is typical of the manufacturer. Ht. 30in. (76.2cm).   *Courtesy Constance King Antiques*

PLATE 99
An unusual Mutzli Teddy in
original chef's uniform. Made of
beige mohair with black button
eyes and a black stitched nose and
mouth. He wears an orange felt
scarf and brown felt shoes.
c.1950. Ht. 5½in. (14cm). Sold for
£368 in 1997.

Courtesy Christie's South Kensington

to twelve year old market.

In Germany, Steiff, whose bears in the early '50s had been marked with a white
fabric label reading "Made in the U.S. Zone", revolutionised all their Teddy
production with a completely modernised design, with short legs and
comparatively larger heads, heralded by the earlier "Teddy Baby". The new changes
in design in 1950 saw the disappearance of many of the earlier Teddy features, such
as the hump and the long arms and legs. Though the larger heads probably appealed
more to children, Teddy lost his traditional character at this time and came more
into line with other soft toys.

Steiff's jubilee celebrations in 1953 engendered "Jackie Baby", with the rounded
ears and short limbs typical of all the cub-type ranges. "Jackie Baby" was made in
three medium sizes and is characterised by a pink horizontal stitch among the black
on his nose and a dark navel on his tummy, exaggerating the young animal appeal
inherent in the design. The first range of this bear was only sold until 1955, though
it was again issued in the 1980s. The Baby Bear of 1955 was available with a tail-
activated head, referred to by collectors as the "yes/no" mechanism.

Of all the 1950s productions, the open mouthed "Zotty" is the most innovative,
though the design departs even further from the traditional Teddy. "Zotty" was first
made in 1951 and was a brave innovation for the new market that had staggered

out of the decade of war. Steiff's designers must have felt the need for a firm statement that the years of economy were well past and the name "Zotty" was derived from *zottig*, meaning shaggy. While not unlike other bear cubs in general shape, Zotty is characterised by his peach-coloured chest and, above all, his open mouth that reveals a wholesome peach interior with brown outlined lips. Zotty has a clipped plush muzzle and a long, shaggy, two-tone effect coat. In the sleeping version made in the '50s, he has closed felt eyes and the limbs are unjointed. The bear looks encouragingly towards the future, with its extravagant long coat and the open mouth that asks and expects to be well fed. Zotty was an optimistic Teddy, looking towards a golden future free from war, shortages and deprivation. Like the children of the 1950s, he anticipated a world that would be bright and prosperous, with food, employment and health care for all.

COLOUR PLATE 194
A British-made bear, with rexine pads, made c.1948. His fur has remained in good condition, as has his growler. Ht. 18in. (45.7cm).
Courtesy Constance King Antiques

COLOUR PLATE 195
A Merrythought Highlander from the 1973 collection. The bear parts that show are mohair and the outfit forms the rest of the body. Ht. 18in. (45.7cm). *Courtesy Constance King Antiques*

CHAPTER 8

A Shoulder to Cry On

While the rest of the world came to life in the "nothing ever the same again" sixties, Teddy Bears remained aloof from worry beads, tie and dye shirts and the *Little Red School Book*. Bears were too traditional in form to adapt to radical changes and even those sold on Carnaby Street, the London mecca of fashion, were brought up to date by the simple additions of Union Jack flags and badges. While good quality, traditional bears were available from large department stores, the High Street versions were almost uniformly dreary, with little shape and more than a passing resemblance to dry sponges. This was a depressing period for Teddy Bears, with few innovations; many small but long established British firms, such as Nora Wellings, ceased trading, while large companies, such as Schuco in Germany, disappeared in takeovers and mergers. The spirit of the decade, with its way-out clothes and eccentric characters, was encapsulated in 1968, when three kapok-filled bears, each with a mask of John Betjeman, were shown by Jann Haworth as "A Valentine to John Betjeman" at the Royal Academy Summer Exhibition.

It was vivid personalities, such as Colonel Henderson, Peter Bull and John Betjeman, who carried the image and the emotions engendered by bears through a decade when manufacturing innovation was at a relatively low ebb and succeeded in inspiring fresh interest among people of all ages. Suddenly the past, antiques, period houses and old toys were sexy and there was an influx of new enthusiasts, who were eager to scour antique shops and markets for interesting acquisitions. Though at first interest in mohair bears was minimal, in comparison with bisque dolls and tinplate toys, they were soon caught up in the wave of interest and eventually developed a small sphere of their own. *The Book*

COLOUR PLATE 196
Pedigree moved its soft toy production to Ireland and this bear carries a pink ribbon label printed blue on white "Pedigree. Made in Northern Ireland" Ht. 18in. (45.7cm).

Courtesy Constance King Antiques

COLOUR PLATE 197
The original artwork for the cover of *Archie and the Strict Baptists*. The artist had known Betjeman from childhood and created a sympathetic and very English interpretation of the subject.
Courtesy Phillida Gili

of the Teddy Bear, by Margaret Hutchings, published in 1964, though primarily concerned with the craft of making bears, included a short history and helped foster an interest in the subject that flowered in the 1990s.

Today, because of the interest in collectable bears, the better quality commercial productions of the Swinging Sixties are beginning to attract good prices, with mohair Chad Valleys, Chilterns, Steiffs and Merrythoughts selling for several hundred pounds, though in general, we are too close in time to be able to pinpoint the real antiques of the future from the toys of these years. Pedigree was one of the main British producers of quality soft toys in the 1960s, continuing to make its wheeled toys as well as the more traditional cub-like bears. Following the changes in design introduced by other manufacturers in the 1950s, Pedigree began to inset separate muzzles and use more synthetic fabrics. Their new designer, Ann Wood, who had worked at the Dean's factory, also adapted some of the older designs. These late Pedigrees sometimes have musical movements or even bells in their ears, in imitation of Merrythought.

Throughout the 1960s, Pedigree made both jointed and the simpler unjointed Teddies, that were ideal for the cheaper end of the market. The unjointed bears relied almost completely for their appeal on the texture of their largely synthetic coats. A few of the '60s bears have plush muzzles, protruding red tongues and,

COLOUR PLATE 198
Hazel Hall's Teddy Bear glove puppet that she last performed with in the early '70s. She was a magician, ventriloquist and musician and performed for forty years, mainly on the South Coast, with her ventriloquist dolls Johnny Jasper and Trixie Truelove. She was married to "Wally Shakespeare", with whom she appeared regularly, and became a member of the Institute of Magicians in 1950. Her bear has plastic eyes and is made of synthetic fabric, with a drawstring at the base to fit the performer's arm. The bear was found among her possessions after her death. Ht. 11in. (27.9cm). *Courtesy Constance King Antiques*

ominously, the foam rubber filling that was later to be scrutinised by safety officers, concerned about the fumes that could be given off in a fire. Most of the bears carry the printed "Pedigree. Made in Ireland" label. Among the most collectable today are the talking Rupert Bear and Simon the Walking Bear, who was battery-operated, though the traditional mohairs with original labels always sell well.

PLATE 100
"Tenderheart Bear", one of ten cuddly Care Bears made in the late 70's. "In a complex world of human communication and emotional expression, the Care Bears are a refreshing new way to help people share their feelings." Each wore a symbol, such as "Funshine" or "Grumpy Bear". They "give voice to the feelings people share". General Mills and American Greetings developed Care Bears, including a "Birthday Bear" and "Good Luck Bear". They were the brainchild of Bernie Loomis of MAD organisation.
Courtesy Care Bears

Triang had been founded by the three Lines Brothers to create quality conventional toys but suffered in the later period from a combination of over-expansion and a tendency to cling to old designs now liked by collectors but which were unable to compete with the cheaply-made toys flooding in from other countries. In 1968, Pedigree was taken over by Rovex Industries Ltd., another Lines Bros. company, and doll and bear production was moved to Canterbury. Though Pedigree was always far more innovative in the area of dolls, their bears appeal today because they remained stolidly British in inspiration and clung to outdated concepts of good taste and quality that now hold great charm for enthusiasts.

In 1972, after the collapse of the Lines Brothers group, Pedigree was among the

PLATE 101
A contemporary photograph of the Merrythought range at the London showroom of Dean and Son Ltd, sole distributors for the British Isles in 1964. In the foreground is Yogi Bear; sitting against the platform is a display size "Cheeky" in silk plush. Yogi was made in velveteen in an 11in. (28cm) size. The showpiece 27in. (68.6cm) Yogi is seen above Pablo the Donkey.

Courtesy Merrythought Ltd.

subsidiaries acquired by Dunbee Combex Marx. I remember visiting one of the toy factories taken over at the time and listening to employees who complained that the design teams were being run down and the whole production had become stagnant. In 1980, after Dunbee Combex Marx collapsed, Pedigree Soft Toys was taken over by Tamewade Ltd. but in 1988 the Canterbury factory closed and the last remaining part of the old firm died. Fortunately, some segments of the original spirit still survive and in Belfast, for instance, Pedigree's ex-production manager set up his own factory in 1971, known as Mulholland and Bailie, selling bears under the trade name "Nylena". Despite an old, well respected name, Pedigree had never taken advantage of the burgeoning collectors' interest that was already becoming apparent in the early '80s, though it is doubtful whether exploitation of this comparatively fringe area of the international toy market would have had any influence on such a massive international operation.

COLOUR PLATE 199
One of the last good quality Chad Valley bears, in golden plush with the label sewn into the side seam under the arm. Printed in blue on white "Hygienic Toys. Made in England by Chad Valley Co. Ltd." He has a stitched nose and plastic eyes. Ht. 23in. (58.4cm).

Courtesy Constance King Antiques

Dean's also underwent many changes in the '60s and the label was redesigned, making later products immediately recognizable. In 1965, the firm dropped the fighting dogs symbol, which was replaced by the various Childsplay printed labels. The Rye factory, which I visited several times in the 1970s, was still essentially old-fashioned, with Sylvia Wilgoss acting as chief designer and attempting to collect early products of the firm as the nucleus of a projected museum. She had joined the company in 1952 and introduced many innovative and charming toys and dolls that were perhaps a little out of touch with the more brash products loved by young children in the 1960s, who were growing up on a diet of cartoons and vivid colours.

Yogi Bear, that most American cartoon bear, who become popular in Britain at the time, was named after Yogi Berra, the baseball player. Created by Hanna Barbera, he

PLATE 102
The co-founder of the London Toy and Model Museum, opened in 1982, with her life-long companion, Lizzie, who was bought for her at Harrods and has accompanied her three times around the world. Lizzie is a good travelling companion, as she is bilingual in English and Thai. "She nearly drowned in a swimming pool on a yacht, but was rescued by my father, Prince Chula of Siam".

Courtesy Narisa Chakra

was drawn by Chick Henderson, an English artist. *Yogi Bear's Own Weekly Comic* appeared in 1962 and in 1972 another comic, *Yogi and his Toy* was brought out. Though Yogi was a superbly drawn cartoon, he was never as satisfactory as a soft toy, as there was an inherent contradiction in a design that called for blocks of solid colour or strong lines, rather than the roundness and gentle feel of a toy. Possibly figures like Yogi Bear had moved too far away from Teddies to be classed among them, but he is collected by many who remember him from childhood, when they were smitten by his cute hat and big, round eyes. Walt Disney animated several bear type figures: Br'er Bear, Bong, Barney and Baloo all have related toys that are now beginning to appear in the collectors' market. Hanna Barbera's Blubber-bear, Boo-Boo, The Hillbilly Bears, Breezy and Sneezy and Fozzy, derived from the Muppets, all riveted children to the television screens but are more in the general tradition of wild bears rather than Teddies and consequently fall outside the scope of the more traditional collections.

In the 1960s, Britain's largest and most important bear manufacturer was still Chad Valley, employing over 1,000 people in seven factories. Though the traditional jointed bear continued to be made, it was joined by a few more innovative designs in a cheap synthetic silk plush, made in conjunction with national events, or for sale with Union Jack souvenir items, that were sold in the Carnaby Street years. Though other manufacturers had abandoned the use of "Sanitary" or "Hygienic" from their labels, Chad Valley continued to use this phrase, even though the period when contaminated fillings were of such concern to parents had passed. In the early '60s, rexine pads were still used on mohair versions, but by 1970 dark brown synthetic imitation suede was in general use. There is a wide discrepancy in price between the Chad De Luxe London Gold Mohair Teddies, which were originally very expensive, and the blended

PLATE 104
Ursa Minor Bears were first made in 1979 from flour, salt and water dough, which was then painted and covered with polyurethane. The first bears were made as gifts for children attending the tenth birthday party of Stuart Gordon's daughter. By 1985, with a Design Centre label, the bears were made of clay and the firm in North Wales was supplying Disney as well as other American outlets. *Courtesy Stuart Gordon and Pamela Coates*

mohair or nylon plush versions. Large Chads of the '60s now command excellent prices, not just because so many people have nostalgic associations with the toys made by this manufacturer but also because the they are among the last high quality, mass-produced Teddies made primarily as toys for children.

By the mid-60s, plastic noses were often used on Chad Valley bears, though these are sometimes removed by the more unscrupulous dealers and collectors and replaced with the earlier type of stitched nose, which gives a more ancient appearance but makes the bears harder to date. In 1967, Chad took over another long-established English firm, Chiltern, and the illustrated "Honey Pot" bear marks this transition, with a Chad Valley Chiltern label sewn on its side. The Honey Pot bear is interesting, as the stretch-fabric covered pot is attached to the bear's paws by velcro and points the way to a possible design development of "holding" bears, that

COLOUR PLATE 200
Musical bears were highly popular and this Chiltern has a Swiss musical movement, key-wound from the back of the torso. It is marked "Chiltern Hygienic Toys. Made in England". Ht. 14in. (35.6cm).

Courtesy Constance King Antiques

COLOUR PLATE 201
The honey-pot bear, marked "Chad Valley/Chiltern, Hygienic Toys, Made in England", on a fabric label sewn into the seam, proving that the bear was made just after the Chad Valley takeover in 1967. The toy is interesting, as velcro was used to enable it to hold the stretch, brushed nylon covered pot. He has a black plastic safety nose and is unjointed. The cub-like musical bear, c.1975, has a stitched in fabric "Made in the Republic of Ireland" label on the left foot. Ht. 13in. (33cm) and 12in. (30.5cm).
Courtesy Constance King Antiques

was not further advanced by Chad Valley.

Which, the consumer magazine, conducted an investigation into Teddy Bears in 1967 and examined thirty-nine typical examples made in Britain. The Teddies ranged in size from 8½in. to 36in. (21.6cm to 91.4cm). Most were covered with a woven cotton fabric with animal fibre or nylon pile. Two were made of woven viscous rayon with nylon or rayon pile and four were made of animal skin. The magazine reported that the fillings were kapok, rag-wool flock, wood wool, foam granules or mixtures. Even at this time, the heads were frequently filled with old-fashioned wood wool, as it has never been bettered for retaining shape. The Rag Flock and Other Filling Materials Regulations for 1961-65 had established the basic requirements for hygienic filling used in British toys and *Which* noted that most of the firms had complied with the new rules. Some of the bears contained chimes, others bleated or growled, while one played "Hush-a-Bye Baby" when its leg was twisted. One wonders how the family pets fared after such an early introduction to juvenile sadism…

Musical bears were especially popular in the 1960s, though they almost invariably played the "Teddy Bears' Picnic" or "The Blue Danube". The Chad Valley bear was especially commended by the *Which* team, as the voice box was contained in a plastic casing that made the toy especially safe. By this time, almost all bear eyes were fixed in place with plastic washers so that the child was not put in danger of sharp wire. *Which* was very critical of the dyes used for Pedigree and Petkin bears, whose paws were not colour fast when washed. Despite claims that the bears were completely washable, the nose and mouth of the Rosebud came off and the Cudlam was unsatisfactory. Despite some criticisms that are interesting in the history of bears, it is obvious that, by 1967, few branded bears posed any significant dangers to children.

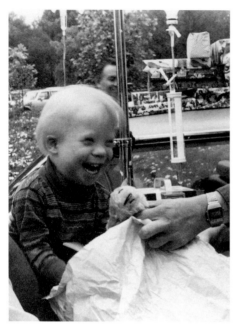

PLATE 105
The therapeutic power of bears, seen in a 1970s American hospital, where a sick child receives a new cuddly Teddy.

Courtesy The United States Bear Force

Dedicated to "T. Edward and Theodore particularly", Peter Bull's *Bear with Me. The Teddy Bear. A Symposium* was first published in 1969, before there was any significant interest in collectable bears. This short work, a serendipity of stories, personal reminiscences and bear history, reached out to people across the world who had previously thought their fondness for bears was somewhat unusual. With good humour, a wealth of curious stories and a style reminiscent of letters from jovial uncles, Peter Bull mixed reports from ursine correspondents with quirky stories and odd snippets from bear lives. He confessed that he would no more think of going away for a night without his own bear, Theodore, than of flying to the moon, and that once the little 2½in. bear was sitting on his bedside table even a hotel became home.

Like John Betjeman, Bull had adored and confided in his Teddy Bear as a small child and was devastated when his mother disposed of his old friend by giving him to a local jumble sale, where he was lost forever. The sixteen year old boy was so scarred by the loss of his confidant that his whole life became centred around the need to find and understand other bears and their owners. Regretting the fact that in 1969 it had become unchic to retain relics of childhood, he was struck by the intensity of feeling many adults expressed towards their Teddy Bears. Despite the natural tendency towards flippancy that, Bull commented, had sent '60s Britain "Gradually sinking giggling into the ocean", the English attitude towards bears was forever coloured by the poetry and thoughts of John Betjeman, who refused to speak to his parents because they had burned his bear when he was seven. Like Betjeman, Bull approached Teddy Bears with a mixture of affection and humour that was peculiarly British and Sixties, as was the Latin version of *Winnie the Pooh, Winnie Ille Pu.*

Peter Bull, in *Bear with Me*, published in 1969, wrote at length about the therapeutic power of Teddies, a theme that was inspiring many people around the world. The toy had become accepted as a companion for the lonely after Elvis Presley has taken his bear as his comforter when conscripted for military service. Several philanthropic societies, directed at people of all ages, sprang up in America and England. Good Bears of the World evolved because Russel McLean, who lived in Ohio, decided that the gift of a new Teddy Bear to children in hospital would provide them with a good friend to keep them company. He was a broadcaster in local radio and persuaded children and the general public to contribute to such a worthy cause. In 1973, James T. Ownby expanded the concept into a much larger organisation "Good Bears of the World", based in Honolulu. Teddies are now given not just to children but even to adults who need comfort in hospital. The United States Bear Force was a similar organisation, giving bears not only to sick children but to soldiers and anyone in psychological need of a bear friend. When the US Marines went into Beirut as part of the United Nations operation, each was given a companion bear by the Bear Force.

COLOUR PLATE 202
The badge of the United States Bear Force, which believes that "everyone has the right to arm bears". The force works in hospitals, schools, rest homes and civic groups.

Courtesy The United States Bear Force, California

PLATE 106
A family of five polar bears made of plastic and produced by Elastolin of Germany in the 1970s.   *Courtesy David Hawkins*

Despite the slow development of a collectors' market and the world-wide interest in bears as an aid to healing, the early 1970s were something of a watershed for commercial Teddy Bears – there were few inventive designs and little interest in antique style examples. At that time, I sold dolls and toys from a shop in Pierrepoint Arcade in Camden Passage, London, a fashionable antiques area, but was only able to carry a few bears in my stock. This was not because bears were expensive but simply because there was such a low level of interest that they were still lying abandoned in outhouses or being thrown away when the house clearance element of the antique trade discovered them. Many of the doll dealers of the time

PLATE 107
Made of ranch and pastel mink, this Teddy was the height of luxury in a period when every fashionable female wore fur coats.

Courtesy Phillips, London

considered them "too dirty and full of germs" to include in their displays and any that were at all damaged were ignored. When I wanted to include a section on Teddy Bears in my first book on toys in 1973, I was politely discouraged, though I did manage a few pages in their own distinct category. I was given some concept of the power of bears by the number of people who commented on my own Chad Valley bear "Rupert"/"Teddy Villers", who was illustrated alongside another large, but short-armed fellow from my stock. Complete strangers at toy and doll fairs and conferences would ask after his health and pedigree, as well as scolding me for not repairing his feet.

At this time, the antique trade was uninterested in the bear collecting fever of such characters as Peter Bull and Colonel Henderson as their interests encompassed examples of all dates and types and were centred mainly on the toy's therapeutic powers. Gradually there was a slow change of attitudes and by the late 1970s old Teddies were being asked for specifically by American collectors. Despite the growing interest, prices were still very low and I was selling button in ear bears for £10-15. Having bought a number of dolls from a North Essex family, I was eventually offered a bear, which was obviously greatly treasured. Aware of his sentimental value and realizing that he was prized so highly by his owner, I paid what was then a silencing £40, to the complete horror of my toy seller friends, who thought him wildly overpriced.

That bear taught me for the first time the degree of affection they demanded of their

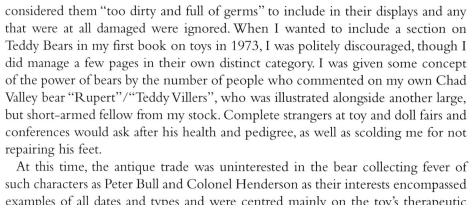

COLOUR PLATE 203
A carton bear, covered with thin, fleecy nylon fabric, with a plastic nose and eyes. He was made as a shop advertisement for Bronnley Soaps and wears the original bow. Ht. 11in. (27.9cm).
Courtesy Constance King Antiques

COLOUR PLATE 204
Old bears began to make their appearance in antique shops from the late 1970s. At that time, buyers were interested more in the character of soft toys, rather than in their condition and manufacturers. This group, taken in the author's shop in 1979, shows a typical selection of mainly 1930s and '50s examples that appealed to early collectors, who searched for friends rather than investments. *Author*

owners. He had sat in the old lady's bedroom for most of her life and she only felt the need to sell him because she had no children of her own. I named the bear "Runnacles" after the family name of the original owner, though I was tempted to call him "Molly", as he seemed to retain the personality of his elderly, tall and benevolent owner, whose parents had bought him for her at Harrods before the 1914-18 War. "Runnacles", because of his excellent condition and good pedigree, having been made by Farnell, has subsequently featured in several books, appeared on television and been reproduced as a line drawing for sweat shirts. He now sits in a case with my own Rupert and a few German bears and bear-related items, though, while I was working on this book, he has sat, muse-like, on a Glastonbury chair in my library.

For commercial bears, the '70s were extremely difficult in Britain and a combination of recession with a significant drop in the birth rate forced several

PLATE 109
When Paddington Bear celebrated his 25th birthday, Coalport issued a special anniversary plate and mug, showing new illustrations of the bear with his birthday gifts.

Courtesy Wedgwood

firms out of existence. The one really bright light was the introduction of Paddington Bear, with his Wellington boots and duffle coat, first produced by Gabrielle Clarkson of Gabrielle designs in 1972. Though *A Bear called Paddington* was first published in 1958, he became famous in the 1960s when his stories were read on the radio and the books were available in all English-speaking countries. The character of the little bear from Peru has always appealed greatly to Londoners, because of his association with the railway station, though his exploits and foibles have universal relevance. His place in the nursery was firmly established when he first appeared in short episodes on television.

Paddington is an alluring combination of child, adult and animal, whose air of puzzlement arouses protective amusement in people of all ages. His red Wellington boots remind us of childhood, while his duffle coat and funny face are reminiscent of elderly politicians and schoolmasters. When Paddington was first published in 1958, duffle coats were almost a uniform for students, though the sou'westers and wellies were worn by children as rainwear, so the adult-child mixture was always evident in his image.

Michael Bond originally wrote the Paddington stories for his wife and perhaps because they were not conceived purely for children, they charm adults and are ideal for bedtime, rather like Milne's Christopher Robin stories. So great was the demand for more tales about the engaging Paddington that a book a year appeared until 1981. Curiously, the American version of the bear, made by Eden Toys from 1975, does not wear red wellies and is quite simply not Paddington to British eyes,

PLATE 110
"Mr. and Mrs. Brown first met Paddington on a railway platform…" The first Paddington Bear illustration.

Courtesy Jane Vandell Associates

COLOUR PLATE 205
Paddington takes a country walk. Made by Gabrielle Designs in the 1970s. He carries his instruction booklet in his pocket and is still a proud possession of his original owner. Ht. 19½in. (49.5cm).

Courtesy Liz Stacey

PLATE 111
From the 1973 Merrythought catalogue, "London Policeman, Guardian for the Nursery floor", 20 and 28in. (50.8 and 71cm). Made in bear brown mohair plush, with a black uniform. "The London Guardsman" is in the same plush with an imitation thick pile bearskin busby, 21 and 30in. (53.3 and 76.2cm). *Courtesy Merrythought Ltd.*

PLATE 112
Two bears made in 1977 by Merrythought. The Traditional Bears in London Gold Mohair blend in the "M" series were produced in eight sizes, from 10 to 48in. (25.4 to 123cm). "Cheeky", made of the same fabric, was produced in six sizes, from 9 to 25in. (23 to 63.5cm). They were both also available in simulated mink. *Courtesy Merrythought Ltd.*

PLATE 113
From the 1973 Merrythought range, "Beefeater Bear", the red costume decorated with braid, 18 and 25in. (45.7 and 63.5cm). The "Highlander Bear" in "Bright tartan kilt with white sporran and smart tammy" (same sizes). *Courtesy Merrythought Ltd.*

PLATE 114
"Winnie the Pooh" characters, made by Merrythought and shown in the 1964 catalogue. Pooh stands 10in. (25.4cm) high and has joints at the neck and arms. There was also a 24in. (61cm) showpiece version. Apart from Tigger, all were made in showpiece sizes. *Courtesy Merrythought Ltd.*

PLATE 115
Made by Real Soft Toys in 1977, this group came out in the period before ultra-soft fillings were developed. The typical '70s bear had short arms and large, cub-like heads to give them a soft, furry appeal.

Courtesy Tanga Wallace Barr

as obviously any bear from Peru would have a pressing need for waterproof boots to keep his fur dry in the London rain and Aunt Lucy would never have let him leave home without them. John Betjeman's *Archie and the Strict Baptists*, published in 1977, is another quintessentially British bear story, about a Teddy that takes to religion but who, unlike Paddington or Pooh, would have held less appeal to children of other cultures.

Though there were some encouraging signs of a bear revival in the late '70s, with Merrythought, Dakin and Gabrielle Designs offering more innovative work, so many firms had gone into receivership that the industry was becoming sadly depleted. The Lines Brothers group, Dunbee Combex Marx, Lesney, Mettoy and

PLATE 116
The 1968 Merrythought "Twisty" range, an exclusive design that enabled the toys to be bent into many realistic poses. The large "Mrs. Twisty Bear", with a white muzzle, and "Mrs Twisty Cheeky" on the right, with a smiling face were in the same sizes – 11in (28cm) and 24in (61cm) showpiece. The four other bears, in the same sizes, are, left to right, "Mr. Twisty Bear", "Mrs Twisty Bear", "Mr. Twisty Cheeky" and "Mrs. Twisty Cheeky". *Courtesy Merrythought Ltd.*

PLATE 117
Teddy Bears' picnics attracted crowds of eager children across Britain and America in the '80s. This event, at the London Toy and Model Museum, was held in July 1985. The child was the winner in a competition for the Best Dressed Bear.

Courtesy Allen Levy

Airfix all joined a depressing list, so it is little wonder that few exciting toys appeared. In 1979, there were 553 British toy making firms, but of these over fifty per cent employed fewer than ten people and were very small by any standards. Bear collectors feel that soft toys are all-important, but by 1982 they accounted for only three per cent of the total toy market. At this time, the adult mascot and collectors' markets were negligible and, with a steadily falling birth rate, many

PLATE 118
Composition bear cubs, made by Elastolin in the 1960s. For a while, plastic and traditional composition figures were made alongside one another.

Courtesy David Hawkins

230

toymakers must have felt depressed about their future prospects.

"The Year of the Child" was celebrated internationally in 1979, giving a boost to the soft toy trade and inspiring many toy-related events, particularly Teddy Bears' picnics and festivals, notably that at Longleat House. Prizes were given for the best dressed, the oldest and the most lovable bears, all of which offered journalists delightful photo opportunities. Suddenly, every child wanted a Teddy Bear of their own, while possessing an antique example gave added prestige. At many of these events, adults were just as eager as children to show off their old Teddy Bear friends and related stories appeared in both local and national papers. Gradually, interest in bears began to assume a curiously different tone, with children becoming noticeably less important: Gund redesigned their bears to appeal more to the adult market, while the North American Bear Co. introduced the Very Important Bear range. Soon, antique bears were appearing more frequently in magazine articles and books, culminating in Patricia Schoonmaker's *Collectors History of the Teddy Bear* in 1979, that charted the history of the bear from original advertisements and press accounts. Other bear-related books soon followed, so that a toy that had remained largely unexplored suddenly became accessible to collectors.

PLATE 119
Marcia Lawson with a few of her bears from the "Show 'N Tell Museum" at Carthage, Illinois, with its many rooms crowded with bears. This was one of the first museums devoted exclusively to things ursine, c.1979.
Courtesy Show 'N Tell Museum

PLATE 120
Teddy Bears' picnics began to become a feature of every carnival and fund raising event in the late '70s. The two coloured synthetic plush bears with large ears are typical of the late 1970s and were often made in the Far East. *Courtesy Jane Vandell Associates*

COLOUR PLATE 206
Still a nursery favourite, the 1997 Golden Bear Rupert. A small finger puppet of the character, which is now seen as an animated series on ITV, is also available. *Courtesy Golden Bear Products*

CHAPTER 9
The Full Circle

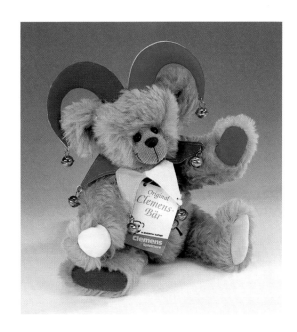

Some of the spirit that had fired Teddy Bear inventiveness before 1910 flared back into life in the early 1980s, aided by growing national economies and a public that was eager to spend, spend, spend. The most extravagant bears ever made belong to this period: gold jewelled Teddies, luxurious mink versions with rhinestone eyes and ornate collars, even lady bears with sequined bras. Replica and collectors' bears were ideal candidates for inclusion in this expensive market and several of the leading toymakers, including Steiff and Dean's, produced their first limited editions in 1980.

Bears were certainly in the spotlight, with Mischa, made by Dakin, used for the Winter Olympics in Moscow and the House of Nisbet's Bully Bear visiting the House of Commons. While several of the old names, such as Pedigree, were lost in the early '80s, their place was soon taken by smaller, but perhaps more artistic, firms. The North American Bear Company introduced its "Very Important Bear Series" in 1980, which was to inspire many artist makers. Canterbury Bears, Little Folk of Devon, Care Bears, Big Softies and The House of Nisbet were all begun in this buoyant decade.

COLOUR PLATE 207
"Care Bears", each with a special message on its tummy. Rather like the Cabbage Patch dolls, the bears have large heads with furrows and short, plump arms. An interesting feature is the heart-shaped foot pads. Left to right: Grumpy, Birthday, Tenderheart, Friend, Cheer and Bedtime. *Courtesy Kenner Parker*

COLOUR PLATE 208
Founded in the years just after the end of the war in 1946 and now run by the son of the original owner, Clemens manufactures a wide range of models. At the back is a fine "Grizzly-Bär", made of acrylic plush. Ht. 24-32in. (61-81.3cm). On the left is a white "Christmas Bear", also in acrylic plush.
Courtesy Clemens Spieltiere

Teddy fever came to a boil in 1984, with all the major manufacturers creating special models or re-issuing antique designs. A survey in Britain revealed that forty per cent of all Teddy Bears sold were bought for adults and this information encouraged toy makers in Europe and America to concentrate on this burgeoning sector of the market. Adult collectors offered a lifeline to many firms which had been concerned about the decline in the infant trade and gave them a new enthusiasm for the quality end of the market. It was in the '80s that bears moved from the nursery into adult life and began to be used as a motif on clothes and fashion accessories. Bears turned full circle at this time and were again seen as amusing and progressive by designers, who repeated the image on everything from smart leather shoes to sheets and wallpaper.

Realising that much heavier advertising and marketing would be necessary if firms

PLATE 122
Like other firms in Britain and America, Dean's became much more interested in the collectors' market in the 1980s. The "Dean's City of London Guilds and Livery Companies Bear Series" was sold under the Dean's Childsplay Toys Ltd. label. With their large heads, the bears are cub-like in style.
Courtesy The Dean's Company

COLOUR PLATE 209
Clemens, in the late 1990s, are concentrating mainly on the collectors' market. A group of golden plush mohair bears in the "Nostalgie" range. *Courtesy Clemens Spieltiere*

were to survive, tremendous efforts were thrown into character merchandising, such as the "Furskin Bears from Moody Hollow", all sold with Xavier Roberts' signature on their paw. Each of the podgy, freckle-faced bears was sold complete with a story book, telling of life in Moody Hollow. Though they were planned as a follow-up to Xavier's Cabbage Patch dolls, the Teddies, despite their individual names, accessories and personalities, never caught on in the same way, though Hank Spitball, Flossie May, the greatest dancing bear in Georgia, and Farrel Furskin, who runs the Post Office, are all heading for the collectors' market of the future. In their first year, 1986, the Furskin Bears outsold the first seven years of the Cabbage Patch Kids, yet never achieved the same fame.

Soon other firms were creating bear families, such as Tomy, with their Sylvanian series, introduced in 1987. These small Brown and Grey Bear sets were aimed at

COLOUR PLATE 210
Laura Ashley's bears first appeared in the 1984 Home Furnishing Catalogue, mainly due to Nick Ashley, who had a great fondness for Teddies. The bear was devised by John Blackburn of Canterbury Bears. It was felt that the bear should not be too brash or commercial, so that it was identifiably Ashley of the mid-80s in feeling. Ashley "Simpla F516 Multi Allspice" was the final fabric chosen for the first bears' paws. The Teddy was called Bernard. *Courtesy Laura Ashley Ltd.*

PLATE 123
Dean's of Pontypool were sustained in the early '80s by the strength of the American collectors' market. Among the toys especially made for the USA was the "Norman Rockwell American Bear" with printed Republican and Democrat ribbons and a box that carried the Rockwell cartoon.
Courtesy The Dean's Company

very young children as well as the pocket money "collecting group" of ten to thirteen year olds, who bought the figures more as ornamental items. Well-made wooden furniture and small bear houses were supplied, as were school and kitchen sets – very much a return to the type of miniature bear products seen before 1925. One interesting advance was the Sylvanian Performing Bears in two shades of brown, which were battery powered and designed to mime in time to voices heard on radio or television. In another collectors' series for children, "Letterbox Bear" appears in the Acorn Green Plush playset. The child's collecting instincts were encouraged by many bear makers in the late 1980s and the 1990s, though the trend is now less strong, with its place taken by television and video related products.

In Germany, Hermann introduced their first special edition collectors' bears, while Steiff threw themselves wholeheartedly into this new field with a 1980 limited edition of the 1905 original Teddy, issued to celebrate their soft toy centenary. Before

COLOUR PLATE 211
A large group of Steiff replica bears, sold in London in 1995, all in excellent boxed condition and with numbered certificates.
Left to right: The large black mohair is a British Collectors 1912 replica, no. 2243 of 5,000, made in 1991. £230.
"Teddy Bär 1906. Blonde 43" No.888 of 5,000. £276.
A black short plush mohair 1907 replica (1988) with a black leather nose. No. 2901 of 4,000. £391.
Wearing bright orange trousers, a beige Golden Gate replica of a late 1930s bear. Made especially for F.A.O. Schwarz, USA, Boxed, no. 750 of 2,000.
A long mohair "1953 Jackie" in the original 13¾in (35cm) size. No. 2421 of 4,000, produced in 1988-89. £207.
A 1955 two-coloured bear with a neck mechanism, produced 1990-91. No. 2,134 of 4,000. £172.
Harrods musical bear, first made in 1909. No. 308 of 2,000. £368.
A gold mohair bear on wheels, first made in 1939. No 3,486 of 4,000. £138.
First produced in 1913, a pink Record "Teddy Rose". No 1,051 of 4,000, produced in 1991-92. £92.
In dark brown mohair, a circus bear with neck mechanism that was first made in 1935. No. 246 of 4,000, produced in 1994. £103.
Courtesy Bonham's, Chelsea

COLOUR PLATE 212

Steiff limited edition replica bears, all in mint and boxed condition and with numbered certificates.
Top, left to right: "Bärle", first made in 1904, "Bear 35 P4" No. 1,544 of 6,000 produced 1991-
92. £322.
A white mohair muzzled bear, first made in 1908. Made in 1989 no. 1,990 of 2,650. £299.
The Polar Bear with neck mechanism was first made in 1931. Produced 1989-90, No. 700 of
3,000. £230.
A pale pink "Teddy Rose", a replica of a 1925 model. No. 5,185 of 10,000, made in 1987. £299.
Front row: A gold mohair "Petsy Brass", first made in 1927. No 3,220 of 5,000. £126.
A white muzzled bear 1908 replica. No. 2,270 of 5,000. £253.
A gold mohair British Collectors replica, first produced in 1907. Produced in 1989, no. 1,303 of
2,000. £747.
A much smaller British Collectors 1906 replica, produced in 1990. No. 941 of 3,000. £345.
The somersaulting Teddy was first made in 1909. No. 2,045 of 5,000, made in 1990-91. £299.

Courtesy Bonham's, Chelsea

COLOUR PLATE 213
The North American Bear Company of Ohio was a market leader in the field of modern character bears. "Scarlett O'Beara and Rhett Beartler" were produced in 1984.
Courtesy North American Bear Company

the Year of the Bear, Steiff, though proud of its long history, had always appeared at international trade fairs as a player in the toys for children league but, aware of the change in attitude and the international interest in their products, a postcard booklet of early bears was published, followed by a facsimile of their 1892 catalogue. The Roly Poly Bear of 1894 represented the last of the Victorian style toys and was reproduced in 1984 as an interesting link in the evolution of the Teddy Bear. It was sold in a world-wide edition of nine thousand. The 1909 replica in mohair was probably of more general interest to collectors, as was the Giengen Teddy set, first made in 1906, with an edition of sixteen thousand. Steiff also celebrated the Year of the Bear with the introduction of the very first fully jointed, machine washable Teddy, intended for children rather than for the international collectors' market.

Inspired no doubt by the tremendous world-wide interest in the new collectors' range, Steiff diversified further in 1985 with such associated lines as costume jewellery decorated with bears' heads and some further limited editions – a 1930s Dicky Bear and a 1905 bear on wheels. In the general children's toy range, there was a Passport Bear, a Petsy Bear with woven fur and a Zotty of the same fabric.

In America, to celebrate the Year of the Bear, Ideal produced porcelain replicas of the first bears they had designed at the beginning of the century, while a completely new firm, the North American Bear Company, introduced Muffy

PLATE 124
"King Edward to Prince William": the author, wearing an original Edwardian dress and carrying a 1908 bear, delivering a contemporary bear to Buckingham Palace on behalf of the United States Bear Force after the birth of Prince William in 1982. *Courtesy Jane Vandell Associates*

Vanderbear, which remains in production. The term "artist bear" had been used since the mid-1970s in America to mirror the structure of the doll market, which differentiates makers of replicas and those who create individual and very personal models. Artist bears influenced commercial American production much earlier than in Europe and craftspeople were exhibiting extravagant and amusing Teddies in the early 1980s. Unconstrained by the conventions of good taste and animal dignity that inhibit the more traditional designers, the first American bear artists displayed brash and refreshingly vulgar creations, complete with spangled lacy briefs and bras. In the very early years of antique bear collecting in the States, the gay community had played a leading role and their influence was also apparent in the first artists' designs. When displayed in expensive gift shops, the curiously dressed new bears soon attracted a following and inspired others to fashion bears as parodies of film stars, singers and even the characters in famous paintings. America certainly led the world in the early '80s, with an ever-growing number of bear artists and exhibitions, all directed towards adult customers.

In recent years, the children's soft toy market has declined dramatically, though it has enjoyed some unexpected peaks, as in the year of the 'Lion King'. Toy Teddies are at

COLOUR PLATE 214
Giant Pooh, with a button-up jacket and Piglet wearing a scarf. Pooh is 31in. (78.7cm) tall. Introduced in 1997 was a range of Pooh squeezy toys, which could be purchased boxed as a group or collected separately. There is also a miniature soft toy range for the children's collecting market. *Courtesy Golden Bear Products*

COLOUR PLATE 215
A range of toys, including bears, in old-fashioned style, made in pleasing earth colours. *Old Bear and Friends* is created by Jane Hissey, a best-selling writer and children's illustrator. The Old Bear stories first appeared on British television in 1993. The ten minute episodes re-create the atmosphere of the books. Jointed "Bramwell Brown" is 12½in. (31.8cm) and "Old Bear" is 17in. (43.2cm). 1997 range.
Courtesy Golden Bear Products

present in one of their periods of relative unpopularity with children, and retailers are finding traditional expensive bears very hard to sell. The problem is largely attributed to the fast decline in the middle class birth rate, the effect of a world-wide recession and the fact that children play less actively and spend an increasing amount of time propped in front of a video or television or strapped into a car seat, with fewer opportunities for crawling, climbing and romping with their Teddies and soft toys.

As the children's market has diminished, the adult mascot and gift area has, fortunately, increased and much of the bear activity has shifted to these outlets rather than toy shops. Collectors' bears are not restricted by the safety regulations that govern playthings and this gives the makers much greater freedom to experiment and mix fabrics, mechanisms and accessories. The possibility of limiting production to a few thousand also helps and gives skilled employees the satisfaction of working on top class models that would be too expensive for nursery use. Because promotion can be targeted at collectors through fairs, clubs and magazines, costs can be controlled without the vast expense of advertising in the general retail market.

The story of The House of Nisbet most characterises the peaks and troughs of

COLOUR PLATE 216
An evocative portrayal of a First World War German Army officer wearing his Pickelhaub and a grey and red greatcoat, made of distressed mohair by the bear artist Marie Robischon, whose work is characterised by this distinctive nose stitching.
Courtesy Marie Robischon

PLATE 125
The actor and great arctophile, Peter Bull, with young William Nisbet, photographed in 1980, when Bully Bear was first introduced.

Courtesy House of Nisbet Ltd.

manufacturing, as its rise and decline were so rapid, and epitomise the successes and failures of the volatile collectors' market. The firm was originally founded to produce costume dolls, particularly for the tourist trade, and was the brainchild of Peggy Nisbet, who exuded some of the personality of a splendid Edwardian Teddy Bear. She was a regal figure in the splendid red outfit she wore for the celebration of her silver jubilee in dollmaking and imposing when one sat and talked with her high up in the delightful water tower that was her home. Peggy had become involved in the toy trade at the time of the Queen's Coronation, when she created her first doll, representing the sovereign in her robes. Once the firm moved from Weston-super-Mare to Dunster Park, there was more space to develop soft toys. In 1976, Peggy Nisbet's son-in-law, Jack Wilson, became chairman and changed the firm's name to The House of Nisbet. Though Peggy said that she regretted the commercialism and push of Wilson, he did breathe new energy into the direction of the company and I talked to him on many occasions about his ambitions for the business, especially as the bears that he loved had become so important in the toy trade.

In an unpublished obituary for Peter Bull, who inspired the Nisbet range of bears, Jack recalled that they met at the first Teddy Bear Rally, held at Longleat in 1979 and hosted by the Marquess of Bath, an occasion that involved fifty thousand bears. Shortly afterwards, at a meeting at Bull's Chelsea home, over a tea of sausages and beans, he stipulated that if Nisbet were to produce a special bear, it had to be designed as a "good listener". The bear eventually met this specification and first appeared in 1980 at the inauguration of the Good Bears of the World Den in the

COLOUR PLATE 217
A figure from the 1997 Royal Doulton "Paddington Bear Collection". The figures are made of resin and are unfired. They are made in China, but modelled by Valerie Annand and are intended for the child collectables market. Ht. 3½in. (9cm).
Courtesy of Royal Doulton

PLATE 126
The well-known actor, Peter Bull, who did so much to arouse and foster interest in Teddy Bears. Seen here reading the Nisbet edition of his famous *Teddy Bear Book* to Bully, Young Bully and Bully Minor in 1983.
Courtesy House of Nisbet Ltd.

House of Commons in London.

The Nisbet "Bully Bear" was created in the firm's workrooms under the supervision of Estelle Hawkins, who worked closely with Peter Bull to fashion a bear based closely on his own "Delicatessen", who later became very famous when he appeared as Aloysius in the television adaptation of *Brideshead Revisited*. "Bully Bear", in his 1980 reincarnation, was much plumper than the original and was in no way a completely imitative replica but more an updating of an old concept. Model 5026 appeared in a world-wide edition of five thousand and sold with his own passport and certificate of identity signed by Peter Bull, who described him as having a "modern and faintly impertinent look".

In 1981 "Young Bully", a founding member of "The Worshipful Company of Peanut Butter Eaters", and "discovered in a sentry box outside Buckingham Palace", was introduced and in 1982 "Bully Minor", representing Bully at prep. school age. The House of Nisbet became even more deeply involved with the world of bears when it re-published Peter Bull's *Teddy Bear Book* in 1983, in a numbered edition that sold six thousand in the first eighteen months. Their *Zodiac Bears*, published in 1984, with the first thousand copies signed and numbered, developed from a cooperation between Bull and the artist Pauline McMillan at "Zodiac, The Astrological Emporium" which Bull ran in Kensington Church Street. The Zodiac Bears were country cousins of Bully Bear and lived in the village of Little Ticking, where there were no humans. The book relates how the twelve bears prepare for the Bear-Day Party that was held annually and it was packed with rich colour illustrations, full of

COLOUR PLATE 218
Made in 1986, the African handcrafted Zakanaka Teddy Bear, made in Botswana by a cooperative funded by a Norwegian aid programme. Ht. 16in. (40.6cm). *Courtesy Design Enterprise London*

the small detail that children love to discover. The project was especially interesting, as the book and the soft toys were designed together as a complementary edition with book illustrator and production team working as a unit. Twelve different fur fabrics were used for the bears, who were given names such as "Polly Hester" (Leo) or "Bella Plush" (Scorpio). The latter was once a famous Hollywood star and intended to raffle some of her clothes from her most famous films in aid of the Home for Battered Bears. The Zodiacs were designed to appeal as much to adult collectors as children and some of the costumes were in the manner of the modern Teddy Bear artists. Peter Bull loved to talk to the workers who were creating his bears and was involved heart and soul in a project that was to become his own obituary. The British Teddy Bear scene was never the same after the death of the actor, Peter Bull, as his larger than life character, his amusing stories and real love of bears brought a vibrancy and eccentricity which cannot be replaced. In all his writing, television and personal appearances, he always linked bears with their owners' lives, problems and delights and showed a real affection for the many children who, like Christopher Robin, whispered the confidences of their bears into his willing ears.

The House of Nisbet perpetuated Peter Bull's "Delicatessen" with a replica that was issued in 1987 to celebrate the bear's 80th birthday and utilized an unusual process for giving modern mohair an antique "distressed" appearance, as did "The Anything Bear" in 1988, a yes/no bear, inspired by a Schuco design and with an up-market embroidered Nisbet label. It is possible that Nisbet by this time was lured too much by the potential of the growing bear collectors' market and had become too American-led, leading to its purchase in 1989 by Dakin U.K. Effectively, the Nisbet family business ceased at this time in Britain, though their bears, because of the comparatively short manufacturing period, are gradually becoming more collectable.

COLOUR PLATE 219
Teddy Beddy Bear, in candy stripes and night caps, made in the mid-1980s by Telitoy.
Courtesy of Telitoy

COLOUR PLATE 220
The book launch of the Zodiac
Bears with Jack Wilson, Peter
Bull and Pauline McMillan, the
illustrator. In the foreground are
the bear characters from the
story. *Courtesy House of Nisbet Ltd.*

PLATE 127
All the signs of the Zodiac. The
twelve bears with their book,
written by Peter Bull and
illustrated by Pauline McMillan
in 1983. *Courtesy House of Nisbet Ltd.*

Colour Plate 221
A cell from the "SuperTed" animation, showing the bear swooping through the air, followed by Spotty Man. The colours and draughtsmanship are unusually good for the period.

Courtesy Abbey Home Entertainments

Alresford soft toys was another logical progression from their collectors' dolls which were first produced in 1977. By the early '80s the business, working from an old water mill near Winchester, Hampshire, was producing bears, and an interestingly costumed series, including a delightful Policeman and Golfer. Their Honey Bears, with U-shaped mouths and raised eyebrows, were unusual, though the standard high quality play bears were the most popular. Alresfords were unusual in that one machinist made the entire animal and they used flat bed sewing machines, rather than the overlock type used by the majority of makers. This meant stronger joins without the possibility of fraying. The animals were filled with super-soft carded polyester and the features embroidered. By 1982, over thirty-five per cent of Alresford products went overseas. All the bears were washable and could be low heat tumble-dried. In response to the collectors' market, a somewhat Edwardian style Bride and Groom were made in 1985, alongside the more conventional products and the Canadian brown and Goldfleck Bruins. Though Alresford Crafts was a relatively short-lived company, trading only from 1970 to 1992, it was interesting as it had developed from the collecting scene itself, with Margaret Jones designing the toys. Originally established to make dolls, bears had taken over by the early 1980s, when there were over one hundred employees. The firm was a complete partnership between John and Margaret Jones, and the firm closed shortly after John's death in 1991. Though their dolls were conceived purely for the collectors' market, the bears were created completely in the play-toy idiom and only during the final years of the company did the burgeoning Teddy Bear market begin to have a real effect on production, which shifted more to this selective collectable area.

As the international bear collectors' market gained momentum in the 1980s, much more effort was expended on interesting new lines and on special editions. Steiff, in their 1994 "Museum Collection", offered a Roly-Poly 1894 and a Bavarian-style limited edition "Giengen Teddy Set" of a baby bear rocked by its mother, set in a box printed with a Bavarian scene. A 1909 replica bear was joined by a new selection of collectors' items, such as gold-coloured brooches, pendants, bags and T-shirts. Though the collectors' editions were attractive, Molly Bear, who lies down ready for sleep and the pink and white or blue and white baby Teddies, intended for very young babies, were probably more interesting as historical developments in the evolution of toys.

A new character, SuperTed, made his first appearance at the British Toy and Hobby Fair in 1983. The character had already featured on the Welsh language television channel S4C and later appeared nationally. SuperTed lived in a tree-

COLOUR PLATE 222
Made by Dean's in 1997, this coal black "Davy", the old fashioned Welsh miner, is made of distressed mohair and carries a brass lamp made by ex-miners. Limited edition of 500. Ht. 13in. (33cm).
Courtesy The Dean's Company

PLATE 128
Alresford Crafts was one of the first British firms to concentrate on costumed character bears. From left to right: Jogger, Golfer, Nurse or Nanny, Fireman, Guardsman and Policeman, 32in (81.3cm). The smaller bears in the foreground are 18in. (45.7cm) high. c.1984.
Courtesy Alresford Crafts Ltd.

house packed with the latest technology, so he could fly anywhere – to protect endangered species, or prevent the theft of archeological treasures. This was a protective bear, who was created to be much softer in approach than other animated characters – a bear with a social conscience and perhaps strangely out of place in the money-money eighties. The character was created by Mike Young of Siriol (Cheerful) Animations to help protect children and animals, always a hard task for any ordinary bear. According to the story, when this bear was first made, there was some fault in him, so he was thrown away and lay neglected in an old storeroom. "Then from outer space a spotty man brought him to life with his cosmic dust" and carried him off to a magic cloud, where Mother Nature gave him special powers – SuperTed has only to utter a magic word and his powers come alive, propelling him across continents, to wherever he is needed.

Like many other modern toys, SuperTed appeared with a host of merchandising spin-offs, from records to "Grow with SuperTed" measuring charts. To feel completely secure, infants could go to bed dressed in SuperTed pyjamas and clean their teeth in front of a SuperTed mirror. All this was a long way from the bedtime stories that Mike Young told his small stepson who was afraid of the dark. At first, twelve eight-minute cartoons were commissioned in English and Welsh and produced in Cardiff's old docklands by the chief animator, Dave Edwards. The animators were somewhat idealistic and determined to create a series of which their own children could be proud. They avoided the mindless aggression, facile plots and crude, robotic movements of so many cartoons and set out to prove that a softer approach could have even greater appeal. The first series was made with the voices of such famous actors as Jon Pertwee, Victor Spinetti and Roy Kinnear. Because SuperTed is just a "reject Teddy", even the

PLATE 129
SuperTed in great demand at a country park Teddy Bears' picnic in 1983.

Courtesy Jane Vandell Associates

PLATE 130
"Tummy Buttons", one of the last innovative Teddy Bear ranges made by Pedigree Dolls and Toys in the early '80s. The child learned how to undo buttons and dress itself by practising on the Teddy's clothes, all strongly made to withstand rough play.

Courtesy Jane Vandell Associates

most underprivileged children could identify with him. By 1984, the SuperTed series had been sold to forty-five countries, while in Britain, a video sold over 2,200 in the first three weeks on the market, suggesting that the softer approach of this environmentally conscious bear had relevance to the lives of ordinary children.

Pedigree was attempting to broaden its appeal in 1986, having always been considered to be primarily a girls' toy manufacturer, mainly because of dolls such as Sindy and her accessories. In the mid '80s, the UK soft toy market was valued at around £25 million and Pedigree, conscious that it had lost ground in the sector, was working to establish its position. The most innovative toy design was "Tummy Buttons", with well-made clothes held in place with a central button. This family of bears also had some educational value, as the baby learned to button its own clothes through dressing and undressing the Teddies. For the traditionalists, the most attractive bear of the year was the De Luxe Sterling Silver coloured mohair bear, though Disney's Pooh, both as a glove puppet and in a 6in. (15.2cm) version, would have held most appeal for the pocket-money market.

COLOUR PLATE 223
"Ralph", designed by John Axe and made in long mohair by Merrythought in an edition of 1,000. 1997 collectors' range. Ht. 15in. (38cm). *Courtesy Merrythought, Ironbridge*

COLOUR PLATE 224
Rupert and Bill Badger, in the Merrythought International Collectors range, with an evocative box lid. 1996 edition.

Courtesy Merrythought, Ironbridge

I first discovered the Aux Nations soft toys in a small shop on the Old Brompton Road in the early 1970s and could scarcely believe the artistry and quality of their mascot and studio pieces. At the time, most toyshops were stocked with poorly constructed, foam -filled animals, setting the French creations completely apart. The firm was established in the early 1960s in Vaison la Romaine to construct top quality toys. "To the Nations" was incorporated with "Nounours", the French equivalent for Teddy Bear, established in 1963 to specialise in the manufacture of high class toys, combining tradition and modernism. At first, the Aux Nations bears were filled with kapok, wool and wood wool, but today non-inflammable polyester and polyurethane fibre are used. All the toys are inspired by live animals and a number of especially commissioned display pieces are created each year, such as a seven foot bear. The 1997 range of sculptured soft toys, intended as much for adults

COLOUR PLATE 225
Frivolous and light-hearted pram or cot bears in plush and French gingham, made by Nounours in their 1997 toy range.

Courtesy Nounours

Nounours toy play bears, with soft, unjointed bodies. Ht. 14-24in. (35.6-61cm). From the 1997
Collection.   *Courtesy Nounours*

as for children, includes superb studio bears some 51in. (130cm) tall when seated.
White polar bears and brown bears are represented in a seated position and there
is a range of smaller, cub-like figures in gold, brown and white. All the Aux Nations
animals are modelled in a gentle, natural style, with great elegance, making them
ideal as ornamental pieces, as they honour the natural dignity of the animals.

Under the Nounours trade name, an extensive range of Teddies intended purely
for children and collectors is marketed. One of the most appealing designs of 1997
is Les Griffes, with the bear or owner's name embroidered on the foot pads, a
refinement that only takes a fortnight for delivery. The mohair bears have
contrasting muzzles and paws and are made in soft creams and browns. Nounours
play bears appear in bright checks and stripes for older children with the softest
pastel shades for tiny infants. In 1997, a new range, La Pelucherie, of the Champs-
Elysées, was introduced, with seated, long-pile bears and some traditional, short
plush, big eared versions, as well as "Ours Couché", floor bears to lie on and fight
with, in brown or white. Aux Nations products represent the finest quality
commercial bears and are displayed in the most exclusive shops around the world.

PLATE 131
The chained bear image still holds appeal for toymakers and this large, well made figure was used
in the 1980s as an advertisement at trade fairs for Dean's Childsplay Toys.
Courtesy Jane Vandell Associates

COLOUR PLATE 227
"Winnie the Pooh in the Armchair" from the Winnie the Pooh Collection. Modelled by Shane Ridge and painted at the John Beswick Studios. Ht. 3¼in. (8.3cm). *Courtesy of Royal Doulton*

COLOUR PLATE 228
"Winnie the Pooh and the paw marks", modelled by Warren Platt from the 1996 range. Ht. 2in. (5cm). A collection of ten figures introduced in 1996 and available with a special backdrop to mark the 70th anniversary of the first publication of the Pooh books. In 1997, five additional models were introduced. *Courtesy of Royal Doulton*

In 1996, the 70th anniversary of the first A. A. Milne Christopher Robin book, Royal Doulton created a range of gift and nursery ware, depicting all the well-loved characters from the One Hundred Acre Wood. The first ten figures, including Piglet and Kanga in a variety of poses, carried a special backstamp for the anniversary. In 1997, a special limited edition tableau, Eeyore loses a tail, showing Christopher Robin, Eeyore, Pooh and Piglet together, was issued. The Pooh collection is made at the John Beswick studios, with the gift-boxed characters modelled by Shane Ridge and Martyn Alcock, who worked closely to the original Shepard line drawings. Those decorated in softer colours will obviously hold most appeal for bear collectors, though they will be joined by plate collectors in their appreciation of Winnie the Pooh by the Christmas tree, not a Shepard drawing, but a sensitive adaptation. Doulton figures always enjoy a strong following among china collectors and once a range is discontinued or radically changed, prices soar.

COLOUR PLATE 229
"Eeyore loses a tail" was modelled by Martyn Alcock and produced in 1997 in a first limited edition of 5,000. The "Winnie the Pooh" range was introduced in 1995 and, in 1996 only, the collection featured a special backstamp in commemoration of the 70th anniversary of the first A.A. Milne book. The figures are hand painted at the John Beswick studios of Royal Doulton.

Courtesy of Royal Doulton

COLOUR PLATE 230

Bears with an interesting provenance have become highly desirable in recent years. The standing gold mohair, 21in. (53.3cm) was made in America by Ideal in the 1930s. He has backed glass eyes and a fully jointed straw-filled body. Known as "Buddy", he was brought to Britain in 1943 by his first owner, who was stationed at a US Air Force base near Warrington. He gave the bear to his fiancée, Penny Aston, before he left to take part in the D-Day landings. He was killed in action. Penny died in 1983 and for a short while the bear was at the Cotswold Teddy Bear Museum. He was sold when the museum was dispersed for £3,450.

The much earlier seated bear, 18in. (45.7cm) high, dating to 1910, with boot button eyes and a straw and kapok filled body, is known as "Wilhelm, the Emperor's Servant". It is reputed that Wilhelm's owner was Max, a servant of Wilhelm II, who left Germany with his abdicating employer in 1918. Max and Wilhelm lived in Holland until 1940, when the bear was brought to England by the owner's son. The bear sold for £2,300 when the museum was dispersed.

Courtesy Bonham's, Chelsea

COLOUR PLATE 231
"God Bless Mummy" in gold mohair made by Merrythought in a collectors' edition of 500 in 1996. Ht. 8in. (20.3cm). *Courtesy Merrythought, Ironbridge*

A curious feature of the last quarter of the century is the bear festivals that sprang up in response to the increasing numbers of enthusiasts who were eager to buy not only antique but also limited edition and artist creations. The first events in Britain were linked to Teddy Bears' picnics and were fund-raising occasions, such as that held at Longleat in 1979. Soon the divergent interests of collectors and children became apparent and collectors' bear fairs were held all over the country. At these events, fine antique specimens are sold alongside reproductions and modern collectors' editions and there are stands selling a whole variety of related merchandise. At some of the larger events, antique valuation services are run by the auction rooms and lectures are given by makers, writers and restorers. For anyone thinking of starting a collection of bears, there is no better way of discovering sources, materials, books and antiques. For those willing to search further afield and become deeply involved in clubs, there are international tours, with visits to collections, museums and important factories, such as Steiff, Hermann or Merrythought.

As the price of good antique Teddies escalates, the number of fakes and misrepresentations also increases. Most are of an obvious kind, with distressed mohair and atavistic body patterns that any collector soon learns to recognise. Much greater problems are posed by the clever fakes, filled with wood wool and sawdust and even including patches and apparently re-covered pads. One dealer friend of many years' experience bought a bear of this kind at a flea market and had it accepted for sale at a leading auction house before she was

PLATE 132
Cartoon-like bears from the mid-1980s range made by Mattel. The Berenstain Bear Family each carried a heart-shaped badge with their names. Papa, with his toothy smile, is especially appealing. *Courtesy Mattel Inc.*

Colour Plate 232
The 1997 range of "Autumn Bears", with their characteristic tartan ribbons, from the
Merrythought Classic Bears, which are intended for children's play.

Courtesy Merrythought, Ironbridge

contacted by the cataloguer and the mistake was revealed. Another clever forger's
ploy was to buy mohair bears of the '50s and '60s, remove the kapok filling and
replace it with wood wool, at the same time re-shaping the bear to give it an earlier
outline. As with any segment of the market, there are pitfalls for the beginner but
anyone who enjoys hunting for a bargain has to accept the losses with the successes.
If a secure purchase is required, then it has to be made from a reputable dealer who
will provide a receipt with a date and comments on the condition and the name of
the manufacturer.

Auction rooms are not covered by the same rules that control the sale of goods
from shops and there is often a disclaimer as to state and date, though even in this
area, rules are gradually being tightened and if a fake is described in the catalogue

COLOUR PLATE 233
"Cheeky Full of Beans", with contrasting inset muzzles and boldly stitched claws. From the 1996 Collectors Range. Ht. 15, 17 and 26in. (38, 43.2 and 66cm).
Courtesy Merrythought, Ironbridge

as "made in 1910", your money would have to be refunded. As this is still a grey area in some salerooms, the new buyer would be advised to study the conditions of sale carefully and also question any stated provenance. To make bears more appealing, they are sometimes given "interesting" family histories or amusing names. For purchasers who are simply buying for fun or because an object appeals, the authenticity of the bear is largely irrelevant but the serious collector or investor has to cast an extremely critical eye on claims as to provenance.

Obviously with such a high level of exposure, many antique bear collectors feel that the market is becoming over-saturated, with too many "limited editions", too many reproductions and an almost weekly increase in the number of bear artists.

PLATE 133
"Petsy" bears in the rounded, cuddly play style form popular in the mid-1980s. Though Steiff were very involved in the collectors' market, they were still mainly producers of soft toys for children.
Courtesy Margarete Steiff GmbH

COLOUR PLATE 234
Royal Doulton produce nursery china that has delighted children for decades. Their 1990s
"Winnie the Pooh" range of nurseryware included an old style Christmas set, introduced in
1996, with the favourite characters grouped around a Christmas tree.   *Courtesy of Royal Doulton*

Curiously, as this section of the market has burgeoned, sales of plush toys to
children have decreased, posing the discomforting question of whether adults now
have a greater need of comfort than their children.

The decline in the British plush toy market for infants is hard to understand in
an affluent period. This commercial market peaked in 1993 because of the interest
in the Lion King, but in 1995 it fell to £77 million and in 1996 there was a further
fall to £64 million. Bears represent approximately 10% of this soft toy market. The
reasons why children own fewer soft toys is hard to understand, but perhaps they
sit, immobile, in front of a television set far too often, perhaps buggies and slings,
rather than prams, result in less play when the child is out of the house, and there

PLATE 134
The Teddy Tidy Team with their cart, an idea devised by Ann Wyatt in the early 1980s to encourage children to Keep The Lake District Tidy. This ranger is Teddy Dinglemire.

Courtesy Ann Wyatt

is also the possibility that more toys are recycled. Combined with a falling birth rate, the number of commercially-produced bears seems to be in a steady decline, while the collectors' market grows in inverse ratio. At Christie's alone, Teddy Bear sales have reached £900,000 a year and Sotheby's, with far fewer auctions, reaches some £80,000. When antique shops, bear fairs, artist models and replicas are considered, sales in the collectors' market must be running hard on the heels of the toy manufacturers. Perhaps soon, those with a real eye for future collectors' items will be looking more at the commercial High Street lines than at the collectors products, as these are likely to be in shorter supply.

Some very cheaply-made and otherwise unexceptional bears arouse great interest at auction because they were owned by a famous or romantic person. The 9in. (23cm) "Mr. Whoppit", made in 1959 by Merrythought, fascinated, as he had accompanied Donald Campbell on his fatal attempt to break the water speed record on Coniston Water in 1967. After a 300 m.p.h. plunge into the lake, Campbell's mascot bear floated to the surface, to be carried later by his daughter Gina on her record-breaking attempts.

PLATE 135
"Klein Archie", created exclusively for The Enchanted Dolls House in 1983 by Steiff in a limited edition of 2,500. Brown mohair with felt paws and leatherette foot pads. Ht. 16in. (40.6cm).

Courtesy Margarete Steiff Gmbh

COLOUR PLATE 235
"Pippin", an unusual bear cub with an "antique" moulded face. In an edition of 500 from the 1996 Collectors range. Ht. 11in. (27.9cm).

Courtesy Merrythought, Ironbridge

At the same 1995 sale at Christie's South Kensington, Peter Bull's miniature bear, "Theodore" was sold. Though comparatively late, dating to 1948, the bear was important because he had lived in Peter Bull's pocket and had been seen on stage and television. Theodore was often referred to by Peter as a "symbol of un-loneliness", who stood above all his other bears in his affection. Theodore was sold after the death of Peter Bull, with his miniature shop, astrological chart, furniture and a tiny Greek dictionary to assist him on his travels, and reached £14,625. Fortunately, most of Peter Bull's other bears were bequeathed to the London Toy and Model Museum, though

PLATE 136
"Cassandra Bears" – soft and cuddly white polar bears in three sizes made by Mattel in California in the early 1980s.

Courtesy Jane Vandell Associates

COLOUR PLATE 236
Bear Brand Stockings were frequently advertised in shop windows by huge display bears wearing top hats. This bear is held by Mo Harding, with her Merrythought Guardsman at THE Antique Toy Fair at the Cumberland Hotel, London, in 1997. *Courtesy Jane Vandell Associates*

Aloysius was also sold. One 1908 Teddy of High Romance was Alfonzo, a rare red Steiff, bought by the Russian Grand Duke George Michaelovich for his five year old daughter. Princess Xenia Georgievna and her red bear were visitors at Buckingham Palace at the outbreak of the 1914-18 War, so the bear and owner remained in London, fortuitously avoiding the Russian Revolution. Alfonzo was treasured by the princess throughout her life and he was sold at Christie's in 1989 for £12,100.

The allure of any antique toy is the surprise of its having survived nursery play: when it is still in fine condition, it has an aura of magic that cannot be replicated.

PLATE 137
Shop display items always hold attraction for collectors, as they are a reflection of the company's self image. The Steiff Teddy watch display, supplied to retailers in 1991, has a specially made stand behind the bear for the watches. The Caran d'Ache German /Swiss piece, made in the 1990s, is more adventurous, with the Schuco bear turning around on one arm. Worked electrically. Sold for £230 and £126 in 1995.
Courtesy Bonham's, Chelsea

No two antique bears are identical, because each has been handled in a completely different way, giving the fur a distinctiveness that contributes to the animal's character. Sometimes the filling material has shifted, altering the very profile of the Teddy, or a nose is a little unstitched, giving an old friend a quizzical look. Even dirt enhances character and I know several examples that lost all their personality once they were cleaned. Recently, it has become fashionable for collectors to wash and blow-dry bears, which can be unfortunate, as many examples seem to lose some of their character and identity in the process.

Artist bears, though almost completely outside the world of the nursery, have a huge following. The term developed in the 1970s, to differentiate the makers of reproductions from those who created something more special and individual, while retaining the conventional Teddy Bear concept that had evolved before the First World War. Regrettably few ultra-modern or progressive artist creations have appeared, because the buyers always demand an atavistic appearance, sometimes even to the length of old boot button eyes and wood wool filling.

This constant harking back to the methods and materials of another age is the intrinsic problem in most bear artists' work: while the object is admired and applauded, the concept arouses some unease. This attitude is completely reflected by the behaviour of collectors in the leading auction rooms, where artist bears are regarded with noticable caution. These are bears to buy because they appeal – as yet they cannot be recommended as investments in the context of the antique market though thousands of makers earn a good living through their manufacture and have created an industry reminiscent of the old German folk workshops. Despite the hype that is lavished on some of the Collectors' Editions sold by leading commercial toymakers, their products are also as yet of doubtful investment interest and sell for relatively low prices when they appear at antique auctions, though they do seem to have a resale value within the collectors' clubs run by manufacturers.

COLOUR PLATE 237
Merrythought produced some fine coloured bears in the 1930s, such as this large blue example with Jane Dymond at her stand at THE Antique Toy Fair at the Cumberland Hotel, London, in 1997.   *Courtesy Jane Vandell Associates*

PLATE 138
Dean's Rag Book Company achieved a realistic effect by fixing a round base stiffened with card to their sheet-printed bears. This well designed sailor Teddy is a 1980's reproduction of an original design.

Courtesy The Dean's Company

An increasing number of commercial toy makers now include a range of artist bears. This Clemens *Till Eulenspiegel,* in mohair plush, was especially designed by Claudia Weinstein in a limited edition of 500. Ht. 10in. (25.4cm). *Courtesy Clemens Spieltiere*

Sometimes an effort is made to massage investment value by issuing special bears in limited editions but even here, to date, the second-hand value is disappointing outside the specialist collectors' clubs. Nevertheless, production for the collectors' market has encouraged many long established firms to create lines of extremely fine quality Teddy Bears that serve to illustrate the ultimate possibilities for manufacturers who are able to combine superb modern materials with long established skills to create bears at which the early makers would have marvelled.

For bear artists who are more progressive, almost any materials can provide inspiration, from antique printed fabrics to fur, patchwork, hessian, leather, metal, ceramics, wools or even Barramundi fishskin. Most of the artist bears have conventional jointing and are made of mohair or mohair mixture fabrics that are now being produced in qualities and textures that would have dazzled the pre-1914 makers. Clubs, special courses and evening classes teach new enthusiasts the basics of soft toy manufacture and it seems likely that each year a new group of artist makers will begin to market their creations.

Occasionally, a truly distinctive and unique Teddy Bear face emerges from the many retrospective models, such as the large-eared Nostalgia Bears, made in Australia by Deborah Sargentson, or the minute, under 2in. (5cm), creations of Elaine Fujita-Gamble in the USA. Many of the new bear artists compete for prestigious awards at conventions around the world and the new trends they inspired have filtered through to the commercial toy bears. Occasionally, long established firms commission individual bears from artist makers, who are able to be more adventurous than staff designers, whose talents are often constrained by committee-

PLATE 139
Thomas Cook's mascot bear "Oliver " seen with Bernard Norman. He was also sold in their retail travel agency shops. The bear was featured in a film called *Runaway*, in which a small boy wanted to run away with his bear. The 1984 publicity campaign "Bear Essentials" featured Oliver with a little girl companion. *Courtesy Thomas Cook*

type decisions and the judgment criteria of accountants and marketing consultants.

There is at present a worrying proliferation of bear artists crowding into an already over-supplied area and some very ordinary bears are offered at inflated prices under the "artist" banner. As with all modern creations, it is only the test of time that will reveal the collectors' pieces of the future, though it is certain that those which survive will have a very special character or feature such as those illustrated in this book. The Limited Edition market, already distrusted in the zone of general collectables, is even more suspect in the bear market, as too many makers have simply adapted a standard bear by adding a hat or ribbon and dubbing it a "Special Issue". Frequently the number of bears in the run of a "limited edition" is even greater than the numbers big factories would have originally expected to sell. This type of marketing has already failed in china and silver and it is seen to have been something of a come-on in the world of Teddy Bears, as the individual pieces are now very difficult to re-sell. If the numbers had truly been limited to, say, five hundred, then the future investment value could have been more interesting.

As in all facets of the "collectors" market, that with regard to limited edition bears is inevitably artificially created, it is very difficult to predict the antiques of the future. Doll artists have been working over a much longer period and as yet few of their creations arouse any interest in the major auction houses, most of which turn away this type of doll. When London sale rooms have attempted to sell artist bears, the prices have again been disappointingly low, as antique and modern bears do not mix well and are purchased by completely different groups of people. The artist bear craze is an end of century phenomenon of "toys for adults" and they are created mainly for people who enjoy the nearness of a soft but attractive animal. This market has been available to some extent throughout the century, from the time when young, glamorous Edwardian women carried bears to the park, to the mascots that adventurers and servicemen and women carried around the world with them in their luggage. When young people leave

PLATE 140
"Sooty", with his characteristic black ears, made in 1982. The bear was attractive for children to handle as it was in the form of a bean-bag. Made by Dakin. *Courtesy Dakin Inc.*

COLOUR PLATE 239
"Mr and Mrs. Twisty Cheeky", carefully re-created from the original Merrythought designs. The figures can be positioned in a variety of attitudes. A 1996 edition of 500. Ht. 12in. (30.5cm).   *Courtesy Merrythought, Ironbridge*

home, "old Teddy", sitting by the bed, takes the harshness out of new surroundings by embodying the comfort and security of the past. As the world becomes harder, people from all walks of life seek solace in soft toys and they are seen lying around the homes of the rich and famous, as well as in the bedrooms of the less privileged. Hugging and cuddling a soft toy is one of the most basic instincts – when there is no plaything around, an infant will replace it with a piece of soft rag or an old blanket. The fact that more large soft toys are now being sold to adults is an obvious reflection of the stresses of modern life, and they must provide comfort to many people who live without pets or close friends. When bears were kept as an affectation, rather in the manner of Sebastian Flyte in Evelyn Waugh's *Brideshead*, or as an adjunct of personality as with Peter Bull or Colonel Henderson, they have a light-hearted connotation that is contributory. When they are a necessary prop for the insecure or unhappy, their presence can be an indication of the loneliness of many contemporary lives.

Most arctophiles buy Teddies simply for the transitory pleasure given by the acquisition of a collectable item. For enthusiasts, the excitement is in the hunt for something special, that almost indefinable appeal of a "bear of character" that teases the eye of the enthusiast and can persuade buyers across oceans to attend auctions or fairs. As there are so many types and qualities of Teddy Bears, they are suited to every income level and attract people of all types and cultures. Some collections are vast and encompass examples of all ages and all conditions, others are almost aesthetic, in their choice of three or four perfect Edwardian specimens, acquired at considerable expense. The days when old bears asked to be rescued from the ignominy of house clearances or charity shops are very long past and they now sit proudly on fine antique chairs and can break price records in the top salerooms.

No other toy belongs exclusively to the twentieth century or has extended such a personal influence on so many people. Dolls have existed since the beginning of civilisation and have been adapted for each generation; metal toys cross the centuries; novelties, such as battery toys, belong to specific and fairly short periods; popular soft toys, such as pandas, rise and fall in a decade. It is only the bear, designed by Richard Steiff, which has survived all the changing tastes of the twentieth century market to offer itself today as a steadfast friend and confidant to young and old.

Chronology

Firms sometimes exhibited their new designs at international trade fairs six months
to a year before they were for sale in the shops.
In the chronology, the date of the first mention is given

1530	Berne city clock installed with a parade of bears.
1555	Woodcut of bears that dance to music.
1620	Automaton bear with clock made in Augsburg.
1760	Hamley's toy shop est. London.
1829	Birth of Jean Roullet.
1831	*The Celebrated Nursery Tale of the Three Bears* by Eleanor Mure published.
1837	*The Doctor*, Robert Southey's version of the Three Bears appeared.
1840	John Kirby Farnell established gift business in Notting Hill, London.
1847	Birth of Margarete Steiff.
1850	Knickerbocker Toy Co. established in USA.
1850s	German sample books show mechanical bears.
1851	Kapok first imported into Europe.
1856	Joseph Cundall changes vixen into a girl, "Silverhair" in *The Three Bears*.
	William Peacock and Sons established.
1860-80	Tin dancing bears under 4in. (10.2cm) high made in America.
1862	First F. A. O. Schwarz shop opened in New York.
1865	Gebrüder Bing established in Nuremberg.
1867	Founding of Roullet et Décamps by Jean Roullet, Paris.
1869	Picture books for young children illustrated by Harrison Weir with dressed bears.
	Invention of Celluloid in USA
1871	International Exhibition in London. A variety of fur-covered animals from Sonneberg shown.
1873	Roullet et Décamps move to 10 rue parc Royal, Paris.
1874	Birth of Mary Tourtel, creator of Rupert.
1877	Margarete Steiff opens first felt shop.
1878	Gamage opens his first shop in London.
	Roullet et Décamps' first catalogue with bears.
1879	Emil Wittzack, Thuringia, making felt soft toys in Gotha factory.
1880's	Artificial silk produced.
1880	Steiff makes first soft toy, an elephant filled with lambswool.
	Edward Prince of Wales admires koala bear in London Zoo.
1881	Eisenmann and Co. founded to deal with British and German toy trade.
1882	Birth of A. A. Milne.
	Birth of Gaston Décamps.
1883	Steiff issue price lists, including toys.
	Steiff toys shown at Export Showroom, Stuttgart.
1889	Association of Roullet and son-in-law, Décamps.
1890s	Nister Wild Animal Stories of bears.
1890	Steiff use wood wool for stuffing.
	William J. Terry established soft toy works in Stoke Newington.
1891	Leven & Sprenger founded in Sonneberg.
1892	Steiff's first catalogue of toys.
	Steiff apply for first patent, DRP 66996
	Steiff shows soft filled bears for young children.
	Steiff advertise small bears in white, grey, brown and black.
	Birth of Alfred Bestall, Rupert's illustrator.
1892-	Steiff offer Roly-Poly bears and bear skittles.
1893	Felt Toy Co. registered by Margarete Steiff.

	Steiff factory registered with Chamber of Commerce.
	Steiff products shown at Leipzig spring fair.
1894	Gebrüder Süssenguth founded in Neustadt, Thuringia.
1895	First cartoon bear cubs in *San Francisco Examiner*.
1896	Eduard Cramer factory established in Schalkau, Thuringia.
1897	Henry and Agnes Farnell establish soft toy firm in Acton, London.
	Birth of Enid Blyton.
	Steiff have their own stand at Leipzig Fair.
	Steiff make advertising display bear, ring-in-nose, designed by Richard Steiff
1898	Gund Manufacturing Co. founded in Norwalk Conn. to make novelties and soft toys.
1899	Steiff register first patents.
	Steiff polar bears and brown bears.
	Steiff riding bears.
	Steiff open London warehouse.
1900	Steiff offer Roly-Poly bears, revolving and bristle bears.
1901	Edward VII accedes to British throne.
1902	Steiff produce "Bär 55PB".
	Steiff making toys of plush, felt and velvet.
	Morris and Rose Michtom make a bear toy.
	Theodore Roosevelt visits Mississippi.
	Clifford Berryman's cartoon of the President with bear.
1903	Steiff use swivel joints for the first time.
	Steiff send consignment of samples to America, including Bär 55PB (P= plush, B= jointed).
	3,000 Steiff bears ordered by Hermann Berg for Borgfeldt, N.Y.
	Richard Steiff designs a Teddy Bear.
	Steiff register pattern for jointed bear at Heideheim.
	Ideal Toy and Novelty Co. established in USA.
	Dean's Rag Book Co. founded in England.
	L'Ours Martin appears in Paris.
1904	Steiff patent joints connected by double wires DRGM 242 399
	Steiff register improved design 'Bär 35PB'.
	Steiff Bär 28PB offered for one year only (20in. long).
	Steiff win gold medal at the St. Louis World Fair and Grand Prix Award.
	Steiff register button in ear trademark in USA.
	Steiff Bär 55PB discontinued.
	Wilhelm Strunz Mechanical Felt and Cloth Toy Co. Nuremberg, making ring in nose bears, in imitation of Steiff.
	Teddy Roosevelt convention badge of a mohair miniature bear.
	"Billy Bluegum", a koala bear, appears in *The Bulletin*, Australia.
1904	Bread plates decorated with bears for Roosevelt campaign.
	"Billy Bruin", a character in "Mrs. Hippo's Kindergarten", *Daily Mirror*, London.
1904-05	Steiff bears have horizontal seam across top of head, sealing wax nose and elephant button (embossed).
1905	Steiff register metal rod jointing DRGM 255 036.
	Richard Steiff evolves a more doll-like bear, known as "Bärle Bär 35 PAB", registered February 12, 10-42in. long,

(plush, disc jointed, moveable) in dark brown, light brown and white.

Steiff use leather squeeze-boxes in some bears.

Dean's London introduce Knockabout Toy Sheets.

"The Roosevelt Bears" begin publication with *The Roosevelt Bears, Their Travels and Adventures*.

1905-06 Steiff introduce printed buttons.

1906 "Teddy Bear" first mentioned in *Playthings* trade magazine.

Several American firms making Teddies.

Women's magazines offer patterns for Teddy Bear clothes.

Teddy Bear printed on fabric for home assembly (USA).

Heinrich Silberstein, Berlin, registers patent for bear with split pin jointing and velvet paws.

Steiff re-registered as Margarete Steiff GmbH.

Gund (New York City) offers Teddy Bears in four sizes.

Buffalo Pottery issue china decorated with The Roosevelt Bear prints (USA).

Tingue Mfg. Co. of Seymour, Conn. "Now largest makers of plush in USA".

"More about Teddy B and Teddy G, The Roosevelt Bears".

Roosevelt Bear postcards appear.

Teddy Bears appear on postcards.

Baker and Bigler, USA. Range of bears.

1907 White, black and brown bears available in USA.

Teddy Bears already adult mascots.

Ideal Novelty Co. described as "the largest bear manufacturer in the country".

Teddy Bear paper dressing figures first published.

Miller Mfg. Co. New York City "The Antiseptic Bear" advertised.

Miller Mfg. Co.'s "The Miller Bear" advertised.

Miller Mfg. Co.'s "The Uncle Sam Bear" advertised.

Bears on tricycles.

Bears somersault on rings.

Performing bears.

Bear on parallel bars.

Bear between two ladders.

Steiff rename firm The Margarete Steiff Toy Factory Ltd.

Steiff introduce hot water bottle cover bear 5335B, a lined body with lacing.

Heinrich Silberstein makes jointed bears.

First American Teddy Bear cartoon strip "Little Johnny and the Teddy Bears" in *Judge* magazine.

First animated bear cartoon of "Little Johnny and the Teddy Bears".

Celluloid jointed Teddy Bears in cinnamon or white (USA).

Bear candy boxes.

Rubber bears.

Fur Jumping Jack Teddy Bears.

Seymour Eaton uses words "Teddy Bear" in poem.

A Roosevelt Bear magazine.

Teddy rocking "horse".

Bruin cages on wheels.

Teddy Bear Shoofly.

Bear buckets and spades.

Gebrüder Bing produces its first Teddy Bears.

1907 Teddy Bear Stuffers go on strike in USA.

Bruin Manufacturing Co. established and use excelsior and silken floss for stuffing. "B.M.C." stamped on foot.

Performers dress as Teddy Bears in circus (USA).

Teddy Bear dressing-up outfits for adults and children.

Mr. Cinnamon Bear by Sara Tawney-Lefferts published.

Teddy Bear book by Alice Scott. Illustrated by Sybil Scott Paley. Published by Dean's Rag Book Co.

The Teddy Bear Two Step written by J. K. Bratton (Now known as *The Teddy Bears' Picnic*).

Teddy Bear shopping bags.

"Teddy and the Bear" cast iron mechanical bank by J.E. Stevens and Co. USA.

"Teddy is not Sissy" article in *The Times* London.

Harman Mfg Co., New York City, advertise Teddy Bears in 9 sizes.

Party game "Feed the Teddy Bear".

Teddy Bear coats the rage.

Teddy Bear stickpins and hatpins.

Teddy Bear notelets in 10 different designs.

Teddy Bear spoons for adults and children.

Teddy Bear dressing gowns.

"Electric Bright Eye Teddy Bears" made by the Fast Black Skirt Co. New York City.

Musical Teddy Bears. 5 sizes 10-18in. in brown or white.

Tumbling Teddy Cubs.

Standard Novelty Co. make black bears with rhinestone eyes.

"The White House Teddy Bears" produced by the American Doll and Toy Mfg. Co. New York City.

"Laughing Teddy " (shows teeth) by Columbia Teddy Bear Mfg. Co.

"Self Whistling Teddy" Strauss Mfg. Co. New York City.

"Teddy Doll". Havana Novelty Co. New York City.

Squeeze musical boxes used.

Dreamland Doll Co. Detroit advertise cinnamon or white in best bear cloth.

Dreamland Doll Co. "Teddy Turnover Doll".

Hecla Bears USA imported plush.

"Paper Dressing Bears" made by J. Ottman Litho Co. 110 West 34th Street New York City.

1908 Farnell (England) make their first Teddy Bear.

Dean's offer printed bears.

Dean's "Three Bears" produced in Knockabout Toy range.

Dean's " Knockabout Teddy Bear".

Chiltern works in operation.

The Toy Trader newspaper established (Britain).

Steiff introduce tilt growlers to bears.

Steiff introduce fabric printed labels behind buttons.

Franz Steiff registers natural movement patents for moving ears and ball-jointed, swivel heads.

Steiff begin to use glass eyes for special orders at extra cost.

Steiff moveable head (tube mechanism) patented, used on polar bears.

Steiff fight in courts over button in ear infringements.

Steiff offer muzzled bears.

Death of Franz Steiff.

The Roosevelt Bears Abroad and *The Bear Detectives* by Seymour Eaton published.

"Bobby and the Woolly Bears" appears in the *Butterfly* magazine, London.

"Willy Winks and His Bears" appears in the *Butterfly* magazine, London.

Mechanical Tumbling Bears advertised, worked by clockwork.

Printed Teddy Bear offered by Art Fabric Mills.

Roullet et Décamps offer electrically powered bears.

Red, white and blue patriotic bears from Art Novelty Co. New York.

Price of plush goes up 30% in America because of bear manufacture.

"Teddy Bear Traveller" appears with case of clothes.

"Yankee Doodle Bear", red white and blue, USA.

Celluloid-faced bears, Hahn and Amberg, USA.

Bisque head sleeping Teddy Bears, Hahn and Amberg, USA.

Arm-wound tumbling bears, Sears Roebuck catalogues.

Wilhelm Strunz of Nuremberg make close copies of Steiff bears.

Wilhelm Strunz using six-sided button in ear with white paper labels.

Globe Teddy Bear Co. Brooklyn established.

Samstag and Hilder dressed and undressed bears: sailor suits, jackets and skirts. Play instruments. USA.

1909 *Tale of Teddy Bright Eyes* published by Humphrey Milford, London.

W. J. Terry described as skin merchant and soft fur toy manufacturer.

W. J. Terry now manufacture cloth, felt and plush animals.

Selfridges department store opens in London.

First British Woolworth's opens in Liverpool.

Steiff Miniature Teddy Bears appear.

Steiff somersaulting bears shown at Leipzig trade fair, light brown, dark brown and white, called Purzel Bär.

Steiff Trapeze bear introduced (to 1911).

Steiff's first miniature bears, under 4in.

Steiff Roly Poly bears with snap fastening arms.

Steiff turned into limited company with capital of 630,000 marks.

Death of Margarete Steiff on 9th May.

Bing mark their bears with button in right ear.

Bing and Steiff in battle over "button in ear".

"Teddy the Terror of Jungleville School" comic strip in the *Family Journal.*

Louis Lindner and Sons, Sonneberg make a variety of skin covered animals.

Fur covered clockwork tumbling bears.

Teddy Bears made by several firms in London.

"Billy Possum" rivals the Teddy Bear.

"Old Mistress Teddy who lived in a Shoe". Morrells, Oxford Street, London.

Peek Frean use Teddy Bears to advertise Teddy Bear biscuits.

Schoenhut produce "Teddy's Adventures in Africa" 53 carved pieces.

Dean's register trademark of fighting dogs.

"Father Tuck's Rope Climbers" include Teddy Bear.

Samuel Finsbury & Co. cotton flannelette printed bears.

Trapeze Bears on chains.

Tree climbing bears.

"Ted the Hunter" printed on fabric to be sewn at home.

The Travelling Bears by Seymour Eaton, published by Barse and Hopkins.

1910 Steiff "Barbara Bear" based on polar bear appears.

Steiff register patent for mechanical bears wound by arm.

Steiff button in ear is registered and patented trade mark.

Steiff "Pantom Bear" designed by Albert Schlopsnies, with strong frames and pull-string voice boxes (to 1918).

Circus displays staged by Schlopsnies at Wertheim's, Berlin.

Margarete and Richard Steiff win personal gold medals at Brussels.

Strunz mark all their bears "Prasident".

Berthold Krauss, Wive und Söhne. 39 years in business, felt and leather animals, arks and menageries.

Décamps register patent on October 12th for somersaulting bear, self-righting.

A Bad Little Bear published by Henry Frowde.

Bertha Caspar, Berlin, best fur and velvet animals.

Teddy in hunting suit from Butler Bros. USA.

Dean's win two gold medals at Brussels World Exhibition.

"The Bruin Boys" appear in Mee's *Children's Encyclopedia.*

H. Leven, Sonneberg, makers of Teddy Bears.

1911 Pintel et fils, France, make first Teddy Bear.

Lyxhayr vegetable fibre filling introduced.

Steiff Frères established in Paris by Otto Steiff.

Albert Schlopsnies appointed to create special display settings (to 1915).

1912 Steiff Bär "Dolly Bear" introduced for American Presidential election with white heads, and green, yellow or red bodies.

Steiff introduce glove puppet Teddy Bears.

Steiff use glass eyes for most bears.

Steiff black bears available.

Steiff Record toys with four wheels introduced.

Steiff Record Bear first made.

Schreyer and Co. (later Schuco) founded by Müller and Schreyer.

Leven of Sonneberg one of the largest toymakers.

"The Bear Family" made of cotton over wire.

Roosevelt fails to be re-elected.

1913 Steiff introduce steering device for wheeled toys.

Steiff add "Record Teddy" to Record range.

Steiff "Autobär" for cars.

Steiff takes George Borgfeldt as US agent.

Max Hermann joins family firm in Sonneberg.

Siegel produces first bears.

Ernst Mechtold, Thuringia, began to manufacture bears. Said to have made first black bear.

1914 Outbreak of First World War.

Richard, Paul and Hugo Steiff in army.

Steiff introduce wooden wheels.

Teddy Toy Co. established in East London.

Schreyer and Co. close factory for war.

W. H. Jones East London established, making soft toys during war.

Harwin and Co. Finsbury Park London making soft toys and bears.

Winnie, an American black bear cub left at London Zoo (dies 1934).

Tim Tubby Toes by Henry Golding, illustrated by M.M. Rudge.

"Doll Bears" made by Louis S. Schiffer New York.

Pull-along bears with metal muzzles.

Britannia Toy Works established.

Jungle Toys established.

1915 Dean's "Kuddlemee Toys". Miss Bruin, a dressed bear.

South Wales Toy Manufacturing Co., Cardiff established. Trademark "Madingland".

The London Toy Co. established Aldgate, East London making Teddy Bears in plush, felt and velvet.

Chad Valley produce first Teddy Bears.

Chad Valley register patent for "Grunter" No. 10663 in July.

Chiltern Toy Works makes first bear, "Master Teddy".

The Travelling Bears series of ten books by Seymour Eaton published by Barse and Hopkins USA.

1916 Ally Mascot Bears by Harwin and Co.

"Big Teddy" and "Little Teddy" appear in Josephine books, illustrated by Honor C. Appleton.

Star Manufacturing Co. making six sizes of bears.

Britannia Toy Works produce Cossack bear in Russian uniform.

W. H. Smith and Sons make Toyland soft toys and mohair bears, Shelton, Stoke on Trent.

Hugg Mee Bears established.

No shortage of mohair in Britain.

Seymour Eaton dies aged 58.

1917 All British Doll Manufacturing Co. produce "Teddy Spring Bear".

1918	End of First World War.

M. Pintel fils et Cie established in Paris to make bears and soft toys.

Toy Trader changes name to *Toy and Fancy Goods Trader*.

1919 Death of Theodore Roosevelt.

Thiennot founded in Piney, France. Use "Le Jouet Champenois" as trademark.

W. J. Terry making bears with webbed paws.

Gebrüder Bing changes name to Bing Werke.

Alcock and Brown carry Harwin Teddy Bear mascots on first non-stop Atlantic flight.

Lines Brothers established London.

Hamiro founded making soft toys. Rokycany, Bohemia.

Art Toy Manufacturing Co. Fitzroy Square London. Made Misska as rival.

"Bobby Bear", first British comic strip bear appears in *Daily Herald*.

Chiltern Works inherited by Leon Rees. Makes bears under 19in.

Steiff make wood fibre bears in five sizes.

Steiff make paper plush bears of curly fibre.

Steiff still suffering from shortage of imported mohair.

1920 Chad Valley open Wrekin Toy Works in Wellington, Shropshire.

Steiff introduce wooden animals.

Steiff introduce dressed bears.

Steiff offer all sizes of Teddies made before the war.

Schlopsnies again working on Steiff's advertising and display.

G. Greiner and Co. take over as agents for Steiff in England.

Duxeen, an imitation leathercloth, patented by Dux, London.

Artificial silk plush used in British toy industry.

Rupert Bear drawn by Mary Tourtel appears in *Daily Express*.

Hermann Spielwaren established by Max Hermann.

"Teddy Tales" appears in *Chicks Own* drawn by Arthur White.

Birth of Christopher Robin Milne.

Zoo Toy Co. established by Joseph Burman. Makes fur, plush and felt mascots, including Teddies.

Steevans Manufacturing Co. (England) ceases trading.

Thiennot of Piney wins bronze medal for Teddy Bear design and Lépine.

Teddy Soft Toy Co., London, patents "Softanlite" kapok filled bears.

F.A.D.A.P. founded at Divonne les Bains, France.

Benjamin Rabier designs first FADAP bears.

Knickerbocker produce their first bears, USA.

1921 Albert Schlopsnies sells his Pi Pe Ro workshop to Bing.

Bing rename soft toy business Bing Artist Dolls and Cloth Toy Co.

Farnell registered as private limited company.

Farnell build Alpha Works.

Agnes Farnell and Sybil Kemp design soft toys.

Germany still has shortage of mohair and elastic.

Christopher Robin bought Farnell bear from Harrods.

Christopher Robin receives Eeyore the donkey as Christmas present.

Ideal (USA) produce walking Teddies in long or short plush.

Chiltern opens second factory at Grove Road, Tottenham.

Globe Teddy Bear Co., Brooklyn, said to be the largest makers of Teddy Bears in the world.

"Whistling Teddies", activated by shaking paw.

Wholesale Toy Co. Finsbury Park patents "Blinka" rolling eyes for Teddy Bears.

Nelson and Sons publish first Rupert book.

W. J. Terry uses "Ahsolight" trademark for first use of kapok by firm.

Schuco adopted as trademark for Schreyer and Co.

Schuco make first "yes/no" bears.

Steiff bears all have glass eyes with black pupils.

Steiff introduce conveyor belt method of working.

1922 First publication of the *Bobby Bear Annual* (runs until 1950s).

Steiff build new factory complex.

Steiff introduce plush bears on metal cycles.

Dean's register "Evripose" joints.

Dean's register "A1 Toys".

Schuco make first bellhop bear.

Schuco registered as trademark.

Schuco make "yes/no" bears.

1923 Chiltern Toys trade name first appears.

Chiltern Toys introduce Hugmee Teddies.

Hug and squeal Teddies introduced.

"Mr. Whitewash", with white plush head from Uncle Wiggily stores USA.

Max Hermann Sonneberg use "Maheso" trademark.

Bear on wheels that growls when put on its back.

Richard Steiff emigrates to America.

Sleeping composition-eyed Teddy Bears.

Chad Valley register "Aerolite" trademark.

Fred Engel becomes president of H. Josef Leven, Sonneberg.

1924 Triang Toys registered as trademark.

A. A. Milne's *When we were very young* published.

Chiltern Toys trademark registered.

Ealontoys Ltd. (East London Toy Factory) make first Teddy Bear in eleven sizes.

The Grand Duchess Olga's Picture Book *The Adventures of Three Small Bears*.

L. Diamant, Spitalfields E.1. produce cheap bears.

Butterick produce sewing pattern of "Deli-Bear" for the Delineator, USA.

"Alice and the Three Bears", a Disney animation.

Jointed wooden bears from Caran d'Ache.

Metal clockwork tumbling bears (Germany).

Umbrella-carrying clockwork bear (Germany).

1925 Chad Valley produces *Happyland* children's magazine.

Farnell produce "Chee-Kee" toy animals from natural skins.

Farnell register Alpha trademark.

"The King's Breakfast", music by H. Fraser-Simpson, words by A. A. Milne, illustrated by Ernest Shepard.

Helvetic Co. musical boxes first used in bears.

Kellogg's printed fabric bear family.

Gaston et Décamps show chocolate-drinking bear at the Exhibition of Decorative Arts.

Teddy Pull Toys, USA, Teddy locomotive, Acrobat, Sailor and Soldier.

Steiff introduce "Teddy Bu" (Boy) with coloured waistcoat.

Steiff "Tali-Bär" mascot for cyclists (to 1926).

Adolf Gund sells firm to Jacob Swedlin and 3 brothers.

W. H. Jones introduces "Hugyu" kapok-filled "Shagylox" (Shaggy mohair soft toys).

Chiltern Toys take over production of "Panurge Pets" Edinburgh.

W. Walter K.G. founded in Lobositz, Bohemia. Made bears and soft toys.

Elastolin takes over Pfeiffer of Tipple-Topple.

1926 *Winnie the Pooh* by A. A. Milne published.

Teddy Bear and Other Songs, verses by A. A. Milne published.

Ealontoys register trademark.

The Saga of Teddy by Marta Tamn-Golind (Sweden).

Nora Wellings opens Wellington factory.

Steiff "Teddy Clown" patented.
Steiff "Urteddy", a clockwork bear on bicycle made.
Steiff "Galop-Teddy" introduced.
Steiff nodding polar bears on eccentric wheels.
Chad Valley produce "Rainbow Tubby Bear" with ruff and hat.
Schuco patent Toys. Tail controls head movements.
Schuco bear cubs with covered metal bodies, Piccolo Bears with scent bottles etc.
Sleeping bears (USA) made by National Cloak and Suit Co.
Singer Bros. (USA) Brown and black bears.
Elastolin registered as trade name (Germany).

1927 *Now we are six* by A. A. Milne published.
Songs from *Now we are six* by A. A. Milne.
5th edition of "Winnie the Pooh".
Exhibition of Ernest Shepard's drawings from *Now we are six*.
Nora Wellings uses "Nora Wellings Productions" label.
"Gee-Line" mechanical velveteen jumping animals made by Gund, New York.
"Anima" wheeled toys introduced by Farnell.
Steiff produce animal purses with zips.
Steiff introduce coloured bears in pink and yellow.
Ernest Steiff, the youngest brother, joins the firm.

1928 "Bobby and his Teddy Bears" drawn by Walter Bell appears in *Sunbeam* comic.
Steiff introduce "Petsy Bear" with large wired ears.
Steiff use Swiss musical boxes in cuddle bears.
More very young songs by A. A. Milne.
The House at Pooh Corner by A. A. Milne.
Chad Valley build new factory at Harborne works.
Agnes Farnell dies.
Farnell opens City showroom in East London.
W. H. Jones (East London) introduce wheeled bears.
Jungle Toys register "The Bingo Bear".

1929 *The Hums of Pooh* song book by A. A. Milne.
"Clown Bear" in tri colours.
Steiff riding animals improved mechanism.
Steiff use metal disc wheels with rubber tyres.
Steiff "Teddy Baby" created.
Chad Valley first use artificial silk.
"Pudgy Baby Animals" USA.
Farnell represented in America and France.
Farnell introduce "Silkalite" artificial silk bears.
Chiltern introduce "Silky Teddy", first artificial silk bears.
Chiltern build new factory, the Chiltern Works, South Tottenham.

1930 Merrythought registers trademark. 20 employees.
Winnie the Pooh soft toys and board game manufactured by Teddy Toy Co. London.
Steiff 50th anniversary.
Steiff "Teddy Baby" patent registered.
Steiff "Dickey Bear" with coloured pads introduced.
Mary Plain stories by Gwynedd Rae, illustrated by Irene Willimason.
Woolnough (USA) produce Winnie the Pooh.
Harwin and Co. London cease trading.
Baby bears made by several manufacturers with bibs and dummies.
Jimmy Kennedy writes words of "Teddy Bears' Picnic".

1931 "Woof Woof" bears sold in America.
Chad Valley take over Peacock and Co. Ltd., London.
Peacock labelled bears produced at Chad Valley factory.
Merrythought produce first catalogue.
Merrythought designer Florence Atwood.
Merrythought "Magnet Bear", "Bingie", "Tumpy" produced.

Lenci, Turin, first bears appear in catalogue.
"Bobby the Bear" trademark registered by Eisenmann.
Farnell introduce "Cuddle Bear" and "Unicorn" soft toys.
Publication of first *Master Rupert*.
Richard Steiff says firm's products must be Americanised.
Hamiro trademark registered.

1932 Steiff introduce dressed bears with long, dangling limbs.
Merrythought introduce electric sewing machines to factory.
Merrythought "Cutie Bingie" (a movie toy).
Merrythought use long curly mohair.
Merrythought Laughing baby bear.
Merrythought Baby polar bear.
Bing goes into receivership and ends bear production.
Bobby Bear Club membership reaches 400,000.
Rupert League formed by *Daily Express*.

1933 Hitler comes to power in Germany.
Merrythought produce 30in. bear.
Merrythought "Chubby Bear", "Baby Bruin" introduced.
Merrythought guardsman, sailor and Highlander.
Merrythought "Bengie Bear", a cot toy.
Merrythought "Bingie" boy and girl dressed bears.
Merrythought sailor and ski girl dressed bears.
Merrythought dressed Grenadier Guardsman bear.
Daily Express Rupert Bear strip in their comic supplement.
"Pady Polar" appears in *Teddy Bear Tail* comic, drawn by Harry Folkard.
Max Hermann, Sonneberg, exhibits group of dressed bears.

1934 Farnell factory destroyed by fire.
Merrythought Highlander Bingie bear.

1935 Rupert League ends because too successful and costly.
Rupert and Bill's Seaside Holiday, the last Mary Tourtel story.
Alfred Bestall (1892-1986) takes over as Rupert's author and illustrator.
Invicta founded by two former employees of Farnell, London.
Farnell opens rebuilt factory.
Farnell introduce "Alpac" range of coloured bears.
Ealontoys moves to Kings Cross.
Merrythought said to be largest soft toy factory in England.
Steiff "Circus Bear" introduced with new snap joints – could crawl, sit or stand.
Long pile alpaca plush bears, USA.
"The Little Bears" set with furniture and story book.
Rubber Teddy Bear hot water bottle.

1936 Australian "Bingo Bears" made of English plush.
Guardsman bears in Schwarz catalogue, USA.
A.L.F.A., Paris, produce first Teddy Bears, unjointed and dressed.
"Kutoy" Norwood, London, soft toys including bears.
Steiff introduce simple woollen Teddy (to 1938).
Hamiro second largest plush manufacturer in Europe. 500 workers.
Merrythought "Bobbie Bruin" with "movie joints".
Merrythought "Chubby Bear".
First Rupert Annual, *The New Adventures of Rupert* published.

1937 "Feedme Bear" designed by Commonwealth Toy and Novelty Co. New York and used as promotion by National Biscuit Co. USA.
Merrythought "Riding Grizzly".
Merrythought "Teddy Doofings", 12-30in.
Pedigree Soft Toys first catalogue for Pedigree Pets.
Steiff "Roly-Bär" new design.
Farnell expands factory.
Farnell bears with Swiss musical movements.

"Eire" used on bear labels instead of "made in Ireland".
A.L.F.A. (France) design bear with upper part that moves while legs static.

1938 "Freckle Faced Bear" sold with copy of his book (USA).
Glove puppet of Freckle, a cartoon-like bear.
Cubbie bears with snub noses, USA.
Merrythought "Jok", "Hiker" and "Dutch" Bears.
"Musical Shag", gold with brown ears. Swiss movement, USA.
Knickerbocker use shaved inset muzzles on bears, USA.
Steiff now measure bear standing rather than sitting.
Nylon first introduced in USA.
Chad Valley receives Royal Warrant of Appointment.
Kirby Toys produce Sun Bears in bright colours (London).

1939 Outbreak of Second World War.
Death of Richard Steiff.
Lambswool Teddy Bears key-wound musical movements.
W. J. Terry ceases business (circa).
Merrythought first use burnished bronze mohair plush.
Merrythought "Bobbie Bear" with voice, Harry Rowntree design.
"Barney Bear" from *The Bear that Couldn't Sleep* by Rudolf Ising. Animation.

1940 Lambskin fleece bears widely available.
Chiltern cease production at Chesham but continue to make some bears throughout the War.
Merrythought diverted to war work.
Hamiro (Bohemia) turns to war work.
Farnell factory blitzed but soon re-opened.
First full colour Rupert Annual published.
Unjointed fluffy bears with flirting eyes. John Plain, USA.
The Bear's Tale animation by Tex Avery.

1941 Schwarz catalogue USA "Autograph Bear".
Schwartz "Feedme Bear".
Schwartz musical bears with Swiss movements.
Schwartz Mama and Baby Bear. Musical.
Snoozing Animals including bears. Pyjama cases. USA.
Zoo Toy Company reduces production.
Yootha Rose makes first toys. Later with Lesley Daiken founds Rottingdean Toy Museum.

1944 Death of Otto Steiff.
Death of Henry Farnell.
Smokey Bear becomes United States Forest Fire Prevention mascot.
Lindee Toys established, Australia. A faun trademark.
British Toy and Hobby Manufacturers Association founded.
Bugs Bunny and the Three Bears animation, USA.

1945 War ends.
"California Cuddle Cub" character bears by Dolls of Hollywood Inc.
Chiltern make soft toys at Amersham works, Chesham.
Adora Toys Ltd., London, make soft toys, trademark "Adora".
Wendy Boston begins manufacturing bears in South Wales.
Chad Valley produce a Clown Bear.

1946 Pedigree sets up in New Zealand.
Pedigree moves soft toy production to Belfast.
Chiltern establish training school at new Pontypool factory.
Plummer, Wandless and Co. founded in Sussex. Sheepskin and soft toys.
Merrythought re-start bear production.
Merrythought archive destroyed in flood of River Severn.
Agnes Brush versions of Pooh and friends.

1947 Pedigree sets up in Canada.

AB Merimex founded by Emil Grunfelt in Sweden to make sheepskin bears.
AB Merimex use "Amica" as trademark.
H. Josef Leven, Sonneberg, taken over by Communist state.
Max Hermann exhibits at Leipzig Fair.
Max Hermann makes first peacetime bears.
Name changed to Max Hermann und Sohn, Sonneberg.
Steiff again allowed to sell in Germany.
Les Créations Anima, Paris, established by Suzanne Vangelder.
Pooh characters cross Atlantic insured for $50,000 and remain at E.P. Dutton, publishers, New York.
Merrythought begin to use amber mohair plush.
Merrythought make "Cradle Bingie".
Fun and Fancy Free animation by Disney, full of bears.

1948 Petz & Co. established in Neustadt. Glass button trademark.
Lefray Toys Ltd. founded in London.
Verna bears, Victoria Australia. Arthur Eaton.
W. Walter KG moves to Mindelheim and includes bear range.
W. Walter KG use "Kersa" metal tags under feet of bears.
Hans Clemens sells bears made of old army blankets in Mannheim shop.
Hamiro confiscated by Czechoslovakian government.
Hamiro archives concealed. Cheap bears still made.
Gund of New York gain exclusive rights to produce Disney and other cartoon characters, including Winnie the Pooh.
Gund use new trademark of rabbit-faced "G".
Ealontoys Ltd. registered name change.
Decca issue "Winnie the Pooh" record sung by Frank Luther.
Velcro invented.
Merrythought "Tummykins" bear (Squeeze box).
"Rupert's Adventures" series begins with *Rupert and Snuffy*.

1949 Nuremberg used instead of Leipzig for German Toy Trade Fair.
Birth of Brumas the polar bear at London Zoo.
Merrythought "Punkinhead" designed for Canadian department store.
B.T. Holmes, son of founder, joins Merrythought.
Sooty first appears.
Clemens Co. founded in Germany.
Dean's produce Brumas with her mother.
Dean's issue first post-war catalogue.
Trudi Giocattoli founds soft toy firm near Venice, Italy.
Subsidiary company Hermann & Co. KG founded in Coburg, US Zone.
Althans founded by Karl and Else Althans in Birkig, Germany.

1950 Orlon first used commercially. US trade name for acrylics.
Cowboy Bear with gun and holster. John Plain catalogue. USA.
M C Z Schweizer Pluschtierchen, Switzerland, use "Mutzli" trademark. Stomach tags of metal.
Steiff resume full bear production after war.
Steiff reintroduce musical animals, including Teddy Bear.
Steiff introduce "Turbo Bear" with waistcoat and bow tie.
Chad Valley registered as public company.
"Barney Bear" appears in *Dandy* comic.
Styrofoam filling patented.
Ganz Bros. Toys founded. Now the largest Canadian Teddy Bear manufacturer.
Blue Ribbon Playthings. Be-Be Ltd, Kettering, included bears.
Merrythought "Tummykins". White patch on stomach.

Musical sleeping bears. USA.

1951   Good Bears of the World starts when Russel MacLean begins to distribute comfort bears in Ohio hospitals.
Steiff "Zotty" introduced.
Steiff redesign their "Original Teddy".
Pedigree established in Australia.
Andy Pandy's Teddy Bear, the first British television bear star.
Ark Toys established Natal, South Africa. Mohair jointed bears, later nylon.
"Rasmus Bear" comic strip, Denmark.
French Toy Fair has over 25 Teddy Bear makers.
Tall Timber Tales animation with the Terrytoons.

1952   Sooty appears on British television.
Sooty made as Chad Valley exclusive.
Zoo Toy Co., London, ceases trading.
Vinyl muzzles introduced.
"Teddy Original" introduced by Gebrüder Hermann K.G.
Schenker established to produce sheepskin soft toys.

1953   Coronation of Queen Elizabeth II.
Chad Valley Warrant transferred to Queen Mother.
"Toffee" from "Listen with Mother" (BBC radio) made by Chad Valley.
"Smokey Bear" made with vinyl head, hands and feet.
US Forest Fire Prevention Campaign introduced.
Merrythought designer Jean Barber joins firm.
"Jackie Baby" introduced by Steiff as commemoration.
"Tara Toys" bears made by Gaeltarra Eireann.
Patriotic bears made for Coronation.
Betty McDermid, New York and her bear Shadrack start a newsletter.
Ideal Toy Co. licensed to produce Smokey Bear.
Hermann family escape from East Germany, relocate in Coburg.
Peggy Nisbet Ltd. founded in Weston-super-Mare.
Steiff 50th anniversary of bears.
Steiff "Nimrod" bear introduced for anniversary.
Steiff "Jackie" jubilee Teddy.

1954   Grisly Spielwaren founded near Mainz, Germany
Schuco produce "Janus", the two faced bear.
Schuco produce roller-skating bear.
Chad Valley produce Brumas bear cubs, standing and sitting.
Invicta, NW. London, closes.
Nylon soft toys available in Britain.
Boulgom make latex foam filled bears.
Sooty appears in *T.V. Comic,* drawn by Tony Hart.
Wendy Boston makes first fully washable nylon plush foam-filled bear.
"Teddy, Haus des Kindes" shop founded in Nuremberg by Artur Hermann.
Ideal produce second version of Smokey.
Jakas Soft Toys established.

1955   Death of Max Hermann.
Colonel Henderson retires from Army and begins researching bears.
Pedigree UK soft toy production moved to Belfast.
Merrythought introduce American compressed air stuffing machine.
Leco Toys registered, Edgware Road, London. Lambskin soft toys and musical items.
R. Dakin USA founded for importing.
Steiff bears with head movements activated by tail introduced.

1956   Dean's move to 18 Tower Street, Rye, Sussex.
Dean's Childsplay Ltd. formed.
Gund move to Brooklyn form New York City.
"Comfy-Glow" registered as trademark for bears by Be-Be Ltd, Kettering.

1957   Schuco produce a dancing bear.
Merrythought introduce "Whoppit".
Merrythought "Cheeky". Mohair or art silk plush.
Merrythought polar bear, white plush with bells in ears.
Merrythought unjointed "Pastel Bear", bells in ears.
Thiennot (Piney) changes trade name from "Les Jouets Champenois" to "Création Tieno".
Chiltern designs by Madeleine Biggs and Pamela Williams.
"Tiere mit Herz" (Animals with heart) trademark of Berg Spielwaren.

1958   100th anniversary of Roosevelt's birth.
Publication of *Paddington Bear* by Michael Bond.
Plummer, Wandless and Co. take over W. H. Kendal. Bears main line with trade name "Tinka-Bell".

1959   Mighty Star Ltd. established Montreal, Canada. Bears, limited editions designed by Laval Bourque.
Death of Bernard Hermann.
Farnell opens Olympia Works in Hastings for bears for export.
California Stuffed Toys founded USA.

1960   Centenary of Chad Valley. 7 factories and 1,000 workers.
Lefray moves from London to Victoria Street, St. Albans.
Yogi Bear by Hanna-Barbera in "T.V. Land".
Walt Disney acquires rights to *Winnie the Pooh.*
Farnell make "Toffee", undressed version.
Farnell use "Mother Goose" trade mark for nylon washable range.
Nora Wellings. Winding-up of production.
Merrythought miniature bears made until 1975.
Merrythought nylon "Cheeky".
Merrythought "Sooty" made until 1962.
Merrythought "Sooty" nightdress case made until 1961.
W. Walter K.G. cease production of "Kersa" bears.
Chiltern's Amersham works closes.
Pintel et Frères, Paris, continue to use kapok and wood wool fillings.
"Gros Nounours", Paul Laydu, France. T.V. series and merchandising.

1961   Merrythought "Chime Bear" made until 1969.
Merrythought "Muff Sooty".
Merrythought "Yogi Bear" made until 1964.
Steiff "New Dralon Petsy", first machine washable.
Malrob Cuddle Toys, Brisbane, Australia. Cheap synthetic fabric bears.
Winnie the Pooh in Latin, *Winnie ille Pu*, the status book of the year.

1962   Merrythought open mouth "Cheeky".
Merrythought "Peter Bear" with velveteen cartoon face.
"Teddy Edward" first appears in books. T.V. character.
Yogi Bear's Own Weekly until 1965.
Jakas Soft Toys manufactures "Big Ted" for Australian Playschool.
Colonel Henderson becomes President of the Teddy Bear Club.
Alfred Bestall retires from illustrating Rupert.

1963   Death of Leon Rees of Chiltern Toys.
Russ Berrie and Co., USA, founded.
Nounours founded in Brittany, France.
Pixie Toys, Stourbridge, closes.
Merrythought Traditional mohair bears 14-32in.

1964   "Shoe Shop Bears" by Margaret J. Baker.
Helena Henderson, Montreal, Canada, makes bears for sick children in hospital.
Margaret Hutchings *The Book of the Teddy Bear* published.
Chiltern and Rees companies taken over by Dunbee-Combex Group.

271

Chiltern and Rees Fairy Foam one piece filling introduced.

Chiltern and Rees first fully washable bear.

Grisly Spielwaren metal button trademark replaced by paper tag.

Merrythought "Cheeky" in gold shaggy mohair.

Merrythought – All bears over 12in. could be fitted with musical boxes.

Merrythought – All bears fitted with patent locked in eyes.

Merrythought Yogi Bear, 11 or 27in., made.

Farnell move all production to Hastings.

Aux Nations founded by Marc Fremont.

Disney obtain rights to produce Pooh and Friends.

Steiff introduce "Zooby".

1965 Dean's change name to Dean's Childsplay Toys Ltd.

Dean's no longer use fighting dogs logo.

"Superbear" appears in *Storytime* comic.

Princess Soft Toys founded USA.

"Teddy Bear", first comic devoted to bears appears in Britain.

"Gwentoys" founded in Monmouthshire.

Celtic Toys, (Ireland) established by Hans Weberpals.

Rupert Bear no longer drawn by Alfred Bestall but by a team.

Merrythought "Mr. and Mrs Twisty Bear" made until 1971.

1966 Lines buy Joy Toys of Victoria, Australia.

"Bamse Bear" Swedish comic strip introduced.

Merrythought "Winnie the Pooh" toys made until 1976.

Merrythought use internal frames for Twisty Bears and Cheeky.

1967 Chiltern becomes a subsidiary of Chad Valley.

Chad Valley/Chiltern label introduced.

Sooty moves to *Pippin* comic. Now drawn by Fred Robinson.

Merrythought new designer Jackie Harper until 1969.

Käthe Kruse introduce plush Teddies Germany.

Pooh Bear made by Joy Toys Australia.

Steiff make "Lully" unjointed baby bear.

1968 Original drawing of Christopher Robin and his toys sold at Sotheby's for £12,100.

"A valentine to John Betjeman" by Jann Haworth, Summer Academy exhibition, London. Three kapok-filled bears, each with a mask of Betjeman.

Australian government begins to lift import tariffs. Most firms fail in the '70s.

Gwentoys Ltd. moves to larger factory on Pontypool Industrial Estate.

Ideal toy Company USA becomes publicly owned. 4,000 employees.

"Pipaluk" the baby polar bear in *Playland* comic.

"The Gretz Teddy Bears" Susanna Gretz, USA. Cartoon type bears.

"Corduroy". Don Freeman, USA.

Albert, the Little Cockney Bear by Alison Jezzard illustrated by Margaret Gordon.

Merrythought "Winnie the Pooh" range, Disney licence.

Merrythought "Mr and Mrs Twisty Cheeky" 11 and 24in.

Pedigree taken over by Rovex Industries, a Lines Bros. company.

1969 *Bear with Me* by Peter Bull published by Hutchinsons.

"Bussi Bär", drawn by Roff Kauka, Germany.

Lefray Toys moves to Abertillery, Gwent.

Gaeltarra Eireann moves to County Donegal.

Gaeltarra Eireann uses "Soltoys" label.

Merrythought make "Pooh in bed".

1970 Schuco ceases trading.

Alresford Crafts established. Margaret Jones designer.

Good Bears of the World founded.

Animated puppet version of Rupert on ITV.

1971 Ultra suede, synthetic fabric. USA.

Collapse of Rovex-Triang.

Nylena Toys established in Belfast. Owned by former Pedigree employee.

"Thumb sucking bear", moulded plastic face and hands, by Avalon Inc. Pennsylvania.

Joy Toys ceases production.

"Yogi Bear" by Merrythought 27in. (1971-73).

1972 Dean's Childsplay buys Gwentoys Ltd. (Soft toys).

Paddington made as soft toy by Gabrielle Designs.

Gamages department store closes.

"Yogi and his Toy" (magazine and toy).

Collapse of Lines Bros. Pedigree taken over by Dunbee Combex.

Robbity Bob Ltd. Auckland, New Zealand. Soft toys and bears.

Merrythought Oliver Holmes, grandson of founder joins firm.

Merrythought London Bears introduced – Beefeater, Highlander, Policeman and Guardsman.

Josef Leven, Sonneberg becomes state owned.

Huenec Pluschspielwarenfabrik begins to make soft toys, including Teddy Bears.

Estimated that in Britain 63.8% of households have a bear.

1973 Good Bears of the World chartered in Berne, Switzerland.

Gund moves to Edison, New Jersey.

Merrythought produce simulated mink bears and bear muffs.

Constance King includes section on antique Teddies in *Toys and Dolls for Collectors*, published by Hamlyn.

1974 Artist bears exhibited by Beverly Port in USA.

Merrythought "Cheeky" in brown dralon.

1975 Eden Toys produce first American version of Paddington.

Walt Disney first full-length feature film of *Winnie the Pooh*.

Nounours buys Aux Nations fine quality toys.

Dusty Bear Monthly established. New English Library.

Merrythought "Flexi Bear" boy and girl.

1976 Wendy Boston factory closes.

Peggy Nisbet Ltd. name change to House of Nisbet.

Death of Jacob Swedlin of Gund, N.J.

Pintel ceases trading.

"Bearfoot" Pillow Pets by Dakin.

Muppets "Fozzy Bear". Fisher Price and Henson Associates.

Merrythought "Winnie the Pooh". Name on jacket.

M. and Mme. Dubois awarded "Oscar of good taste" for Aux Nations animals.

"Rupert and the Worried Elves" by John Harrold for the *Daily Express*.

1977 Sigikid, Bayreuth, Germany. Plush animals in toy range.

Merrythought "Bedtime Cheeky" wears pyjamas.

Archie and the Strict Baptists, John Betjeman, published by John Murray.

1978 Chad Valley taken over by Palitoy.

"Bear in Mind". Mail order company established Concord, Mass. USA.

"Sleepy" small bears with sleepy eyes. Thiennot, Piney.

North American Bear Co. established. Makes Teddy from old sweatshirt.

North American Bear Co. introduce "Albert the Running Bear".

75th Anniversary Bear. Ideal Toy Co. USA. Also booklet.

Big Softies established by Valerie and Ted Lyle. Life-sized animals.

1979 International Year of the Child.

Start of British bear events, e.g. Longleat House.

Gund launch "Collectors Classics".

Gund redesign bear range to appeal to adult market.

North American Bear Co. introduce first V.I.B. series.

Golden Bear Products established, Telford, Shropshire.

GPO issues Winnie the Pooh stamps UK.

Soltoys Ireland ceases production.

Collectors History of the Teddy Bear written by Patricia N. Schoonmaker, but published 1981.

1980   Canterbury Bears established.

Collapse of Dunbee Combex Marx, including Pedigree.

Tamwade take over Pedigree.

Dean's Rye factory closes. Move to Pontypool.

Steiff make first replica bears. 1905 model, 11,000 run.

Steiff produce "Molly Teddy", unjointed baby bear.

Dakin produce "Mischka" for Moscow Olympics.

Little Folk established in Devon, to make Acrylic plush bears. Now making mohair bears for the collectors' market.

Death of Karl Theodor Unfrecht, founder of Grisly Spielwaren GmbH, Mainz.

"Winnie the Pooh and Friends". Paper doll book from Whiteman & Co., USA.

Lefray takes over Real Soft Toys.

"Honey Bear" made by Bunjy Toys, South Africa.

Mink Teddies sold by Fortnum and Mason.

"Bully Bear" by House of Nisbet visits the House of Commons.

1981   "Bully Bear" and "Young Bully" launched by House of Nisbet.

Term "bear artist" is first used in UK.

"Aloysius" is a star in *Brideshead Revisited* on television.

Sheepskin Products Ltd. founded in Auckland New Zealand. "Widest range in the world".

Merrythought simulated mink "Cheeky", champagne coloured.

Canterbury Bears first exhibit at Earls Court Toy Fair.

Dean's enter collectables market.

Dean's make Norman Rockwell inspired designs with Democrat and Republican ribbons.

Dean's introduce "Porridge Bear".

1982   London Toy and Model Museum opens with special bear collection.

"Woody Bears" with carved wooden heads and paws by Robert Raikes.

Dean's use green embroidered label until 1986.

"Fuddo" a black bear from Sally Bowen's book, made by Hermann, Germany.

"Bialosky Bears" made by Gund.

"Bully Minor" made by House of Nisbet.

Philadelphia Zoo's first Great Bear Rally.

Big Softies begin to manufacture Teddy Bears.

Mutzli introduce "Jubilee Bears".

Merrythought introduce special edition Collectors Bears.

Merrythought collaborate with Tide Riders Inc., New York, to export Collectors range to USA.

Merrythought introduce blue and pink plush "Cheeky" bears.

Ideal Toy Co. sold to CBS Toys.

Applause division of Knickerbocker Teddy Co. bought by Wallace Berrie.

Disneyland '82 "Grad Night Pooh". California Stuffed Toys.

Film on Alfred Bestall and Rupert for Channel 4 television.

1983   *Doll & Toy Collector* magazine introduces regular feature on antique bears.

Care Bears introduced.

Merrythought introduce "Edwardian Bear".

Merrythought introduce "Aristocrat Bear".

Merrythought "English Rose Garden Bear".

North American Bear Co. produce "Hug" by Ted Menten

North American Bear Co. introduce "The Vanderbear Family".

Gund produce 85th Anniversary bear.

House of Nisbet publish new edition of *The Teddy Bear Book* by Peter Bull.

"SuperTed" animation and related merchandise appears.

Steiff produce "Richard Steiff 1905" replica.

1984   Death of Peter Bull.

Steiff Teddy "Petsy" first fully jointed machine washable bear.

Steiff "Roly-Poly" bear replica of 1894 toy. Edition of 9,000 world wide.

Steiff "Giengen Teddy Set" 1906 replica 16,000 edition.

Steiff "1909 Teddy Bear".

Steiff "Mr. Cinnamon Bear", based on 1903 "Bärle".

Hermann introduce special edition collectors' bears.

"Valentine Bear" by Wallace Berrie. Collectors edition of 6,000.

House of Nisbet "The Zodiac Bears" collectors limited edition.

House of Nisbet "Sailor Girl" special edition of 1,000.

House of Nisbet "Bully Bear goes to Harrods" special edition.

House of Nisbet Honiton and Nottingham lace bears.

"Muffy Vanderbear" introduced by North American Bear Co.

Merrythought introduce "Champagne Plush Cheekie".

Ideal introduce porcelain replicas of first bear produced.

British survey reveals that 40% of bears bought for adults.

Boots produce Winnie the Pooh hot water bottle cover.

25th anniversary "Silver Bear" by California Stuffed Toys.

"Asquiths", the first British Teddy Bear shop opens in Windsor.

1985   Designated "International Year of the Teddy Bear".

Dakin & Co. produce "No Frills Bear" in calico.

Dakin & Co. make "SuperTed".

Dakin & Co. 30th anniversary bear "Bentley Bear".

Christies hold first auction devoted to bears in December.

Christies achieve record £1,800 for Steiff bear, first to sell at over £1,000.

Teddy Bear Artists Guild of America founded.

Rupert Collectors Club publishes "The Nutwood Newsletter".

Malrob Cuddle Toys, Australia, ceases production.

Karl Bär, Neustadt, makes replica Schuco models.

"Mybear" new concept by Jere B. Ford Inc. Maine, USA.

Vermont Bear Co. "Bear Buns".

Vermont "Sunshine Foggle Bear".

Vermont "Bearzar and Family of Friends".

House of Nisbet "Bully" family of jointed bears.

Applause USA include Robert Raikes designed Bears.

"Tiny-Tees", bears with T-shirts. Santa Barbara, CA..

Shelmar Imports. Russian mechanical wind-up bears.

Charles Zadeh Inc., New York City, "Bearly People".

Charles Zadeh Inc. "Buddy Bear".

R. John Wright, USA "Christopher Robin and Friends".

Merrythought "Bearington Family".

Merrythought "Softie Bear" and "Softie Polar Bear".

Merrythought limited editions for Tide Rider Inc. USA, including "Noel Bear".

Steiff replica 1905 bear on wheels. Edition of 12,000.

Steiff 1930 "Dickie Bear". Edition of 20,000.

Steiff "Passport Bear".

Steiff "Petsy", woven fur.

Steiff "Zotty", woven fur, ear-rings, etc.

Gund Inc. "The Last Elegant Bear".

Gund Inc. "Bialosky Bear".

Mighty Star Inc. New Jersey, "Polar Puff".

1986   Plaintalk takes over Dean's Childsplay Toys. Becomes The Dean's Co. Ltd.

First Teddy Bear museum in the world opens in Berlin.

House of Nisbet 10th Anniversary. Two Limited Editions.

Merrythought muff and purse bears.

Merrythought "Magnet Bear" replica.

Merrythought "Bear in a Balloon".

Merrythought new 5in. miniature bear.

Merrythought "Highlander" and "Policeman" dressed bears.

Merrythought "The Elizabethan Bear" in London gold and brown.

Merrythought "HR" designs with plastic nose.

Merrythought Giant bear made to ride in carriage for wedding of H.R.H. Prince Andrew.

Steiff "Teddy Clown" replica. Edition of 10,000.

Steiff "Jackie Bear" (1953) edition of 10,000.

Applause Inc. "After Eight" bear.

Applause Inc. "Nicolette" Christmas edition bear with moulded plastic face.

Sears Roebuck "Winnie the Pooh Centennial Bear, 1886–1986" Disney.

Pedigree "Tummy Buttons", "Valentine", "Happy Easter".

Teddy Bear Review launched in USA.

1987   Big Softies, Otley, Yorks, "Tough Ted" by Simon Bond.

House of Nisbet "Delicatessen" Peter Bull's bear made as replica for his 80th birthday.

House of Nisbet include new designer bears by US artists, e.g. Beverly Port and Ted Menten.

House of Nisbet invent new distressing process for mohair.

John Adams, Wargrave, Berks. "Winnie the Pooh" soft toys.

Bandai, Guildford, "Little Softies", Mapletown range.

Bedford Bears, Sandy, Beds. Traditional mohair and synthetic jointed bears with humped backs.

Blosson Be-Be, Kettering. Musical and talking bears.

Blisswood miniature bears.

Carriergrams. Miniatures with messages.

Cowan de Groot, London. "Gummi" and "Care Bears".

Flamingo Toys, Ringwood, Hants. "Live Bears", jointed plush.

Golden Bear Products, Telford "Teddy Beddy Bears".

The Teddy Factory, Wirral. Traditional bears.

Steiff "Teddy Rose" replica, edition of 10,000.

Steiff "Polar Bear" 1909 replica edition of 3,900.

Canterbury Bears, each fully jointed bear an individual.

Canterbury Bears produce "Gregory".

Canterbury Bears allowed to use City's coat of arms on label.

1988   Amsterdam Zoo holds first Netherlands Teddy Bear Festival.

Chad Valley trade name bought by Woolworths.

Dean's go into voluntary liquidation. Bought out by Managing Director.

Teddy Bear Museum opens in Stratford on Avon.

Pedigree Canterbury factory closes. Company ceases trading.

Merrythought open exhibition in Ironbridge shop.

Golden Bear Products take over right to "Tough Ted".

Golden Bear Products said to be largest maker in Britain.

Gund Inc. "90th Anniversary Bear".

Aux Nations awarded "Ourson de l'Exportation".

Steiff "Teddy Blonde" 1909 replica.

Steiff "Teddy Rose" 1925 replica, edition of 10,000, see 1987.

1989   Steiff "Jackie Bear" 1925 replica, edition of 4,000, see 1986.

Steiff "Black Teddy" 1907 replica, edition of 4,000.

Steiff "Seesaw with Teddy Bears" 1924 replica edition of 4,000.

Steiff "Dicky" replica of 1930 bear made for Schwarz.

Steiff "Petsy" replica of 1927 bear limited edition.

Sotheby's sell "Happy" a 1926 Steiff for £55,000.

Dakin & Co. acquire House of Nisbet.

F.A.O. Schwarz open new San Francisco shop.

"The Golden Gate" commemorative bear for Schwarz.

Nounours, France, buys "Ajena", cheaper range of soft toys.

"Countrylife New Zealand", Rabbity Bob Ltd. Antique style bears and limited editions. Largest NZ. bear maker.

Effanbee USA. "Gregory" by Carol Lynn Rossel Waugh and "Eureka" by Linda Spiegelhohre. Bear artists.

Official Steiff history published, *Button in Ear*, Jurgen and Marianne Cieslik.

Lion mark introduced in Britain for UK Safety Standard.

BBC produce first televised Rupert series.

1990   Hermann Spielwaren 70th Anniversary, produce "Jubilee Bear".

Hermann Spielwaren produce "German Reunification Bear".

Hermann Spielwaren produce replicas of old Leven designs.

Ursula Hermann writes history of Hermann Spielwaren.

Leven buildings and titles handed back to Fred Engel's family by state.

Steiff "Teddy Rose" replica, 10in. size, edition of 8,000.

Steiff "Petsy Bear" Brass 1927, replica edition of 5,000.

Steiff "Record" 1913, replica edition of 4,000.

Steiff Teddy with muzzle 1908 replica edition of 6,000.

Steiff grey/brown flecked bear 1926 replica edition of 5,000.

Canterbury Bears produce "Clan Bear".

Canterbury Bears produce Tenth Anniversary Bear edition, of 500.

Canterbury Bears making 50,000 bears a year.

Merrythought 60th Anniversary "Diamond Jubilee Bear".

Merrythought "Magnet", lavender tipped replica.

Winnie the Pooh wristwatch. Disney.

Hamiro's factory in Rokycany reopens for new Miro products.

Teddy Bears of Witney produce replica of "Alfonso" Princess Xenia's bear. Edition of 5,000.

Hugglets Teddy Bear Magazine appears.

Rupert and the Woolgatherers by Ian Robinson, his first story.

1991   British Teddy Bear Association founded.

Canterbury Bears Collectors Society formed.

Canterbury Bears produce "Sopie" especially made for Gund (one of eleven designs).

Dean's introduce new range of collectors' bears with wood wool stuffed heads.

Dean's re-introduce the old Dean's Rag Book Company logo of fighting dogs.

Sigikid collectors limited edition plush animals appear.

A. A. Milne's *Winnie the Pooh – the colour edition* published.

Giocattoli "Original Trudi. Hand Made" collectors bears and limited editions, Italy.

North American Bear Co. produce replica of "Aloysius" from *Brideshead Revisited*.

Hermann Spielwaren produce two 1929 replica bears, editions of 3,000.

Steiff "Bär 35PB", replica edition of 6,000.

Steiff "Somersault Bear", 1909 replica edition of 5,000.

Steiff "Snap apart Teddy", 1909 replica edition of 5,000.

Jakas International limited edition range and "Big Ted" (Playschool) replica.

Nelvana produce animated Rupert series for ITV.

1992   Death of Dora Margot Hermann.

Sigikid, Mistelbach, enter the replica market.

Sigikid "Miro" limited editions introduced.

Hermann Spielwaren introduce Leven replica bears.
Hermann Spielwaren introduce "Columbus Bear".
Hermann Spielwaren introduce "Europa Bear".
Miro make replicas of Hamiro 1920s and '30s bears.
Steiff Collectors Club formed.
Steiff celebrate 90 years of Steiff bears.
Steiff produce "Record Teddy Rose", edition of 4,000.
Steiff "Black Bear", 1912 replica, edition of 9,000.
Steiff "Music Bear", 1929 replica, edition of 8,000.
Steiff "Dicky Bear", white, 1930 replica.
Steiff "Teddy Baby", maize, 1930 replica.
Gund buys French firm Anima.
Gund becomes US distributor for Canterbury Bears.
Alresford closes after death of John Jones in 1991.
Berg Spielwaren introduce limited editions.
Big Softies introduce "Good Companion Bears", also collectors and limited editions.
Merrythought introduce "Touch of Silk" Collectors range.
Merrythought "Birthday Bear" for Karin Heller, Germany.
Merrythought introduce "Mr. Whoppit", replica.
Merrythought introduce "Gatti", Titanic survivor replica.
Merrythought introduce "Bingie", replica.
Merrythought introduce "Mr. and Mrs Mischief".
Karl Bär makes Steiff replicas.
Clemens introduce Collectors range for 40th anniversary.
Berg, Austria, introduce "Toothache Bear".
Thiennot 1920 replica bear, limited edition.

1993   Les Créations Blanchet, France, limited edition replicas of original bear cubs.
F.A.O. Schwarz produce "Truffles".
Steiff "Ur-Teddy Bear", 1926 replica, edition of 4,000.
Steiff "Bärle 35 PAB", 1905 replica, edition of 6,000.
Steiff "Brown Bear", 1907 replica, edition of 5,000.
Steiff "Teddy Baby Boy and Girl", 1930 replicas.
Sigikid "United Europe Bear".
Christies sell blue Steiff for £49,500.

1994   Hermann Spielwaren replica of 1930s bear, edition of 2,000.
"Teddy Girl", sells at Christies for £110,000.
Steiff limit replica editions to 7,000.
Steiff "Circus Bear", brown, 1935 replica, edition of 4,000.
Steiff "White Teddy" 1908 replica edition of 7,000.
F.A.O. Schwarz New York. John Wright 250 limited edition of "Wintertime Pooh and Piglet".

1995   Big Softies "Simon", edition of 100.
Big Softies "Carnival Bears".
Merrythought "Micro Cheeky Bears", including "Mounty" and "A Forty-Niner" for American market.
Royal Doulton produce "Winnie the Pooh" china.
Steiff reduce limited editions to maximum of 5,000.
Steiff "Blonde Bear", 1909 replica.
Steiff "Teddy Baby", 1929 replica, edition of 3,000.
Steiff UK limited edition of 14in. bear. White label with unusual red ink. Edition of 3,000.
Steiff 6in. "Petsy".
"White Dicky" and caramel and white tipped "Zotty".
"Classic range" 1928 "Petsy" and 1938 "Bear on wheels".
Hermann Spielwaren new range of boxed and numbered miniatures 2-4in., editions of 3,000.
Hermann Spielwaren "Miniature Jester" and "Bedtime Bear".
Hermann Spielwaren "Beary-go-round" edition of 500.
Dean's Michaud collection.
Dean's "Ebenezer" charity bear.
Dean's Artist Showcase range.
Canterbury Bears "Dressing Gown", miniature edition of 1,000.
Canterbury Bears 6in. "Baby Tartan Bears" and "Little Bluey".
Canterbury Bears 5in. claret coloured "Morag", edition of 500.
Bing "Sir Bing the Banker" and "Sir Cony the Cave Bear".
Bing 6cm bears.
Rupert's 75th anniversary.

1996   Merrythought replica of dressed musical Alpha Bear, edition of 500.
Alpha Farnell replicas, edition of 500.
Merrythought Little Sleepy head with comfort blanket, edition of 500.
Merrythought Home Guard in uniform, edition of 1,000.
Merrythought Billy the Bakers Boy in Ironbridge apron, edition of 500.
Merrythought John Axe Jeremy Junior & Goldie, edition of 1,000.
Merrythought Back pack bear, edition of 500.
Merrythought Paleface muff.
70th Anniversary of *Winnie the Pooh*.
Royal Doulton collection of 10 *Winnie the Pooh* figures.
Steiff "Record Petsy", 1928 replica, edition of 4,000.
Steiff "Snap Dicky", 1936 replica, edition of 5,000.
Steiff "Teddy Bear", caramel, 1951 replica, edition of 5,000.
Steiff "Teddy Bear", white, 1921 replica, edition of 4,000.
Dean's Collectors Club "Humphrey".
Dean's Collectors Club "Irving", musical edition of 500.
Dean's Collectors Club "Hamish", "Angus" and "Little Willie", editions of 1,000.
Dean's "Son of Nigel", edition of 2,000.
Christies sell "Teddy Edward", star of "Watch with Mother" for £34,500.
Christies sell a Steiff with photograph of owner for £18,400.
Christies sell 1920s Steiff for £17,230.

1997   Merrythought "Stowaway" in a wooden box, limited edition of 750.
Merrythought "Bearheart" with a tail, edition of 750.
Merrythought "Love in a Mist' pair, edition of 750.
Merrythought Georgie Girl with long legs, edition of 250.
Merrythought Chess in black and white, edition of 750.
Merrythought Baby Baggy Bear (beans in torso), edition of 750.
Merrythought new mohair Shropshire Bears.
Merrythought Brandy bear with contrasting muzzle.
Merrythought Heritage Bears – a new Chef Bear.
London auction rooms turnover £1,000,000 for antique bears per year.
"Noah's Ark", first special Aux Nations shop, in The Hague.
Nounours, Brittany make 10,000 soft toys a day.
Nounours "Les Griffes" have new owner's name embroidered on pad.
"La Pelucherie of the Champs Elysées", Aux Nations.
Royal Doulton add five models to *Winnie the Pooh*.
Royal Doulton first limited edition of "Eeyore loses a Tail". First in series of annual tableaux.
Steiff red Hong Kong Bear. 11in. English and Chinese edition of 2,000.
Clemens "Virgil" edition of 500.
Clemens now concentrate on collectors' market.
Clemens range of Claudia Weinstein limited edition bears.
Sigikid offer Gisela Hofmann Bear of the Year.
Sigikid "Der Bär aus der Box", edition of 1,000.
Sigikid Artist Bear Collection introduced.
Golden Bear Jane Hissey's "Old Bear and Friends".
Golden Bear "Teddy Toes".
Golden Bear "Giant Pooh".
Golden Bear "Rupert" and "Rupert Finger Puppet".

Bibliography

Axe, John, *Magic of Merrythought*, Hobby House 1986.

Bailly, Christian, *Automata the Golden Age*, Sotheby's 1987.

Betjeman, J., *Archie and the Strict Baptists*, John Murray 1977; *Summoned by Bells*, Murray 1972.

Bielosky, P. & A., *Teddy Bear Catalog*, Workman 1980; *Teddy Bear Catalog* Revised ed., Workman 1984.

Brown, Michelle, *The Teddy Bear Hall of Fame*, Headline 1996.

Bull, Peter, *Bear with Me*, Hutchinson 1969; *Bully Bear Goes to a Wedding*, Bull and Irving 1981; *The Teddy Bear Book*, Nisbet 1983.

Cieslik, J. & M., *Button in Ear*, Cieslik Verlag 1989.

Clise, *Ophelia's Voyage to Japan*, Potter 1989.

Cockrill, P, *Teddy Bear Encyclopedia*, Dorling Kindersley 1993; *Teddy Bears and Soft Toys*, Shire 1988; *The Ultimate Teddy Bear Book*, Dorling Kindersley 1991.

Crisp, Marty, *Teddy Bears in Advertising Art*, Hobby House 1991.

Fawdry, K. & M., *Pollocks History of English Dolls and Toys*, Ernest Benn 1979.

Hebbs, Pam, *Collecting Teddy Bears*, Collins 1988.

Herridge, *Every Bear's Life Guide*, Ebury 1983.

Hillier, Bevis, *Young Betjeman,* John Murray 1988.

Hillier, M., *Teddy Bears a Celebration*, Ebury 1985.

Hockenberry, D., *Enchanting Friends,* Schiffer 1995.

Keyes, Josa, *The Teddy Bear Story,* Windward 1985.

King, Constance E., *Antique Toys and Dolls*, Studio Vista 1979; *Toys and Dolls for Collectors*, Hamlyn 1973; *Encyclopedia of Toys*, Hale 1978.

Menten, T., *The World according to Hug*, Delilah 1984.

Mullins, L., *Teddy Bears Past and Present*, Hobby House 1986.

Newman, Bruce M., *Fantasy Furniture*, Rizzoli 1989.

Nicholson, *Teddy Bears on Paper*, Taylor 1985.

Pearson, Sue, *Bears*, De Agostini 1995.

Perry, George with Alfred Bestall, *A Bear's Life, Rupert*, Pavilion 1995.

Picot, G. & G., *Teddy Bears*, Weidenfeld 1988.

Pronin, A. & B., *Russian Folk Arts*, Barnes 1975.

Schoonmaker, Patricia, *Collectors History of the Teddy Bear*, Hobby House 1981.

Sieverling, Helen, *3rd Teddy Bear Price Guide*, Hobby House 1988.

Waring, P. & P., *Teddy Bears*, Treasure Press 1984.

Werkmäster, Bengtsson Peterson, *Teddy Bears*, Barron's 1988.

Wilson and Conway, *Steiff Teddy Bears Dolls and Toys*, Wallace Homestead 1984.

Index